PROFITING FROM THE PLAINS

T0313908

PROFITING FROM THE PLAINS

The Great Northern Railway and Corporate

Development of the American West

CLAIRE STROM

UNIVERSITY OF WASHINGTON PRESS

Seattle and London

University of Washington Press
P.O. Box 50096
Seattle, WA 98145-5096
www.washington.edu/uwpress

Library of Congress Cataloging-in-Publication Data
Strom, Claire.
Profiting from the plains : the Great Northern Railway and corporate
development of the American West / Claire Strom.
p. cm.
Includes bibliographical references and index.
ISBN-10: 0-295-98663-8 (pbk. : alk. paper)
ISBN-13: 978-0-295-98663-0
1. Great Northern Railway Company (U.S.)—History.
2. Railroads—Great Plains—History.
3. Hill, James Jerome, 1838–1916.
4. Businessmen—Great Plains—Biography.
5. Agriculture—Economic aspects—Great Plains—History.
6. West (U.S.)—Economic conditions.
7. United States—Economic conditions—1865–1918.
I. Title.
HE2791.G775S77 2003   385'.0978'09041—dc21   2003050738

This book is dedicated to my daughter,

Phoebe Helga Margaret Strom

She was not yet born when I started my research and will be eleven by the time it is published. She has, therefore, through no fault or choice of her own, lived with James J. Hill and the Great Northern Railway all her life. I thank her for that, and for the joy and grace she has brought to my life.

CONTENTS

ACKNOWLEDGMENTS

AS HISTORIANS MOVE to a greater understanding of the role of subjectivity in their discipline, it is increasingly interesting for me to read acknowledgment pages. Now wanting to know whom the author knows can be replaced, or maybe merely justified, by an academic curiosity regarding the intellectual networks that influenced the author's perceptions and insights. With that in mind, I proffer those who influenced my thinking and who deserve more than just this public thanks I can give.

Let me start with my professional thanks. Many librarians have contributed countless hours over the years helping me with my research. Particular thanks goes to the interlibrary loan librarians at Iowa State University, the University of Wisconsin—Baraboo/Sauk County, and North Dakota State University. I also received considerable assistance from archivists at the James J. Hill Reference Library; the Minnesota Historical Society; the Special Collections and Archives at the University of Minnesota; the North Dakota Institute for Regional Studies; the North Dakota Heritage Center; the Merrill G. Burlingame Special Collections and University Archives at Montana State University; and the Manuscripts, Special Collections, University Archives Division of the University of Washington Library.

Generous grants from the Rock Island Arsenal Historical Society, the James J. Hill Library, and Brigham Young University supported my research.

In addition, I want to thank my copyeditor Mary Ribesky and editors Julidta Tarver and Marilyn Trueblood at the University of Washington Press for their professionalism and courtesy in dealing with both me and my manuscript.

I also have many personal debts. Linda Cameron, Dick Duncan, Peggy

Hamant, Susan Hardman, Jeff Holmes, Jil Hopland, Ann Kaplan, Ann Melhus, Ann Miller, Richard Strom, and Nancy Tracy encouraged me in the early days of this project when I was an interpreter at the James J. Hill House interested in Hill's agricultural endeavors. During the last decade, the friendship, humor, and affection of Alice Bishop, Pat Coleman, Karen Danbom, Dale Floody, Dan Flores, Ken and Mary Grant, Mike Haaf, Carole Kazmierski, Shelley Orngard, Wendi Pasco, Ann Regan, Gene Robkin, Jane Turner, John and Jane Whitney, Lisa Williams, and my colleagues at North Dakota State University have helped me in countless ways to stay grounded and focused.

Matt Klingle, Mike and Heather Koop, Melissa and Dan Thomason, and Rosa, Tres, Lucy, and John Thompson opened their homes to me for prolonged stays during various research trips, while remaining gracious and companionable.

My thanks is also due to Adrian Bennett, Ham Cravens, David Danbom, John Dobson, Doug Edwards, Phil Frana, Dick Kottman, Eileen McCormack, Mike Malone, Cameron Saffell, Dorothy Schweider, Coll Thrush, Cherilyn Walley, and Jim Whittaker for generously sharing their ideas and expertise.

Six people were most influential during the creation of this book. My parents, Maggie and Dennis Bray, have always encouraged my curiosity. They have supported me and my studies unselfishly, both emotionally and financially. Jay Taylor steered this work through my graduate years. He taught me to look for and understand the larger context of my story as well as led me to relevant historians and their works. Modupe Labode carefully read the manuscript twice, exposed me to different ways of thinking about history, and has become a dear friend. Jim Norris provided a keen critical eye while I revised and expanded the manuscript for publication. More importantly, our love for each other enhances my days. Finally, Tom White has guided this project from the beginning. He took me seriously when I was researching just for fun, encouraged me to go back to school, provided support and insight at numerous conferences, and continues to help me maintain a sense of humor and perspective in my academic life.

PROFITING FROM THE PLAINS

1 / Introduction

In late 1869, Louis Riel, the Canadian métis, led a rebellion against English control of Manitoba and seized Fort Garry at the site of present-day Winnipeg. The situation was dire for the Hudson's Bay Company, which depended on Fort Garry as a hub for the fur trade and on the métis as labor for that trade; for the colonial government in Ottawa, which was trying to forge a united Canada; and for businessmen in St. Paul, who had recently acquired a considerable portion of the trade, carrying furs out of the hinterland. Exacerbating the situation was the lack of information coming out of Fort Garry and the post's inaccessibility in the depths of a northern Great Plains winter.[1]

In March 1870, a young St. Paul entrepreneur, whose profits were threatened by Riel's rebellion, offered to journey up the Red River Valley to find out what was happening and to report back to all parties concerned. The Canadian government agreed, and James J. Hill set out on his trip. He started by train, taking the St. Paul & Pacific Railroad to St. Cloud, which was the end of the line. He proceeded another hundred miles by coach, stopping repeatedly to dig out from snowdrifts. At Benson, Minnesota, he contracted with a métis guide to take him to Fort Garry. Using sleds and dogs, they moved up the Red River Valley. Hill grew increasingly frustrated by the pessimistic talk of his companion, who did not believe that they would ever make it to the Fort due to the hazardous weather conditions. Finally Hill abandoned his guide near the present-day site of the University of North Dakota in Grand Forks. The next day he started a seventy-mile trip, snowshoeing through the frigid landscape, up to the home of a local family, the Cavaliers.[2]

Hill reached Fort Garry and interviewed Riel and others to gain as clear an understanding as possible of the complex situation. He then set off again down the Red River for St. Paul in April, with the terrain made even more difficult by the onset of the spring thaw. He started the trip with a new métis guide, several ponies, and a cart. All went well until the guide, while pushing the cart out of some mud, dislocated his shoulder. After a cold night under a piece of canvas, Hill relocated the man's shoulder using his underclothes as a rope and a box elder stick for leverage, and they continued the journey. Further along, Hill fell through some rotten ice while crossing a river. "All of a sudden [the ice] gave way, and as I didn't know how deep the water was I had occasion to think of all the good things and all the bad things I had ever done between the time I started down and when I struck ground, with the water reaching to my vest pockets. It was hard work getting back to the ice again. The ice kept breaking as I tried to clamber out; but at last I got on to a small pile of earth heaped up by a beaver when the water was not so high." Reaching St. Paul again at last, Hill telegraphed the British government in Ottawa with details of the situation at Fort Garry. He also started planning ways to expand his trade along the Red River, such as using flatboats, construction of which started that very summer.[3]

For the rest of his life, Hill loved to tell this story. Over time the narrative probably was conflated with other episodes in his life and exaggerated, as favorite personal legends often are. He told it frequently in private, and all his friends knew the story well, but he also regaled graduating classes and other audiences with it well into his seventies.[4]

The story represented to Hill, as well as to his various audiences, the essence of the American male's interaction with the West. It had the vital components, with incompetent and untrustworthy non-whites, an unforgiving, harsh environment, and a white man triumphing over all vicissitudes through his own ingenuity, strength of character, and rugged individualism. This was the West as most Americans in the late nineteenth and early twentieth centuries saw it. More importantly, this was how they perceived their interactions with the western environment and peoples. Through these American traits, the West would attain successful development and enduring prosperity.[5]

This legend of western development through individualism has been exploded by numerous historians. From Limerick to Athearn, from White to Nash and all the western historians in between, the acknowledged forces in western development have been capital, corporations, and the federal government. All of the extractive industries of the West, including furs, mining, lumbering, cattle ranching, and oil, needed capital investment for success, and that capital was usually only accessible outside of the region. Although many individuals tried to make their fortunes fur trading or gold mining, and a few did, sustained and substantial resource exploitation only occurred after considerable capital had been tapped. So it was that John Jacob Astor and the American Fur Company dominated the fur trade from New York, while Frederick Weyerhaeuser from Wisconsin controlled the lumber.[6]

For all or most of these industries to succeed, they needed effective communications with the East. It was difficult to make a profit trailing cows to Ohio, or sailing copper to New York. Rail connections were needed instead. This, in turn, required federal intervention.

Shortly after the Mexican War and the discovery of gold in California, Americans acknowledged the need for transcontinental lines. Only railways could unify their newly expanded nation, created by purchase, war, and conquest, and develop the new lands. Americans also recognized the inherent problems in building these lines. Railroad construction in the settled South and East had been financed by haulage. A company would connect two towns, and the resultant revenue would float the line's extension to the next population center. Municipalities sometimes provided cash incentives to run roads to certain towns, but such inducements had little effect on the basic financial structure. Such earlier financial strategies could not apply, however, to the expansive, unsettled spaces of the West. Few towns existed, haulage potential was small, and distances were prohibitive.[7]

Thus, despite the political and economic necessity of linking the nation's coasts, the project appeared financially unfeasible. Laying tracks across the Great Plains and over the western mountain ranges, with little hope of business-generated revenue until reaching the Pacific and its gold, required a vast reserve of money. Therefore, as early as 1845, Asa Whitney proposed that the federal government subsidize transcontinental lines. By the 1850s most national politicians, led by Jefferson Davis, acknowledged the necessity of government support. However, a cash-poor government was not in the position to offer monetary incentives to railroad builders. Instead it offered land, which it had held in abundance since the Louisiana Purchase of 1803.[8]

Early federal efforts to subsidize railroads through land grants faltered due to sectional conflict. In 1850 the federal government gave midwestern states public domain, with a mandate to sell the land and use profits to subsidize construction of the Illinois Central. The all-encompassing sectional strife of the 1850s, including South and North vying for the first transcontinental road, stymied further land allocation and railroad construction. In 1862, freed from congressional conflict by the Civil War, President Lincoln approved the first grant of land for transcontinental railroad construction to the Union Pacific Railroad.[9]

Land subsidies resulted in transcontinental lines gaining tremendous power in the Great Plains and Far West. Federal land grants, designed to prevent the acquisition of huge, uninterrupted acreages, offered alternating sections of land on either side of the tracks. State governments also courted railroads with immense, often untraceable, land holdings. Frequently consolidating these grants, the railway corporations utilized their landed wealth and transportation dominance to spur migration, determine town sites, control local and state politics, and direct economic development.[10]

Many Americans opposed this federal allocation of land to large corporations, as it represented a break with traditionally accepted land ideologies and policies. The role of the public domain had been debated since its creation in 1781. Vaguely defined as the possession of all citizens, the land was seen variously as a source of federal income, an opportunity for individual profit through speculation, and a solution to the "Indian problem." However, until the advent of Progressive conservation and its tenet of administering the public domain in perpetuity for the benefit of the populace, few questioned that the fundamental federal land policy hinged on distribution and settlement. Rather, the ideological debate centered on whether the federal government was entitled to make a profit from land sales or simply administer the land transfer to individuals. In 1862, with the Homestead Act, the federal government finally assumed the mantle of altruistic guardianship.[11]

Thus, the innovation of railroad land grants met with considerable resistance. Despite frequent sales of the public domain to large corporations, starting in 1787 with the transfer of one million acres to the Ohio Company, the federal government had never *given* land to a private corporation until the railroad grants of the mid-nineteenth century. Public dissatisfaction with these grants grew, especially after the Civil War, when farmer opposition to railroad monopolies and freight rates became increasingly organized through the Patrons of Husbandry, also known as the Grange.[12]

This general anti-railroad antagonism was exacerbated by corporate practices. As with all companies, the early transcontinental railroads aimed primarily to make profits for their shareholders. They differed from eastern lines only in their methods of producing revenue. With little to haul in the unsettled Great Plains and mountain states, the railroads could not depend on freight. The vast land grants—the Northern Pacific received an area the size of New England in 1870—required considerable effort to convert into cash, and so the lines initially adopted other tactics. They generated income and profit through oversubscription of stock, created dummy corporations to siphon off money, and cut corners in the construction of the lines. These methods proved very profitable and made several large fortunes in the first phase of transcontinental railroad construction. The exposure of some of these fraudulent practices, most notably the Crédit Mobilier scandal, which muddied the Union Pacific as well as dozens of politicians, resulted in the federal government ending land grants to railroads with the Texas and Pacific Act of 1871.[13]

The boom time for railroad construction ended shortly thereafter in 1873 with a national depression. This panic resulted directly from an over-issuance of stock for the Northern Pacific Railway and the subsequent failure of Jay Cooke's banking house. After 1873 surviving transcontinental lines had to rethink operations. Those with land grants, like the Northern Pacific, focused on selling real estate. Railroads founded after 1871, however, received no public domain and needed to find new and different methods of generating revenue.[14]

James Jerome Hill, a young Canadian, inherited these complexities of western transportation. Born in Ontario in 1838, Hill moved to the United States in 1856. After drifting around the East for a few months, he settled in St. Paul, Minnesota Territory. St. Paul, a small entrepôt on the Mississippi River, supplied army posts in the region and carted furs to market. Arriving in this growing center, Hill started work as a shipping clerk on the Mississippi levee. He accumulated knowledge and capital, which he used to invest in a variety of enterprises from coal to furs.[15]

By 1878 Hill had amassed a considerable fortune and was well positioned to benefit from the bankruptcies following the crash of 1873. With other investors, he purchased the St. Paul & Pacific, which possessed land grants in Minnesota and eastern North Dakota. But, when he reorganized the line as the Great Northern Railway in 1889 and pushed westward across the Great Plains, the line received no additional government land.[16]

Bankers, wary of investing money in transportation ventures that had proven so capital intensive, required proof that the Great Northern would pay its way. Consequently, and unlike most other transcontinental lines, the Great Northern had to make profit as a railroad from the start. Thus Hill built a durable line over the flattest available grades and worked hard to promote commerce in both directions. Like the older eastern lines, the Great Northern had to rely on freight to generate much of its revenue.[17]

In the East this strategy had largely relied on extant industries. Lacking established economic resources, Hill and his line had to adopt more diverse tactics. The corporation had to develop an economic infrastructure throughout its territory from which it could profit. Given the geographical location of the railroad, Hill assumed that this base would be mainly agricultural, with hopefully some industry in the form of mining and lumbering. The Great Northern, therefore, developed a program to settle the land and promote types of agriculture that would result in maximum railroad use. The marginal quality of much of the land in the northern tier exacerbated this challenge, with the environment shaping, and often contesting, the direction of development intended by Hill and the Great Northern.

The environment was pivotal to agricultural success, just as it was to most early western economic development. Most of the major western industries were extractive, taking their profits directly from the land. Agriculture, although not directly extractive, was equally dependent on the environment, flourishing best on fertile soil with a temperate climate and a sufficiency of rainfall. Unfortunately, by the late nineteenth century, the area left for agricultural development was the Great Plains. The plains provided few of the essentials for agriculture, except good soil (in places). The climate swung between harsh extremes, and the annual rainfall classified the area as semi-arid. Despite these realities, both the Great Northern Railway and other institutions at work on the plains, such as the federal government, saw the area as best suited to farming.

The reasons for promoting farming on the plains were only partly pragmatic. Most of the justification was grounded in cultural assumptions of the day. Without extensive mineral deposits or trees, agriculture looked like the best economic bet for development. The assumption was that development, any development, was necessary; that the plains were worthless unless they generated income. Therefore, the Great Northern's interest in agriculture related directly to profit, a fact that the first general manager of the line, James Hill, never hid: "I know that in the first instance my great interest in the agricultural growth of the Northwest was purely selfish. If the farmer was not prosperous, we were poor." This symbiotic relationship embroiled him, and the railroad, in agricultural development and education throughout his career.[18]

While agriculture seemed like the only possible alternative, it also fit nicely into the ideological vision of most Americans. The rapid industrialization and urbanization of America had precipitated a cultural crisis in the late nineteenth century. Relieved of the distractions of the Civil War and Reconstruction, many middle-class Americans increasingly turned their attention to the causes of the apparent moral decay evident in their cities. Many discovered a nation that had moved far from the agrarian vision of the founding fathers and toward a decadence approximating that of the Old World. The solution was seen, almost universally, in a return to older, rural values; a shoring-up of modern America through strengthening its democratic foundation: the Jeffersonian yeoman. Although reformers agreed on the aim, the means provided occasion for considerable debate.[19]

This crisis spawned a number of reform movements. From the rural radicalism of the Populists to the patronizing moderation of the Country Life Movement, these culminated in the early twentieth century with the birth of Progressivism. Each group of reformers sought to preserve the ideals seen as embodied in the American farmer and farming life, using a variety of methods. Initially, the reformers tried to revitalize the lives and economies of rural people. Over time, however, the reformers altered their focus to cleansing the cities and translating the traits of the Jeffersonian yeoman to the urban environment. The nation finally adopted a Progressive rather than reactionary response to the problem of moral decay in America, finding ways to revitalize democracy that incorporated the changes brought about by industrialization and urbanization. Despite this, for a period of about twenty years, the problems of rural America moved to center stage, and, in their solution, reformers sought the salvation of the nation.[20]

The paradox confronting reformers was the continued flight of rural dwellers to the cities. Farmers and reformers alike wanted to maintain a rural population in order to uphold a Jeffersonian base of yeomen. They firmly believed that this would sustain vital democratic traditions and provide an uplifting example for urban America, yet demographic trends continually undermined their plans. Hence, the reformers tried to stem this rural exodus by improving life on family farms, economically, socially, and materially, thereby making it more attractive and stable.[21]

By promoting the development of an agricultural economy for the Great

Plains, James J. Hill and the Great Northern Railway thus planned to simultaneously generate income and save the nation. At the time, few people foresaw any obstacles to this goal, even in the environmental characteristics of the region. The late nineteenth century was a time of great optimism concerning human abilities. One aspect of the burgeoning Progressivism of the time was the confidence that all things could be controlled and understood through scientific study and the rational application of knowledge. Thus, while the plains might not naturally provide an environment conducive to agriculture, one could, and would, be engineered. A synchronicity of time and space, therefore, led the Great Northern Railway to attempt to develop the Great Plains agriculturally.

So far, the story of the Great Northern Railway and western development conforms to historiographical traditions, with the corporation's needs driving economic change. Although profit to the company remained primary throughout, the influence of individuals cannot be discounted. James J. Hill, the leader of the company, had considerable personal influence over the stance of the corporation. Rarely acting against the Great Northern's interests, Hill still managed to leave a distinct personal imprint on the railroad's promotional endeavors from the 1880s until his death in 1916. Equally so, the farmers that the corporation was trying to reach, although largely anonymous, were individuals whose decisions profoundly affected the success of the railroad's program.

Hill adopted a number of techniques intended to influence farmer activity on the plains. Working personally and through the railroad corporation, he financed research and demonstration programs, affiliated his energies with other organizations that he perceived as moving in the right direction, and lobbied for appropriate action on the part of state and federal governments.

Part of his approach to the intricacies of educating farmers involved consciously distancing himself from the usual portrayal of agricultural educators. The late-nineteenth-century trend toward specialization and expertise had resulted in a variety of groups laying claim to the title of agricultural expert. Sociologists, college professors, scientists, federal officials, and businessmen contested the nature of agricultural expertise and, by implication, the right to chart the future of American agriculture. Farmers clearly wanted to benefit from the scientific and educational advances of their day and supported the right of their profession to academic standardization. They resented, however, the attempted usurpation of their expertise by university scientists and others. Hill wanted to avoid appearing as a patronizing conveyor of elitist knowledge and, consequently, sidled up to farmers as a peer rather than a superior. He created an image of himself as sympathetic to his identified audience by stressing his background as a western pioneer and his current status as farm owner. He solidified his authority by stressing his business success and the links between the railroad and agriculture.[22]

Hill plunged into this struggle for agricultural dominance through corporate necessity and developed his own conception of farming expertise. He concurred with the Progressive belief that agriculture needed to be more scientific and businesslike, and he supported the need for experts to establish fundamental agrarian principles. At the same time, as a self-made man, he believed that expertise could be established through means other than formal education. Thus, he viewed himself as an agricultural expert because of his practical experience and business acumen.

The conflict over agricultural expertise was decided largely during Hill's life. By 1916 university experts had clearly gained ascendancy. Farmer deference to this group had been forged sporadically and regionally, based on a wide number of variables that included personalities, location, and economics. Although pockets of resistance remained, it was generally, if begrudgingly, acknowledged that academics would dictate the future of American agriculture. In refusing to concede defeat, Hill was, by the time of his death, an anachronism, succoring his claim to expertise with outmoded principles.

In discussing the agricultural development of the northern Great Plains, therefore, many factors must be considered. Obviously, corporations such as the Great Northern were vital. They brought capital into the region and, in the case of railroads, provided necessary transportation of goods to and from markets. In these corporations, individuals sometimes exercised a dominant influence, whether resulting from powerful personalities, majority shareholding, or, in James Hill's case, both. In addition to corporations, other organizations had an interest in the farming future of the plains. State governments wished to increase their state's populations and economies by any means available and were certainly attuned to the possibility of a densely settled hinterland. The federal government still paid homage to Jefferson's yeomen and saw the plains, through utilization of the Homestead Act, as the obvious location to promote this democratic and societal reinvigoration. The new state universities were sometimes a tool of, and sometimes independent of, both state and federal governments. These institutions tried to please all their paymasters (which on occasion included the Great Northern), but administrators were also concerned about their institutions' reputations and upholding Progressive notions of trained expertise. The farmers also had considerable influence on the outcome of any development scheme. Wanting to maintain their own autonomy while simultaneously maximizing their profits, these people represented a fickle, complex, and ill-defined force in plains development. Finally, the environment played a crucial, and largely unacknowledged, role in all the agricultural schemes. All the optimism and greed of human participants ultimately depended on the environmental feasibility of their projects. Despite their Progressive assertions, their power to alter environmental realities was decidedly limited.

2 / Trial and Error, 1878–1893

From its inception as the St. Paul & Pacific Railroad, the corporation that would become the Great Northern Railway focused on the environmental possibilities of the line's hinterland, trying to shape western development in the most advantageous way. (See Table 2.1 for a timeline of the Great Northern.) In 1878 entrepreneur James Jerome Hill, fur trader Norman Kittson, and financiers George Stephen, Donald Smith, and John S. Kennedy bought the St. Paul & Pacific, a bankrupt road joining the Mississippi River with the Red River of the North, running from south of Breckenridge, Minnesota, to Winnipeg. They initially conceptualized the project as a local line connecting St. Paul with Winnipeg through the Red River Valley, foreseeing their profits coming from two sources: the sale of the road's land grants and the haulage of valley products. The first priority after purchase, from the perspective of the investors, was to save the line's state land grants, which totaled upwards of 850,000 acres, from forfeiture. To do this, the buyers contracted with the Minnesota state legislature to complete the St. Vincent Extension to the Canadian border by the end of 1878 or lose the land. With Hill acting as general manager, they successfully met this challenge.[1]

The other way to profit from railroad ownership was by hauling goods, and here the timing and location of the purchase of the St. Paul & Pacific proved auspicious. The Red River Valley in the late 1870s was a flourishing grain basket. The valley floor had been formed by the vast, post-ice-age Lake Agassiz, which had increased in size as glaciers retreated northwards, finally spilling into Hudson Bay. As the lake drained, it left two smaller lakes, Manitoba and Winnipeg, with the Red River flowing north into the latter. The current valley extends about 325 miles north to south between its source

TABLE 2.1. Significant Railroad Dates

1878	Purchase of the St. Paul & Pacific Railroad by James J. Hill, Norman Kittson, George Stephen, Donald Smith, and John S. Kennedy.
1879	Creation of the St. Paul, Minneapolis & Manitoba Railroad, which incorporated the St. Paul & Pacific Railroad. James J. Hill assumed position of general manager.
1889	Formation of the Great Northern Railway. James J. Hill named as president.
1890	999-year lease of St. Paul, Minneapolis & Manitoba Railroad by Great Northern Railway.
1893	Great Northern Railway reaches Puget Sound.
1896	Permanent alliance of Great Northern Railway and Northern Pacific Railway.
1901	Creation of holding company, Northern Securities, including three-fourths of Great Northern Railway stock and nearly all of the stock of the Northern Pacific Railway.
1902	Suit filed against Northern Securities by Attorney General Philander Knox.
1904	Northern Securities Company disbanded by the Supreme Court, although roads remain linked through stock ownership and known collectively as Hill Lines.
1907	James J. Hill becomes first chairman of the board of Great Northern Railway. His son Louis Hill assumes presidency.
1912	James J. Hill retires from Great Northern Railway. Louis Hill becomes chairman of the board, and Carl R. Gray is named president.

in Lake Traverse, currently in southwestern Minnesota, and Lake Winnipeg, and is 75 miles across at its widest. The soil is fertile, glacial till overlain with a porous mixture of clay, sand, and gravel, which provides an easily drained subsoil. Flowing through the old lakebed, the river meanders over a wide flood plain, distributing its load of rich alluvium in between gravel ridges formed by the beaches of the old lake. The land was perfect for agricultural development: flat, treeless, and stoneless, awaiting only a sedentary population and transportation links to markets.[2]

Immigrants to the Selkirk settlement, located at present-day Winnipeg, had grown wheat in the valley as early as 1820, but without a large local market or transportation to reach more distant centers, agrarian development stalled. Consequently, the valley's early economic development centered on the fur trade, as Red River oxcarts, steamboats, and finally railroads moved pelts down the river to St. Paul. By the 1850s the British Hudson's Bay Company shipped furs out of the hinterland via St. Paul, which became the second largest fur market in the United States after St. Louis. Hill entered this trade in 1860 as a young freight agent working with the well-established fur trader, Norman Kittson. In the early 1870s they extended their involvement through a monopoly of steamboats on the Red River.[3]

A financial disaster dramatically ended the dominance of furs in the economy of the Red River Valley. In 1873 the overextended Northern Pacific Railroad went into receivership, bringing down the banking empire of Jay Cooke and precipitating a national panic. James Buell Power, the general agent of the land department of the Northern Pacific, believed that the only way to salvage the line was to sell off parts of its enormous land grant. Therefore, to maximize the sale price of the land, Northern Pacific personnel had to demonstrate the land's fertility and potential. In 1874 Power convinced George W. Cass, the Northern Pacific's president, to personally purchase 13,440 acres in the Red River Valley and turn it into a model wheat farm for advertising and promotion. In addition, many Northern Pacific bondholders took advantage of their right to exchange their now worthless securities for large acreages of railroad land. Power did his best to ensure that those who obtained land, at least lots adjacent to the railway, had some intention of working it. Most buyers were organized speculators who pooled their resources to secure large acreages and hire the men necessary to farm them. Thus, what became known as the Panic of 1873 resulted in corporate manipulation of western development, as the Northern Pacific found ways to make the land profitable in order to sell it.[4]

These so-called bonanza farms, or agribusinesses, created by financiers and speculators, were capital intensive. They utilized newly introduced farm machinery such as double gang-plows and steam-powered engines, both of which could be fully profitable only operating in economies of scale. The Red River Valley, with its flat, uninterrupted landscape, offered a perfect environment for these machines, encouraging farming on an enormous scale. Bonanza farms varied in size from 1,000 to 61,000 acres, with large individual fields averaging one section or 640 acres. On these farms, usually run by managers, huge labor forces raised enormous crops of wheat. One farm, for example, employed a crew of one thousand in 1884 to produce a total yield of 600,000 bushels of wheat.[5]

Along with the establishment of bonanza farms by speculators and corporations, the general prosperity engendered by the wheat boom in the Red River Valley attracted small-scale farmers to the region. During the 1880s the amount of land homesteaded in Dakota Territory increased from 2.25 million acres to a peak of 11 million acres in 1884. At the same time migration to the Red River Valley increased dramatically, with some counties more than doubling their population between 1880 and 1885. By 1890 North Dakota had 27,611 farms of which only 389 were over 1,000 acres in extent. Thus, whilst the majority of land in the valley was owned by large-scale operators, most of the farmers in the area were smallholders who, nevertheless, hoped to profit from commercial agriculture.[6]

Power's scheme to rescue the Northern Pacific Railroad through the promotion of specific land use worked. The convergence of the fertile plains of the river valley, development of large-scale farm machinery, new milling processes that made Minneapolis the milling capital of the nation, a high European demand for American wheat, and improved transportation resulted in a massive land boom. Land sales in the valley skyrocketed. The resulting influx of capital refloated the Northern Pacific, track construction resumed, and the line reached the West Coast by 1883.[7]

The smaller St. Paul & Pacific Railroad also profited from this land boom. In May 1879 the "Associates" formed a new corporation, the St. Paul, Minneapolis & Manitoba Railroad. The St. Paul & Pacific provided the basis for this new company, which also included other smaller railroads, some of which had been purchased at a foreclosure sale. The new line sold nearly 180,000 acres of the original St. Paul & Pacific land grant by mid-1879. James Hill, as general manager of the line, paid particular interest to settling the land, wanting to attract farmers rather than speculators. He was helped by James Power's experience when he came to work for the St. Paul, Minneapolis & Manitoba in 1881.[8]

The bonanza farm boom, engineered by the Northern Pacific Railroad, thus indirectly benefited the rival St. Paul, Minneapolis & Manitoba through land sales. In addition, the latter corporation determined to maximize the railroad's share of the haulage of wheat to the Minneapolis mills. To do this, Hill focused on interlacing the Red River Valley with branch lines. The Northern Pacific management had viewed the valley as a temporary source of revenue through land sales, while their overall strategic focus was the completion of their transcontinental connection. St. Paul, Minneapolis & Manitoba personnel, on the other hand, viewed the valley as vital in the

MAP 1. Rail routes in Minnesota

development of what historian Russell Kirby calls a "city-hinterland sym-biosis." The corporation aimed to establish permanent economic bonds with the valley and its communities, which would provide a solid foundation for further expansion. Hill's railroad, in other words, became a vital economic and cultural link in a broader national process of industrial revolution that bonded country to city in an ever more intimate relationship.[9]

The St. Paul, Minneapolis & Manitoba Railroad succeeded in establishing branch lines throughout the valley to maximize haulage. By the early 1880s the Red River Valley alone generated more traffic for the road than the original St. Paul-Winnipeg connection. In the crop year 1878–79 the railroad handled just over two million bushels of wheat from the valley; within less than a decade, wheat shipments had increased to over thirty-seven million bushels. This rate of haulage acted as collateral for the subsequent financial backing the St. Paul, Minneapolis & Manitoba received in order to push its tracks further west.[10]

The dependence of the corporation on income generated in the Red River Valley remained high, even as the line moved west. Determined to expand their railroad enterprises, Hill and his colleagues created the Great Northern Railway in 1889, and in January 1890 the new corporation established a 999-year lease on all properties of the St. Paul, Minneapolis, & Manitoba Railroad. Despite loans obtained from New York financiers and Dutch investors, the Great Northern focused on maintaining and increasing the income-producing capacity of existing lines to help finance the push to Seattle. Without any further land grants, the only way that the Great Northern could make money was through haulage. Consequently, the corporation and its first president, James J. Hill, continued to try and mold the economy of the line's hinterland in a way most profitable to the railroad. Given the ecology of the Red River Valley, this economy would necessarily be agricultural. So, from the beginning, Hill found himself enmeshed in agricultural concerns, recognizing the symbiotic relationship between successful development and the prosperity of the Great Northern Railway. His interest in farming improvements continued until his death in 1916 and always remained linked to the economic needs of the railroad that he had created.[11]

Despite the profits that the corporation gained from the bonanza boom, Hill believed that large corporate farms did not utilize the environment of the valley in a way most beneficial to the railroad. American railroads had traditionally produced the most income when operating in densely settled regions. Extensive land grants and company bankruptcies testified to the problems of financing railroad construction in the sparsely settled West. Consequently, for security, most railmen wanted to create networks similar to those in the East, but this usually meant heavy investment in settlement promotion and town building.[12]

Hill, on behalf of the Great Northern, thus fought against the agricultural tendency toward large, capital-intensive, single-crop farms, although they reflected the national trend toward industrial consolidation and corporate growth in which he was a leader. Instead he promoted the more traditional, diversified, small-scale, commercial family farm, run by the same yeoman farmer lauded by Thomas Jefferson in the eighteenth century. The company sent immigration agents to Europe, targeting British and Scandinavian immigrants, and arranged for editors of foreign language newspapers to tour the valley. Subscribing to the Social Darwinism of the age, Hill hoped that these "superior" peoples would be able to replicate the dense, rural settlements of their homelands.[13]

Hill was not alone in this preferred mode of agricultural development, joining many contemporary agricultural experts, academic and otherwise, in America as well as Canada. Settlers, politicians, agricultural scientists, and businessmen wanted the plains states to emulate the small, diversified farms of eastern America and Europe, which would hopefully allow them to achieve a similar prosperity. Thus, in the years leading to 1891, in which Hill completed what he saw as his "Great Adventure," running the line to Puget Sound, his agricultural focus remained the Red River Valley, where he tried to establish a land use pattern that would provide his railroad with a large, secure, and stable income.[14]

In the early years of his involvement in railroading, Hill tried to promote diversified and scientific agriculture through his own personal endeavors. He consistently aimed at greater profits for the railroad corporation through increased haulage, which would benefit him as an employee and shareholder. After the formation of the Great Northern Railway Company in 1889, Hill ceased to draw a salary and instead earned income only from his shares in the line, which made increasing corporate revenue a more pressing concern. To augment haulage through farming diversification, Hill launched a number of projects, ranging from developing his image as a farmer to funding a farming newspaper and giving away cattle. He financed most of these early schemes from his personal funds. Hill thus merged the private and the corporate, using one to benefit the other. The use of private funds did limit his financial involvement. Although interested in promoting diversified agriculture, Hill was unprepared to invest a large percentage of his personal fortune, spending far less money in these years on his agricultural projects than on his private art collection.[15]

Hill always acknowledged that his interest in agriculture stemmed from the needs of his corporation, but his promotion of small, diversified family farms also resonated with his own personal history. Although impossible to separate the two, it is clear that his land use advocacy on behalf of the Great Northern reflected both a reasoned understanding of how to maximize railroad profits and a highly personalized belief in the optimum human environment. Thus, his ultimate rejection of bonanza farming as an effective permanent land use of the Red River Valley resulted from the needs of the railroad tempered by his own distrust of monocrop agriculture. He thought that a single crop, as exemplified in the wheat-dependent bonanza farms, would prove too vulnerable to climatic and economic vicissitudes. This belief partially reflected his Canadian origin. In the late 1850s Ontario farmers suffered from the wheat midge and winter desiccation of fall wheat. In response they began to diversify by supplying animal products for the expanding urban market. Hill, who had witnessed this transition to an apparently more sustainable, profitable agricultural system, became committed to the advantage of diversified agriculture over monocropping.[16]

To realize his ideal economy of dense, diversified rural settlement, Hill first needed to establish himself as an agricultural expert so his opinions would carry weight. Rejecting the Progressive current, which identified expertise only after formal education, he tried to forge an identity for himself as a traditional gentleman farmer. He also needed to devise effective means of disseminating his ideas to the farming community along his railroad. Hence, from an early period, his transportation network was also an agricultural information network that aimed to control the development of the West in a way most financially beneficial to itself.

Hill's struggles to create an agricultural identity revealed an inherent culturally conservative streak, as the gentleman farmer image had long-established, Old World roots. The gentleman farmer was a phenomenon most associated with the agricultural revolution in England. Such farmers, emerging first in the early sixteenth century in southeastern England, tended to hold much more land than they could personally farm, and so they used their capital to employ labor to work the land. Sometimes they acted as foremen, and sometimes they refrained from manual labor altogether. These large-scale farmers sold their surpluses to growing urban markets, thus increasing the capital base of their operations. As various agricultural innovations were introduced in England during the seventeenth and eighteenth centuries, gentlemen farmers had the money to implement these new methods, and they stood to profit most from those that favored economies of scale. In many respects these individuals were on the cutting edge of change in their time. The gentlemen farmers had the money and time to invest in agricultural experimentation, and they actively participated in the diffusion of new ideas. This class of farmers disseminated new crops, such as sainfoin and turnips, bred better farm animals, and introduced technologies such as floating water meadows. The gentleman farmer then crossed the Atlantic with the early colonists, becoming first established in the southern colonies, where capital-intensive, commercial agriculture quickly emerged as the dominant economy.[17]

In the late eighteenth century the concept of agricultural development dovetailed, too, with the messages of the Enlightenment. Faith in man's reason and in his ability to observe and understand the world about him set a good ideological stage for rich southern farmers to experiment and improve their operations. Farmers such as Thomas Jefferson and Edmund Ruffin imported stock from Europe, tested soils and fertilizers, and experimented with different crop rotations. They also founded agricultural societies and newspapers and sponsored private research. They were confident that their research would ultimately benefit their people and nation. This progressive ideology, ability to finance experiments and improvements, and unquestioning immersion in commercial agriculture distinguished the gentleman farmer in early America. Equally important, the gentleman farmer gained the majority of his income from his land.[18]

The gentleman farmer concept had also taken root in Canada, Hill's native land. During Hill's lifetime prominent Ontario farmers, such as Charles Arnold and William Saunders, not only established reputations for their practical experiments but also helped Ontario's provincial government create its agricultural policy. Yet, unlike earlier English and American gentlemen farmers, some of these men did not earn their primary living from farming.[19]

Impressed as much by their social stature as their economic success, Hill followed these early models to establish his credentials as a practical and experimental farmer. Hill had been closely connected to farms all his life, having been born on one in Ontario. Once in Minnesota, he and his family rented a farm for a few years in the 1870s. In 1880 Hill bought his first farm, Hillier, on Lake Minnetonka. The next year he purchased Humboldt in the Red River Valley, and in 1883 he started acquiring the land north of St. Paul that would become North Oaks. Some of these farms supplied Hill's family with supplies while acting as country estates, an important part of the gentleman farmer image, although his farms, with the exception of

Humboldt, never supplied a substantial percentage of his income. At Hillier and North Oaks, Hill experimented with stock raising and breeding, and from North Oaks he developed ties with other like-minded breeders and farmers throughout the nation.[20]

The Humboldt farm, initially at least, had little to do with image creation and much to do with personal profit. Hill, determined to benefit from the bonanza farming boom, bought land from the St. Paul & Pacific grant at a price considerably under cost, therefore profiting from his corporate position. Managers ran Hill's land using techniques common on the huge bonanza farms, although, with only about three thousand acres in cultivation, the farm was considerably smaller than most. Toward the end of his life, Hill changed how this acreage was used, trying to establish a cattle raising station, but initially Humboldt provided personal profits and the assurance to potential settlers that the general manager of the line was willing to invest in the area.[21]

The farms around St. Paul, however, represented Hill's first forays into agricultural experimentation. At Hillier, west of Minneapolis, Hill launched a traditional gentleman farmer program. Given his concerns about monocropping in the Red River Valley and his advocacy of diversification, he inclined toward stockbreeding. In 1882 Hill bought two carloads of "fancy breeding cattle and sheep" from Scotland and experimented crossing Angus heifers with Shorthorn bulls. He exhibited the resulting breeds at fairs throughout the region. Thus, as a gentleman farmer, Hill tried to establish stock bred from pure lines, where the bulls would provide quality beef and the cows a large quantity of good milk. Hill believed that improved production would make diversification more attractive to the region's farmers by increasing profitability. This program later dominated much of the work at the North Oaks and Humboldt farms. Ultimately Hill aimed at increasing the number and improving the quality of cattle (with a lesser emphasis on sheep and hogs) along his line, therefore maximizing revenue for both the farmers and the railroad.[22]

Hillier failed to serve Hill's purpose for very long. He soon recognized that the scope of his agricultural interests could not be accommodated on 160 acres. Therefore, in 1883 Hill purchased North Oaks. The new farm, ten miles north of St. Paul, proved "commodious," being three thousand acres, which Hill increased to five thousand within a few years. The establishment of North Oaks dramatically halted plans for the Hillier farm. The livestock moved to North Oaks in September of 1883, and Hillier was rented out.[23]

North Oaks was more of a multipurpose farm than Hill's other rural prop-erties, its closeness to St. Paul allowing the family to use it as a second res-idence, but its primary function was still agricultural. From 1883 to 1893 it operated as a stock farm and as a base for Hill's search for the perfect dual-purpose cow. Hill's initial approach to this problem continued his earlier work at Hillier. He tried to develop beef cattle with good dairy qualities. Overall he favored Scottish Shorthorn and Angus beef cattle, breeding them to try to increase their milk yield. He believed he was successful and wrote in 1885 of beef cattle producing "from 26 to 28 quarts a day from grass for six months at a time."[24]

To start a herd with the best bloodlines available, Hill imported addi-tional purebred cattle from Great Britain. In 1886 he shipped six Shorthorn cattle and thirty-five Polled Angus over from Liverpool. Perhaps because of his Canadian connections, he chose to bring the stock in through Canada rather than New York. The cattle spent the winter in quarantine in Quebec because of cases of pleuro-pneumonia in the herd and did not reach the farm until May 1887.[25]

Hill also wanted to determine the optimum feed for maximized livestock production. Feeding experiments started in the early years at North Oaks. In 1886 Hill wrote to the editor of the *Farmers Advocate and Northwestern Stockman* that a combination of turnips, beets, cabbages, hay, and oilcake provided better winter feed than corn. Two years later the *National Livestock Journal* discussed Hill's use of root vegetables, clover, and corn as feed.[26]

This use of root crops for forage had its basis in England, as Hill acknowl-edged in his letter, and had come to him by way of Canada. Ontario farm-ers regularly grew a sizable amount of root crops for fodder, dominantly mangel-wurzels (related to rutabagas) and turnips. Indeed, the total acreage of Ontario farmland invested in root crops in 1895 represented 20 percent of the land planted in wheat. In contrast, North Dakota's root crop in 1896 only represented 0.02 percent of its wheat acreage. Hill ordered seed for rutabagas and turnips from Toronto, trying to grow plants that had adapted to a harsher environment.[27]

Hill's farming interest at this time was not just limited to cattle. The North Oaks letterhead from 1887 listed Hill as an "Importer and Breeder of Short-Horn, Aberdeen-Angus and Jersey Cattle; Cleveland Bay Horses Shropshire and Highland Black-faced Sheep. Cob Ponies; Berkshire Swine." He bred purebred pigs, buying "Pilot," a prizewinning Berkshire boar, from a farmer in Edmonton in December 1887, and he sold many purebred Berkshire pairs throughout this period at ten dollars per pair. In 1888 his interest turned to poultry, and he acquired some Mammoth Bronze turkeys, some Black Cochin cockerels, and some Plymouth Rock cockerels. He also had various breeds of sheep and horses. The work at North Oaks involved a significant financial turnover. In 1888 Hill's income from the farm was $30,673.66, which was offset by expenses totaling $32,614.78. These sums, however, were paltry for Hill, who, three years later, spent $123,500 on paintings for his new art gallery.[28]

Most people interested in improving American agriculture agreed that maintaining blooded stock was more productive than raising native cattle, but many farmers simply could not afford to buy purebred cattle. Hill and other agricultural educators countered that buying purebred stock was, in fact, cheaper than raising scrubs (native, unblooded cattle) because it maximized livestock profits. Hill backed his assertions with hard figures. "An animal weighing 1600 or 1800 pounds, worth 6c a pound can be raised for less money than one weighing 1300 pounds that will sell for 4 1/2c per pound." The problem for small-scale farmers was not that they disbelieved or even disagreed with Hill's thinking and numbers, but simply that they lacked the upfront capital to invest in purebred stock.[29]

Although Hill's contention that raising purebred stock was more profitable that raising scrubs reflected the beliefs of late-nineteenth-century science, he strayed from mainstream, contemporary wisdom by stressing dual-purpose cattle as a supplement to grain income. He believed in the possibility of crossbreeding cattle to create an optimal strain whereby the cows would give large quantities of quality milk and the steers would yield high-grade beef. This would obviate two problems in the Red River Valley. First, although raising beef cattle on the plains had proved immensely profitable to some investors, quality stock was usually too expensive for a small-scale, commercial farmer or homesteader. Second, attempts to introduce dairy herds in the northern tier of the plains states had been largely unsuccessful for a number of reasons, including the vulnerability of dairy cattle to extreme cold. Dual-purpose cattle were cheaper than blooded beef stock and hardier than most available dairy breeds, thus offering both an adaptation to the economic potential of the type of farmers Hill was seeking to attract and a biological adaptation to climate conditions.

Although diverging from mainstream scientific opinion in his support of dual-purpose cattle, Hill was not operating in complete isolation. Most university scientists rarely advocated dual-purpose cattle, favoring instead either a dairy or a beef focus, but scrub cattle usually provided both subsistence milk and meat for farm families. Consequently, a strong minority of agricultural experts, including some at universities, showed interest in dual-purpose stock because of its strategic importance to smallholders. The recovery of Ontario's agriculture that Hill had witnessed in the 1860s and 1870s, pivoting as it did on diversification, must have been another important influence on some researchers. With their emphasis on mixed farming, Canadian farmers had found most success in using dual-purpose cattle.[30]

Diversification through dual-purpose cattle represented one of the first identifiable components of Hill's agricultural philosophy, and all his later university friends would espouse it as well. Professor Thomas Shaw, a fellow Canadian, head of animal husbandry at the University of Minnesota and later an agricultural expert for the Great Northern and Northern Pacific, advocated dual-purpose cattle. His successor at the university, Andrew Boss, another of Hill's friends, experimented with dual-purpose herds as late as 1930.[31]

Dual-purpose cattle had a pragmatic appeal for subsistence and other less affluent farmers. These animals required less time and labor than blooded stock, were cheaper, and involved less risk than launching a full-blown dairy or beef operation. Support for dual-purpose cattle continued long after Hill's death. During the Great Depression, when farmers struggled for financial security but had little capital to invest, the University of Minnesota's Agricultural Experiment Station produced a bulletin evaluating the variables involved in raising beef cattle and dual-purpose cattle. The authors concluded that a dual-purpose herd involved "less risk than a beef herd," with less initial investment, less skill to maintain, and marketing options for both milk and beef. However, such herds "do not offer possibilities of as large profits as may be obtained with either a beef or a dairy herd" as they produced less milk and lower-quality beef.[32]

Ultimately the difference lay in the class of farmer the scientist aimed to serve. The proponents of dairy and beef cattle, such as Theophilus Haecker at the University of Minnesota, boosted agricultural specialization, seeing a single agricultural focus as the ultimate method of maximizing a farm's profit potential. As these men promoted monocultural farming, they favored cattle bred for one specific purpose rather than generic, all-purpose animals. Like many agricultural scientists, Haecker's research and advice was geared toward the richer landowners of the region, the ones who could mobilize considerable political and financial support for the universities. Agricultural specialization, however, was beyond the financial reach of most of the families attempting to settle the plains. These smallholders and their advocates, men like Andrew Boss, pragmatically supported advancement of cheaper, multi-use stock. Boss argued that dual-purpose stock presented the most efficient and profitable solution to farmers when seen in the context of a diversified agriculture. As these smallholders constituted a majority of farmers along the Great Northern line, they were of vital importance to the corporation, and their potential success held out the possibilities for high levels of railroad haulage. James Hill was thus more interested in types of agriculture that would profit this group. He advocated the use of livestock in a program of diversification intended to appeal primarily to smallholders, farmers with little available capital. Having witnessed the success of diversification in restoring agricultural productivity in Ontario, Hill argued that the forage available in Minnesota would produce a "beef and dairy yield equal in value to the entire wheat crop of the state."[33]

Disagreement over dual-purpose cattle represented part of a larger argument concerning the role of science in agriculture and agricultural education. In the late nineteenth century scientists professionalized, using tertiary educational credentials to maintain their dominance. Most small-scale farmers met this elitism with disdain, believing that agricultural research was fundamentally based in practical skills. The conflict often focused on the work of the agricultural experiment stations, where opposition from farmers and politicians often stymied attempts to conduct "pure" research. The same antagonism existed among the stations' faculty, as formally uneducated farm boys reached professorial positions and clashed with trained professionals. The former tended to stress practical research and educational outreach; the latter emphasized modes of ideal production, irrespective of cost, and resented the demands of farmers on their time.[34]

These problems of research and education in agricultural science developed during Hill's career and would influence many of his decisions. In general, he sided with the old-school farmers, researchers, and teachers, whose methods were consistent with the gentleman farmer model, but who targeted the yeoman farmer. Hill's alliance was evident in his continual promotion of dual-purpose cattle, his desire to establish small-scale diversified farms, and his advocating practical farmer education through demonstration farms.

During the 1880s, Hill therefore involved himself actively in the business of farming to gain the knowledge necessary to qualify as a farmer and so place himself in a position to influence the economic development of the Great Northern's hinterland. He dealt with much of the agricultural correspondence for his farms himself. He ordered supplies, paid farm bills, established retail arrangements, and hired staff. For this acquired knowledge to operate as an effective educational tool, however, he needed to turn it into a reputation.[35]

With the purchase of good quality stock, involvement in agricultural shows, breeding and feeding experiments, and correspondence with other breeders and the agricultural press, Hill used methods he had seen in Canada to establish himself as an agricultural expert. North Oaks gained a reputation for quality stock among other breeders. Hill had large annual sales that were featured in all the major stock magazines. Hill's status as a gentleman farmer was also acknowledged through competition. From 1885 onward, Hill entered animals in the Fat Stock Show in Chicago and consistently walked away with prizes. Thus Hill did manage to acquire a regional reputation for breeding quality stock. From the perspective of the corporation, however, this reputation was useless, as it resonated only among extant stockbreeders who had, unlike the majority of farmers, the financial ability to sustain their convictions.[36]

Hill's agricultural influence extended to other groups interested in agricultural development as well. An active member of the Minnesota State Agricultural Society, he donated money, built railroad tracks to its fairgrounds, and gave regular public addresses. He viewed the society and its fair as vehicles for buttressing his credentials and extending his influence over area farmers. He exhibited his cattle at the state fair starting in 1886, although he refused to compete. He wanted his stock to inspire other farmers by its excellence rather than win prizes. By this point, many members of the society acknowledged his expertise, and Hill received eleven votes for president of the organization in the annual election, even though he was not on the ballot.[37]

By the late 1880s, Hill had established a reputation as an expert among a group of rich farmers, businessmen, and agricultural scientists in the Midwest. He achieved this by developing his farms into model, scientifically run, diversified establishments and by publicizing his accomplishments. However, as with his cattle sales, Hill's involvement with the Minnesota State Agricultural Society did little to benefit the Great Northern. Once again, most of the men involved had little influence with respect to agricultural change. Like Hill himself, many of them were businessmen and politicians. Some, like Clarke and Carson N. Cosgrove, maintained herds and demonstrated interest in breeding experiments, moving toward a gentleman farmer role, while others had no agricultural connection at all.[38]

A more important and more difficult goal in spreading Hill's ideas throughout the railroad's territory was determining methods to convey his knowledge to the smallholders and homesteaders along the line, convincing them of his expertise and qualifications. Hill needed to find ways to convert his reputation into an influential educational tool. Having established himself as an expert among a farming elite who had money to attend stock shows and time to invest in the Minnesota State Agricultural Society, Hill needed different tactics to reach grassroots farmers. He chose to approach them as equals. Unlike many academic experts who, as he put it, "don't know enough to put a crop in the ground or to hoe a row of turnips," Hill offered practical expertise.[39]

Although he publicly supported universities, Hill aligned himself with the farmers. In speeches promoting his prime interests—diversification, crop rotation, and soil conservation—he relied on his farming experiences to establish his agricultural authority. He regularly referred to his farms and described himself as "farming by proxy." This helped distinguish him from professors, and thus he avoided being implicated in attacks on effete, book-learnt, agricultural scientists.[40]

Initially Hill approached the matter of farmer education simplistically. Following the traditions of the eighteenth-century gentlemen farmers, he believed that the example of his successes would be sufficient to convince others of the efficacy of his notions. Part of his educational approach during these early years involved leading by example. Hill encouraged local farmers to visit his operation at North Oaks. In addition, he allowed the farm to be used for practical demonstration by the agricultural classes at the university. He also spread his expertise and knowledge through letters to farmers. At this time, Hill still answered much of his agricultural correspondence personally. This involved exchanges with other interested parties about the advantages of different breeds and the exchange and collection of a variety of seeds.[41]

In reality, however, Hill often preached to the converted, and therefore his impact remained highly circumscribed. Farmers who showed interest in visiting North Oaks, agricultural students at the university, and breeders exchanging information represented a group of agriculturists already convinced of the importance of the need for a scientific, or at least quasi-scientific, approach to farming. On the other hand, most farmers in the region lacked the time, money, and inclination to visit a rich man's farm or to correspond with him. These yeomen farmers continued to practice the types of agriculture that seemed most productive to them. In addition, many resented the implied allocation of blame. Hill, like other rural reformers, thought the nation's farming crisis resulted from inefficient farmers. Many farmers countered that the undervaluing of their occupation in American society at large represented the core issue.[42]

Having engineered an agricultural reputation by the 1880s, Hill tried to encourage farmers to diversify their agricultural practices through personal philanthropy. Again, his prime motive was maximizing the haulage potential of his railroad. Hill was not blind to the conditions of the small-scale farmer. He understood the role of money in facilitating change and knew that many farmers lacked the capital necessary to purchase quality cattle to maximize livestock productivity. His initial response to this dilemma was in keeping with the gentleman farmer image. As early as 1883 he contemplated breeding quality animals at North Oaks for annual distribution to poorer farmers. He planned to start small: dispensing only four yearling bulls the first year, offspring of the blooded stock he had just imported.[43]

By the summer of 1884, as he realized that breeding the necessary cattle would be too time-consuming, his philanthropic horizons expanded. Instead, he distributed his prized, imported cattle directly, giving away 143 purebred bulls from 1884 to 1885. The distribution of cattle geographically mirrored his broader corporate agenda. Hill's concern was to improve the general quality of stock throughout the catchment area of his line, and so he gave bulls to farmers along the St. Paul, Minneapolis & Manitoba Railroad in thirty-one counties of Minnesota and North Dakota. Farmers received bulls on the condition that for four years they allow their neighbors access to the bulls' services for a nominal one-dollar charge (which would hopefully cover the cost of keeping and caring for the animal). The animals also had to be cared for according to specific guidelines and, if sick, to receive treatment from a veterinarian chosen by Hill. Thus, when the bull given to P. S. Lay fell ill in November 1885, Hill arranged to have the animal shipped to Grand Forks so his chosen veterinarian could perform surgery.[44]

Hill's generosity in this matter continued through the end of the decade. In 1885 he gave away about a hundred bulls. He had thousands of applications from farmers, and the next year he spent $34,111.11 on the purchase and distribution of bulls. In 1890 Hill assigned the Grand Forks veterinarian, now superintendent of the North Oaks farm, the task of distributing two carloads of Angus and Shorthorn cattle and one carload of Berkshire pigs along the line west of Larrimore, North Dakota. To encourage the use of gift cattle for stud, Hill offered prizes at county fairs for their offspring, as well as for the best grade cattle.[45]

Hill's philanthropy proved considerably less effective than he had hoped, neither benefiting the Great Northern nor diversifying the farm economy of the line's hinterland. Farmers often neglected the donated cattle. They either failed to realize the time and effort necessary to raise quality stock or were not prepared to invest in them. Farmers tried to treat quality stock the same way they had always treated their scrub cattle, maintained for home production. As historian David Danbom contends, although they understood the theoretical benefits of diversification, many northern Great Plains farmers remained primarily interested in grain production. Livestock did not receive necessary attention and time, and farmers did not plant sufficient forage and fodder crops. Inevitably, Hill's cattle failed to thrive or produce profit.[46]

At a time of relatively high grain prices, farmers were loath to turn valuable grainland over to pasture and forage crops. In fact, farmers voiced considerable opposition to Hill's distribution scheme. Many of the farmers chosen to receive the blooded stock donations made the necessary promises and then proceeded to slaughter the bulls for family consumption.[47]

These farmers' unwillingness to invest time, money, and effort into Hill's beef and dairy promotion may well have stemmed from a realistic understanding of the economic and geographical limits of their operations. These limitations caused an insuperable marketing problem for either dairy or beef production. First, unlike states such as Wisconsin and New York, northern Minnesota and North Dakota lacked urban markets for their dairy products. Second, even after the blizzard of 1886–87 that destroyed many herds in the West, farmers aiming to produce cattle would have to contend with a well-established western beef industry. An embittered Hill, talking from a perspective of nearly thirty years, recognized these farmer concerns, although still denying their validity: "They said I was trying to ruin the reputation of the State; that it was not a cattle state. It was not a live stock State; it never would be. It was the home of No. 1 hard wheat and was always going to be the home of No. 1 hard wheat. They . . . condemned me."[48]

Farmers used far more complex criteria when making agricultural decisions than Hill ever acknowledged. Sometimes these decisions coincided with the ideas he advocated. Pigs were a case in point. Along with distributing cattle, Hill gave away hogs on terms similar to those for bulls. From the small-scale farmer's perspective, at least those within the geographical range of Hill's railroad, hogs made far more economic sense than cattle. Unlike cattle, especially dairy, pigs were easy to maintain and required little time, space, or special feed. They also had a quick market turnaround. A shoat was marketable within six to eight months of birth, and they could be transported to market alive. In raising pigs for market, farmers thus avoided the problems with spoilage that so plagued dairy farmers until the advent of refrigerated railcars. Hill came to recognize the relative merits of his distribution programs and continued to give away hogs into the new century. He ceased donations of cattle, however, in 1890.[49]

Another technique Hill adopted in the 1880s that was designed to reach a wider agricultural audience was sponsoring an agricultural newspaper. *The Farmer* started publication in the spring of 1886 under the editorship of one George W. Hill (who had no relation to James J. Hill's family), and it had its base in the Minnesota state fairgrounds in St. Paul. Hill completely financed it, but within a year became concerned about its lack of success. By April 1887 the newspaper had a subscription list of only six thousand farmers throughout the Upper Midwest, yet the paper had cost Hill over $56,000.[50]

Worried that Hill would stop financing the paper, George Hill tried to explain its lack of success. Much of the high cost, he concluded, could be attributed to the one-time expense of starting a new newspaper, including purchasing equipment. He asserted that the low number of subscriptions resulted from class antagonism, saying "It would be useless to deny the deep prejudice existing among a very large section of the farming class against a paper which does not join with them in or rather lead them in the direction of unreasoning antipathy to the other classes of the community and in proving that all their ills are largely the result of their own shortcomings." Unwittingly, perhaps, George Hill had hit upon one of the key reasons that farmers were unwilling to adopt changes proposed by outside reformers: the implication that farmers themselves were to blame for the problems of rural life.[51]

The paper had, over the year of its existence, delimited fundamental schisms within the region's farming community. As George Hill pointed out, the paper had established itself as the "exponent of certain general principles," promoting intensive, diversified farming, conducted on a scientific, or at least a professional, basis. Articles regularly discussed crop rotation and promoted dual-purpose cattle, while reporters visited successful "modern" farms and investigated various stock feeding regimens. The paper's editors also discussed political matters that concerned farmers, providing, for example, detailed coverage on the action taken to prevent pleuropneumonia at state and national levels. As James Hill was one of the leaders in the fight against this disease in Minnesota, these editorials also helped to highlight his understanding of farming and activism on behalf of the rural community.[52]

The Farmer also frequently addressed issues raised by farmer organizations, such as the Patrons of Husbandry and the Farmers' Alliance. The paper was extremely careful not to alienate farmers by dismissing or attacking these organizations. Instead, it rationally discussed the planks of the movements one by one. Of course, *The Farmer* deemed most of the farmers' ideas, especially those relating to railroad regulation, as unnecessary and harmful. It did, however, support the Grange's bid for a separate agricultural college in Minnesota, arguing that the University of Minnesota had failed to provide hands-on, practical farming education, relying too much on theoretical studies. A farm paper launched in 1886 at a time of considerable Grange influence in Minnesota had a doubtful chance of surviving without fully endorsing the farmers' movements, but George Hill's assessment of the lack of success probably had a considerable degree of validity. Additionally, most late-nineteenth-century farmers were traditionally nonliterate in learning techniques and cautious of outside recommendations. As late as 1913 a survey by the University of Minnesota discovered that although 84 percent of rural households took farming journals, only 50 percent read them, and only 43 percent "expressed any confidence in scientific farming methods."[53]

Discouraged, James Hill proposed shutting down the paper in the summer of 1887. The editor protested, claiming that it would be more expensive to close the presses than to keep them going while looking for a buyer. Hill acquiesced, and the paper continued through 1888. In September of that year, the Orange Judd Publishing Company of Chicago took over the paper, moved it to Chicago, and renamed it *The Orange Judd Farmer*. Orange Judd had been a successful agricultural editor for several decades when he became involved with James Hill. At the helm of *The American Agriculturist*, Judd had been one of the first writers to convert scientific jargon into a readable style, thus making the work of agricultural scientists accessible to literate farmers. Hit hard by the depression of 1873, his paper failed in 1879. He moved to Chicago and wrote for *The Prairie Farmer* before buying *The Farmer*.[54]

Despite Judd's takeover, James Hill remained financially involved in the paper, although he lost his interest in the weekly's content. Because he had entirely floated *The Farmer*, the paper owed him outstanding bills for advertising and subscription, and the collection process proved long, convoluted, and largely fruitless. Consequently, as late as February 1891, Judd still owed James Hill $15,000. By the spring of 1891, all correspondence between the Orange Judd Publishing Company and Great Northern officials had ceased, and it never resumed.[55]

Hill also attempted to reach a wider audience of yeomen farmers, at least in the Red River Valley, through the St. Paul, Minneapolis & Manitoba Railroad's drainage schemes. This project, financed by the corporation rather than by Hill himself, had multiple goals. In the short term it aimed to improve the railroad's lands and maximize sale prices. Over the long term, the scheme would demonstrate to local farmers the advantages of improving agriculture scientifically, and their subsequent adoption of these methods would increase production, thus also benefiting the railroad.

The Red River Valley on the Minnesota side divided into three topographical regions running north to south. The two regions to the west (closest to the river) and east (furthest from the river) had sufficient gradient and natural streams to remain well drained. A middle region, however, did not. This posed a particular problem when combined with the climate. Farmers in this area, if they planted too early, faced their seeds being destroyed as the saturated ground froze. One solution, which had been commonly and successfully used throughout the Midwest during the previous decade, was to lay tile drainage systems throughout the valley. These buried, u-shaped tiles were placed in networks under the fields, and helped channel excess water through the soil to drainage ditches and then back into the river.[56]

In addition to endangering crops, flooding in the middle reaches of the valley also posed a problem to railroad operation, as the waters could wash out the tracks. To prevent this, the St. Paul, Minneapolis & Manitoba cut forty-five miles of ditches in Kittson, Norman, Polk, and Clay Counties in 1879 and 1880. Later, to improve the land of the St. Paul, Minneapolis & Manitoba for potential purchasers, the railroad's engineers built outlet canals at the cost of several thousand dollars. These canals connected closed watercourses, such as the Sand Hill and Wild Rice Rivers, to the Red River, incorporating these existing waterways in the corporation's drainage network.[57]

The combination of tile drains and canals successfully drained the railroad's land, but, by acting unilaterally, the corporation's ecological engineering caused problems. By determining the boundaries of its drainage schemes according to land that the St. Paul, Pacific & Manitoba owned rather than by a broader ecosystem rationale, the corporation channeled much of the excess water on to other farmers' fields—fields that, in some cases, had no prior history of flooding. The project antagonized neighboring farmers, who sued the railroad for the flooding of their land. According to Hill, the charges were generally unfounded, as the farmers' lands "were benefitted by the better drainage facilities," but the suits "aggregated an amount of nearly $100,000, and the Company was forced to a heavy expense in defending them." In the end, many of the verdicts went against the railway.[58]

In its first decade of existence, therefore, the railroad that would become the Great Northern Railway tried to influence farming practices along its line through the efforts of James J. Hill, but it failed. Hill wanted farmers to practice more diversified and scientific agriculture and sought to guide them in this transition through a variety of projects. First, he established his own reputation as a successful farmer and hoped that this would result in emulation. Second, he invested his own personal finances to promote more cattle raising in the railroad's hinterland. Third, he launched his own weekly paper to propagate his views on agriculture. Finally, he used railroad land as a showcase for the benefits of drainage. All of these early agricultural endeavors failed to meet his expectations, primarily due to the general unwillingness of small-scale farmers to accept Hill's expertise as superior to their own and, consequently, their refusal to follow his prescriptions.

Hill recognized the failure of his agricultural promotion schemes and altered his strategy accordingly. The drainage attempts in the Red River Valley and Hill's cattle donations represented the last large-scale efforts, for at least twenty-five years, by the railroad or its personnel to improve agriculture unilaterally. From 1890 on, both Hill and the corporation were cautious to operate in conjunction with other governmental, academic, and local organizations when promoting on-site improvements. Hill used this new tactic of cooperation to simultaneously borrow credibility from other, more recognized experts and to deflect any potential liability or blame in the case of failure.

This strategy first became apparent in the continuing problems of drainage in the Red River Valley. Hill backed out of private corporate drainage attempts, but some locals noted the good effects of the St. Paul, Minneapolis & Manitoba's few miles of ditch, and indigenous interest in drainage grew. Hill took advantage of this interest by sponsoring a drainage convention in Crookston, Minnesota, in 1886. At this meeting Hill suggested that drainage projects should be funded directly from assessments of the lands that would benefit from them. This made locals nervous, as no one could provide an estimate of the final cost. Thus the convention decided that the first order of business was a topographical survey of the valley to determine the potential for drainage. Hill paid half the survey's cost (five thousand dollars) and obtained the services of a trained hydraulic engineer to undertake the work under the direction of Charles G. Elliott, a drainage engineer from Illinois. The survey results demonstrated the feasibility of drainage in the valley and called for 275 miles of ditch at an estimated cost of $750,000. The reconvened convention decided to push for state intervention to finance and complete the work.[59]

Under the guidance of Hill's lawyer and pointman in the valley, Ezra Valentine, concerned citizenry lobbied the Minnesota state government to pass the appropriate legislation. In 1893 the legislators responded with a law to conduct drainage work in "the counties of Wilkin, Clay, Norman, Polk, Marshall, Kittson, Grant and Traverse" and appropriated $25,000 a year for four years. In addition, the legislation specified that no money should be paid out of the state treasury for any work until the Great Northern Railway Company had deposited $6,250 toward the drainage each year.[60]

Although pleased with the act, Hill was unhappy about the state appropriation of company funds, pointing out that "the Great Northern Company cannot and will not allow the State to appropriate money for it to pay." He acknowledged that the company should pay for any benefit to land it owned, but argued that the Great Northern owned no land in the valley. The territorial government had granted public domain to the Minnesota & Pacific Railroad, which had been assumed first by the St. Paul & Pacific and then by the St. Paul, Minneapolis & Manitoba. In September 1889 Hill had formed a new company, the Great Northern Railway. The Great Northern established a 999-year lease of the St. Paul, Minneapolis & Manitoba, so that they could operate in conjunction, but legally they remained separate corporations. Therefore, the Great Northern officially had no interest in drainage work along the St. Paul, Minneapolis & Manitoba line. Hill finessed the potential conflict with the state by paying the money on behalf of the St. Paul, Minneapolis & Manitoba, which had "a large block of land on the Sand Hill River, South of Crookston, that would be benefited by the opening of that river." The work went ahead, with Erza Valentine and N. D. Miller, chief engineer of the Great Northern, being appointed to the Board of Audit by Governor Knute Nelson.[61]

His experiences in Red River Valley drainage taught Hill a new strategy by which to obtain agricultural change. By working through businesses and a group of influential local farmers wealthy enough to benefit from technological advances, and by mobilizing the power of state legislation, Hill achieved successful drainage in the Red River Valley. Hill realized the value of cooperation with other institutions in implementing agricultural change, a change that, according to him, most of the average farmers in the valley had done "what they could to prevent." He also discovered the efficacy of using his pointmen, who were usually well known locally, to promote agricultural change.[62]

Through the drainage of the Red River Valley, Hill refined his methods of agricultural education. His attempts to educate farmers using personal or corporate example had had very limited success. The farmers who displayed interest in his ideas were those already open to progressive concepts of agricultural development and who had already embarked on improving their methods. Hill's carefully cultivated persona as a scientific gentleman farmer influenced only those with the money, interest, and knowledge to invest in agricultural improvements. Hill's attempts to reach the bulk of farmers directly through local example resulted in lawsuits against the railroad. What he did discover was the efficacy of promoting ideas through local organizations and of utilizing institutional power to effect change.

As with his drainage ventures in the Red River Valley, Hill found that, while he failed to promote farm diversification through the distribution of blooded stock, he had considerable success working in conjunction with other institutions. To protect his cattle schemes, Hill participated in a national campaign against pleuro-pneumonia after a number of his imported cat-tle caught it in 1886. The same year the disease erupted in the Chicago stock-yards, causing a nationwide panic. In 1884 the U.S. Congress had passed legislation empowering the Bureau of Animal Industry, a branch of the United States Department of Agriculture (USDA), to purchase and destroy animals suffering from certain diseases, including pleuro-pneumonia, and in June 1886 it appropriated $100,000 for the work. This funding proved insufficient, and various state laws hamstrung the work of USDA officials, preventing the purchase of diseased animals.[63]

Hill became involved in the fight for effective diseased animal control legislation in 1886. In November of that year the national Consolidated Cattle Growers' Association appointed Hill to the Committee of Congressional Legislation. The Association then prepared a bill, known as the Miller bill, to increase appropriations for work against pleuro-pneumonia and to give the USDA greater powers to purchase and destroy diseased animals or to impose and enforce quarantine restrictions. Hill and other members of the committee began lobbying congressmen to vote for the bill. To do this, Hill used *The Farmer,* which published many articles advocating federal control over pleuro-pneumonia. By March 1887 the bill had passed, and the new act gave the Bureau of Animal Industry half a million dollars to perform the work, with a fifth of the funds available immediately. In the next Congress, two other bills regarding pleuro-pneumonia were introduced to ensure continued funding of the program.[64]

The work proved a great success. Utilizing the power of the federal gov-ernment and the expertise of its employees, the Bureau completely eradi-cated pleuro-pneumonia in the United States by 1892 at a total cost of $1,509,100. Once again, as with drainage in the Red River Valley, Hill learned the benefit of working with other institutions in promoting agricultural change. In neither case, though, did Hill truly control events or dictate results, a disadvantage he would later realize.[65]

Working from an eighteenth-century English tradition transmuted through nineteenth-century Canada, Hill had established himself as a gen-tleman farmer. Using demonstration and philanthropy, as well as *The Farmer,* Hill tried to convince farmers along the St. Paul, Minneapolis & Manitoba Railroad to follow his example by practicing intensive, diversified farming, with a focus on dual-purpose cattle.

Hill's choice of image proved outdated, as the audience he needed to reach no longer deferred to this sort of expertise, if they ever had. After the Civil War the American elite had altered their approach to rural pastimes. No longer did the status of gentleman farmer legitimize privilege. As the nation moved away from its rural past, so agricultural pursuits ceased to legitimatize power, prestige, and influence, and became increasingly choices of leisure. Hill was not alone in his agricultural interests. Some of his contemporaries also invested time and money in rural activities. Leland Stanford bred racing and trotting horses at his Palo Alto farm. He enjoyed watching horses on the track and studying the mechanisms of equine locomotion through photography. George Vanderbilt established a model farm at Biltmore, where he bred hogs and prizewinning Jersey cattle. Unlike Hill, though, these men did not try to influence the average farmer. They had little vested interest in solving the problems of rural life and instead "farmed" for self-gratification rather than for power, prestige, or influence. Hill also valued the country estate connotations of his North Oaks farm, but his prime aim was to create an image of himself as a successful scientific farmer. He intended to use this image to persuade farmers to adopt agricultural techniques that would increase their profit margin and that of the railroad. With much available land, high wheat prices, and good climatic conditions, most farmers simply ignored him.[66]

By the time the Great Northern Railway reached Puget Sound, Hill had abandoned many of his early attempts at agricultural education. While keeping North Oaks, he sold all of its cattle, letting the farm become more of a country retreat than a working stock farm, although he still bred horses, pigs, and sheep. Hill's involvement with newspapers also ceased. He had lost faith in farmers, remarking darkly that he "would be glad at any time to help enlighten the farmers, but they seem determined on self destruction, and perhaps the remedy will come quicker by letting them have their own way for the present."[67]

On the other hand, Hill responded to failure by refining his tactics. As described above, the most successful of Hill's early agricultural ventures were those which involved other institutions. In promoting drainage in the Red River Valley, Hill antagonized farmers when he acted alone or through the railroad, but he often succeeded through more subtle and indirect means. Through promotion and expenditure, he found he could influence local and state authorities to move in desired directions. Hill's participation in the fight against pleuro-pneumonia, which used a combination of grassroots pressure and federal force, demonstrated the efficacy of cooperation. Hill learned his lesson well and would continue to forge links with other organizations to achieve his agricultural ends over the next few decades. He would, however, gradually find that the gains made through this form of cooperation were frequently offset by the loss of personal and corporate control in determining the direction of rural development and change. By 1893, therefore, although in a good position economically (so much so that his railroad was one of the few to survive the crash of that year), James Hill entered the new decade abandoning his old agricultural policies and programs and having to create new ones.

3 / Cooperation and Success, 1893–1902

Business and political affairs surrounding the Great Northern Railway distracted the corporation and its president from manipulating western development for a few years after the Panic of 1893. Unlike such competing lines as the Northern Pacific and the Union Pacific, the Great Northern company avoided bankruptcy. Its success was due in large part to a strong economic infrastructure in the Red River Valley and an unusually well-built railroad, with flat grades and quality equipment that pared operating costs to a minimum.

The mid-1890s posed a personal political crisis for James J. Hill. By inclination a low-tariff Democrat, he had consistently supported Grover Cleveland, despite the president's initial failure to approve the St. Paul, Minneapolis & Manitoba's right-of-way across western North Dakota and Montana and his refusal to mobilize government forces against Eugene Debs's American Railway Union strike of 1894. In 1896, faced with the dramatic growth of the People's Party and the double presidential nomination of William Jennings Bryan, Hill changed affiliations, backing the Republican nominee William McKinley and contributing ten times more to McKinley's campaign, $100,000, than he had ever given to Cleveland. He also worked with Marcus Hanna, McKinley's genius campaign manager, to gain a Republican victory in the Upper Midwest. The struggles Hill faced economically and politically during the first half of the 1890s served to distract his attention from his endeavors to educate farmers.[1]

Hill was also engrossed in expanding his railroad enterprise at the end of the century. The second bankruptcy of the Northern Pacific in 1893 gave the Great Northern a chance to acquire interest in that road and thus eliminate its major competition in the Northwest. Backed by J. P. Morgan, Hill embarked in 1895 on a plan to bring the Northern Pacific under the umbrella of the Great Northern. Initially the corporation aimed to completely subsume the Northern Pacific, placing it under Hill's management. This scheme, dubbed the London Agreement, was drawn up by Hill and various English bankers in 1895. The idea of uniting the lines, however, met with opposition from Henry Villard, president of the Northern Pacific, and that railroad's personnel who objected to being engulfed by the Great Northern. The Morgan/Hill faction also feared substantial political opposition to the takeover because of the anti-monopoly fervor of the 1890s. Hill persuaded a friend and business associate, Thomas Pearsall, to file a test case for a merger. The ambiguous results convinced Hill and Morgan that uniting the two lines might prove difficult. In 1896 they scrapped the London Agreement in favor of the London Memorandum. This eliminated most of the competition between the two lines, forging a "permanent alliance, defensive." Instead of a corporate merger, therefore, they settled for an agreement between the two companies aimed at maintaining high prices. The London Memorandum, unlike the straightforward merger proposed in the London Agreement, was definitely a "combination in restraint of trade" and violated the Sherman Anti-Trust Act of 1890, but it had the advantage of being relatively inconspicuous.[2]

Hill found the new agreement less than satisfactory. Power rested in Morgan's hands, and the Great Northern did not even have a seat on the board of directors of the Northern Pacific. Over the next four years Hill worked to increase his control both by stock purchase and by badgering Morgan. Morgan's increasing respect for Hill's abilities and the death of Charles H. Coster, the general manager of the Northern Pacific, in March 1900, gave Hill his opportunity. By late fall the Morgan group relinquished working control of the Northern Pacific to the Hill faction, which immediately implemented the de facto amalgamation of the lines through personal ownership of stock and company cooperation. They completed the merger on November 12, 1901, creating a holding company, capitalized at $400 million, known as the Northern Securities Company.[3]

The alliance with the Northern Pacific increased Hill's ability to influence regional development in the northern tier of states. Like the Great Northern, the line ran from St. Paul to Tacoma, Washington, but took a more southerly route, thus giving Hill a monopoly of transcontinental lines in the northern United States. Furthermore, the Northern Pacific's branch lines added density to Hill's operations, making his persona more visible and giving him and his agents greater access to the settlers throughout his roads' hinterlands. But, while Hill's involvement bridged the two railroads, the corporations remained technically separate, and Hill never displayed the same interest in or control over Northern Pacific operations as he did with the Great Northern.

By the mid-1890s, with McKinley elected and the London Memorandum signed, Hill renewed his interest in the agricultural development of the West. The completion of the Great Northern in 1893 and the effective settlement of the Red River Valley had dramatically expanded the nature and geographical area of Hill's interests, but the ultimate goal of railroad profit remained fixed. He still pushed for diversified, commercial smallholding along his line, seeing it as the optimum agricultural method both in moral terms and in terms of haulage generated. He envisioned a paradise, but for the railroad to profit it had to be a densely populated paradise. "If you put a railroad in the garden of Eden and had none but Adam and Eve patronize the road, it would be bound to be a failure," he reportedly opined.[4]

Although this settlement pattern had been somewhat approximated in the Red River Valley, the idea of establishing small-scale, diversified family farms throughout the arid West was environmentally unsound. Much of the land west of the Missouri River was too dry, and the climate was too extreme to foster traditional homesteader crops such as corn and wheat. The federal government had recognized this problem in 1877 with the passage of the Desert Land Act. This act, however, did not abandon the concept of yeomen farmers in the West, but rather placed its faith in science and in human capacity to alter the environment. The act gave settlers in eleven affected states and territories more land: 640 acres, or a full section, four times as much as they could obtain under the 1862 Homestead Act. The act's sponsors intended the excess acreage to provide the settler with an incentive, in the form of future profits, to irrigate the land. By the late 1890s, with his line crossing the northern Great Plains and the Columbia Basin, Hill followed the pattern set by the Desert Land Act, choosing to promote irrigation as a means to achieve the settlement pattern he desired. He was somewhat behind the times, however, as by this point, failed attempts at individual irrigation were giving way to cooperative ventures.[5]

The ideal of dense agricultural settlement was politically, as well as environmentally, flawed. In the 1890s, the arid West, especially the northern Great Plains, was still dominated, politically and economically, by stockmen and mine owners from the front range. The businesses these men engaged in provided little haulage for the Great Northern, and in promoting an alternative development plan founded in agriculture, Hill set himself up for conflict. Thus, by traversing Montana and Washington states, the Great Northern became embroiled in issues of environmental manipulation and political dominance, which ultimately propelled the corporation into national debates about land use and resource control.

Hill's goal of increasing the haulage of the Great Northern and its profit margin stayed the same, but he adapted his strategy to reflect lessons he had learned. Hill acknowledged his earlier failures to convince farmers of his agricultural expertise and thereby influence them directly. Building on the success of the drainage commission in Minnesota and the legislation against pleuro-pneumonia, Hill now combined the weight of his political and economic strength with his agricultural expertise and mobilized to aid other institutions, which he saw as furthering his agricultural goals. Working behind the scenes, he sought to use his own, and the Great Northern's, clout to influence agricultural education and development programs, as well as to shape legislation. Sponsoring programs for farmer education, drainage, and irrigation, Hill bolstered his claim to expertise through the use of professional scientists and government officials. He remained closely involved with the projects he sponsored and chose them carefully, rejecting any scheme that did not promise benefit to the Great Northern.

The failure of Hill's early attempts to alter farmer land-use patterns to the benefit of the corporation necessitated a rethinking of his agricultural strategy. Rather than acting unilaterally and personally, Hill increasingly mobilized corporate funds to back agricultural schemes that he viewed favorably. Additionally, Hill proved far less willing to act as the front man and tended to favor schemes whereby the Great Northern provided funds and advice to various institutions and organizations and their experts, who actually carried out the educational work.

Hill's new deference to formal expertise did not represent a complete break with past tactics. He still cultivated his image as a farm expert by giving speeches on agricultural issues to farmers, farmers' organizations, and students. He also maintained his involvement in agricultural organizations such as the Minnesota State Agricultural Society and its fair. In every case he stressed the importance of diversification and scientific agriculture to increase production and income.[6]

After 1893, therefore, Hill ceased to act independently, preferring to adopt a more covert style. Consequently, he placed less emphasis on his personal prowess as a farmer. This change was reflected in his use of his personal farms. The North Oaks farm, just ten miles north of his main residence in St. Paul, increasingly functioned as the family's country estate rather than as an experiment station. Hill's children spent a considerable amount of time living at the farm, while the animals kept at North Oaks were intended for family pleasure rather than for financial profit or farmer education. By 1893 Hill had disposed of his Aberdeen Angus herd and, within two years, cattle breeding had completely ceased at North Oaks. In 1896 the *St. Paul Pioneer Press* described North Oaks as much more like a country estate than a working farm. "At North Oaks today carriage horses are bred, dairy cows are kept, sheep feed upon the pastures, swine fattened on the mast of oaken forests, elk and deer browse upon the growth of a woodland enclosure and a herd of buffalo roams through a large range."[7]

Along with adapting his farm usage away from public suasion, Hill increased his support of more mainstream agricultural educators. In subsidizing programs run by other institutions, such as the state government and the University of Minnesota, Hill acquiesced to a modern, almost Progressive notion of expertise based on formal education. Hill did not acknowledge that other experts were more knowledgeable than he. Rather, he hoped that they would prove more effective in conveying information to farming audiences and implementing improvement schemes. Consequently, their expertise would complement his.

This deference to other experts first emerged over the issue of drainage in the Red River Valley. Hill helped establish a state program of drainage that expanded in 1897 and culminated in the 1901 creation of the Minnesota State Drainage Commission. Although railroad financial involvement had ceased by this point, Hill kept a close eye on the work through Erza Valentine, one of his pointmen in the valley and the president of the Board of Drainage Commissioners. Valentine reported annually to Hill on the state of drainage and in return received an annual pass on the railroad to carry out his work.[8]

In addition to working with state officials on drainage in the Red River Valley, Hill also contributed to the University of Minnesota's attempts at outreach education in the valley. In 1888 the university hired Willet Hays, later federal assistant secretary of agriculture under James "Tama Jim" Wilson. The university mandated Hays to increase grassroots support for the institution. To achieve this, Hays developed an innovative new program to extend the institution's agricultural experiment stations and its high schools throughout the state.[9]

Embarking on this effort in 1894, Hays needed to investigate possible sites around Minnesota for these stations. Seeking free railway transportation, he approached the Great Northern head offices in St. Paul. On his second visit, Sam Hill (James's son-in-law) ushered him into Hill's office. Immediately, the older Hill started to indicate on a map a proposed gift of land near Crookston, Minnesota. "Why, Mr. Hill," Hays protested, "I am hardly in a position to consider gifts of land, for the board of regents has not even formally considered this project." Hill placed his hand on Hays's shoulder and said, "Young man you go ahead."[10]

Hill got his way. The university received the 476.61 acres from the railway on the condition that the land always be used as an experiment station. Hill persuaded the Minnesota legislature that year to authorize the establishment of branch stations for the university. Hill's donation of land for the Northwest Station at Crookston also freed a state appropriation of twenty thousand dollars for buildings and equipment as well as the purchase of land for the Northeast Station in Grand Rapids, Minnesota.[11]

Hill understood that the land eventually would be used as a branch agricultural school as well as an experiment station. Hays had explained his dream to the railroad man, and the idea of the school figured greatly in Hill's motivations for giving the land. Through his generous combination of gift and action, Hill gave substance to his belief in the importance of agricultural education based on scientific principles. The donation also underscored his desire that the state organize agricultural education and that actual farms should figure prominently in this education.[12]

The gift of land to the university supported Hill's own agricultural education ideas and offered the potential for increased production in the valley. He hoped that, unlike the early drainage work by the railroad, the university could effectively demonstrate the benefits of tile drainage. In addition, the donation proved a timely philanthropic gesture on behalf of a railroad that competed with other regional lines for business in the area.[13]

The donation not only facilitated drainage experimentation, but also reinforced Hill's belief in the effectiveness of demonstration farms as a learning tool, moving the onus from his own farm at North Oaks to the state institution for higher learning. The reliance on demonstration farms as the best method of teaching agriculture reflected Hill's theoretical agreement with many farmers and other advocates of more traditional educational methods. Since the 1850s a majority of farmers considered model farms, run at a profit, to be the perfect way to instruct agrarians. They could visit these farms and witness new machinery, modes of bookkeeping, and husbandry that they could utilize on their own lands. Conversely, these farmers saw little need for the expertise of agricultural science to teach farming and had little faith in extant university demonstration farms that consistently operated at a loss.[14]

For all his advocacy of modern, scientific farming, Hill remained wary of academic experts. To him, demonstration farms were the key to agricultural education, and he thought that each county should have a demonstration farm. As he said, "This model farm would be simply a tract of land conforming in size, soil treatment, crop selection and rotation and methods of cultivation to modern agricultural methods. Its purpose would be to furnish to all its neighborhood a working model for common instruction." He saw practical demonstration as more effective than "a lifetime [of] reading books or listening to stump speeches."[15]

While the gift of land augmented Hill's image vis-à-vis the Red River Valley settlers and, perhaps, gave the Great Northern a competitive edge over the Northern Pacific, it proved unsuitable for most desirable types of cultivation and therefore damaged Hill's relationship with the University of Minnesota. Although he had admitted that the land was wet, this was an understatement. When James Boss of the University of Minnesota Experiment Station in St. Paul first arrived at the site in the early spring of 1895, he described it as "a discouraging proposition for farming, and a very much better one for ducks." Like much of the land in the middle reaches of the valley, the donation was boggy and prone to flooding, and the Great Northern had not invested any money in its drainage. Hill, focused on profit, would have been unlikely to give away land to improve an intangible image that he could have sold for hard cash. Consequently, he passed an agricultural nightmare over to the university.[16]

The university approached the Northwest Station with Progressive resolve, an optimistic faith in human abilities to solve all problems. Unwilling to adapt in any way to constraints imposed by the environment, scientists and administrators invested time, money, and energy engineering the landscape to fit their needs through a lengthy and expensive process of soil drainage. Experiment Station Superintendent Conrad Selvig reported that annual flooding delayed seeding, endangered the foundations of the buildings, and provided material discomfort to the university personnel on the site. Floodwaters also washed unwanted seeds onto the experiment farm, which germinated among the crops, giving, according to Selvig, "the exceedingly unfortunate impression that the Farm suffered from chronically careless management." Only in 1908, after laying fifty thousand feet of drainage tile and constructing one and a half miles of open ditch, was the site finally drained effectively.[17]

For thirteen years, therefore, the University of Minnesota's scientific credentials were challenged by its inability to control the environment of the Northwest Station. The station became "an unwanted waif" to the administrators in Minneapolis, contributing nothing to the university and costing a great deal in money and reputation. The state legislature, which was called on to provide much of the funding for drainage, called the site a "white elephant." Institutional anger at this untenable gift was focused on human rather than ecological targets. Crookston's first superintendent, a Hill protégé named Torger Hoverstad, wrote annual reports to the dean of agriculture that exuded "hope and idealism," but the slow and difficult progress of draining the site resulted in his being fired in 1906.[18]

Hoverstad was not the only victim of institutional frustration with the problematic environment at the Crookston station. Hill's relationship with the university also suffered. As the costs of maintaining the site multiplied, many university personnel viewed the railroad baron less favorably. Conversely, the university actions regarding the station did little to endear the institution to Hill. Hill had given the land with the understanding that it would be used as an agricultural school and a demonstration farm. The nature of the land placed the university's focus on drainage rather than on education, leading to a twelve-year delay in founding an agricultural school and little demonstration taking place until 1908. The university's failure to drain the land increased Hill's skepticism about its commitment to agricultural education and its claim to agricultural expertise.[19]

Consequently, with nature exacerbating relations between the university and Hill, the gift of the Crookston land marked the extent of Hill's formal relationship with the university for many years. The gift also presaged Hill's future relationships with other institutions, as the frustrations engendered by the site were deeply embedded in the different goals of the corporations, represented in this case by Hill and by the university. Despite this, Hill maintained personal contact with many of the University of Minnesota's faculty, especially those who agreed with him regarding the importance of diversification and the nature of agricultural expertise. Agricultural experts such as Andrew Boss and Thomas Shaw empathized with Hill in both practical and theoretical arenas.[20]

The conflict over expertise was not limited to an external battle, pitting academics against farmers and other amateurs. Agricultural scientists at land grant schools throughout the Midwest and West disagreed amongst themselves about their roles and methods of implementation. Those recipients of lengthy formal education tended to perceive their mission as one of pure research, with little or no educational component. On the other hand, those who had achieved professorial positions before the new emphasis on academic credentials remained more loyal to the original mandate of land grant schools. They thought that their work should combine applied research with a strong educational mission, acting as a bureau of information for farmers of their state. Because of their personal backgrounds, this latter group, like Hill, rejected the mysticism and elitism that the new generation of scientists wove around their expertise. This internal academic conflict concerning expertise, in conjunction with the struggles raging externally among the universities, farmers, federal bureaucracy, and corporate entrepreneurs like Hill, did not find resolution until the second decade of the twentieth century and the creation of the federal Extension Service.[21]

Hill also found himself antagonizing the other main institution of tertiary learning in the Red River Valley, the North Dakota Agricultural College. In 1897 that College decided to resume experiments in sugar beet growing, which had started five years previously. President John H. Worst wrote to Hill inquiring if he knew of any limestone quarries along the line. Milk of lime is used in sugar manufacture to remove nonsugars from the beet syrup. Hill's reply was discouraging. Completely ignoring the question of limestone, he asserted that he had no doubt that sugar beets could be successfully grown in Minnesota and North Dakota. He believed that the business, however, could never be profitable and that no one would invest the necessary money in establishing a factory. With its cheap labor and government subsidies, Hill asserted that European sugar would always undercut the American product. President Worst replied that the investigation was still important. It would determine if, indeed, sugar beet growing was feasible but impracticable due to high labor costs, a situation that he stated might change as "inventive genius [overcame] the cheap labor of Europe through horse power and machinery on these level fertile prairies."[22]

As with the University of Minnesota, the root of Hill's conflict with the

North Dakota Agricultural College lay in a conflict of interests. Worst, adopting the Progressive notion of the importance of scientific inquiry for its own sake, could not convince Hill to participate. Hill clearly placed financial viability before the increasingly dominant notion of scientific expertise centered on pure research. He saw no value in experimentation that led to no immediate financial prospects for the state and no haulage for his railroad. If American sugar could not sell, why investigate its production? If the situation changed (which it did after the First World War), then scientific expertise could be applied to the problem.

Despite his continuing interest in engineering the economy of the Red River Valley in a way that maximized railroad profit, Hill also wanted to generate an income from the rest of the Great Northern's line. This posed new problems, as the Great Northern, unlike other lines with which Hill was involved, such as the St. Paul, Minneapolis & Manitoba and the Northern Pacific, did not receive land grants from the state or federal government. Therefore, Hill and other railroad personnel had to be flexible in designing corporate development programs, ensuring that each one matched the economic realities of the line it was intended to serve. While haulage rates were important to all rail lines, some had other sources of income. Haulage had played a vital part in funding the building of the Great Northern, and, upon completion of the line, became its only means of profit. Consequently, the railroad's personnel needed to invest a large amount of time in finding effective ways to exploit, not just sell, territory along the line. Settlers were important and encouraged, but it was crucial, in the case of the Great Northern, that settlement proved permanently successful, not transitory. Once the Great Northern had reached the Pacific Coast, therefore, Hill became embroiled in the complexities of farming a much more diverse and arid landscape than he had confronted in western Minnesota and eastern North Dakota.

The first problem faced by Great Northern personnel in increasing haulage along the line was the decline of foreign immigration to the United States, and especially to the northern Great Plains, in the late 1890s. Immigration did not pick up until well into the new century. By that time, the Canadian government had started a propaganda campaign to attract American farmers. This campaign appeared especially successful in areas just south of the international border, with Minnesota and North Dakota contributing one third of the emigrants. Although many of these Americans eventually returned home, and the net permanent migration numbered no more than two hundred thousand, concern about this exodus ran high during the late nineteenth and early twentieth centuries. Low wheat prices compounded and contributed to this problem of attracting settlers. Prices had fallen in the 1880s with the influx of plains' wheat onto the international market and did not recover, remaining low throughout the rest of the century. In 1893 wheat prices fell still further and did not start to rise again until 1897.[23]

To try and counter this out-migration, Hill, as front man for the Great Northern, focused on developing and marketing the line's hinterland as a feasible environment for small-scale, diversified, commercially viable farms. To do this, he stressed the potential of irrigating the plains and other parts of the arid West and of growing crops other than wheat. Avoiding the problems of operating unilaterally, he worked through a number of companies on the Columbia Plateau in Washington and behind the scenes altogether in northern Montana.

The Columbia Plateau presented a new geographical and climatic challenge for the Great Northern. The plateau encompasses part of southern Washington and northern Oregon between the Rockies and the Cascades, along the Columbia River. It is a region riddled with streams and rivers, as water flows out of the two mountain ranges into the Columbia. The valleys are separated from each other by more exposed benchlands. The climate is generally dry, but without the extremes of cold experienced on the Great Plains. Indian agriculture had started in the protected valleys and, with the white settlement of the mid-nineteenth century, a pattern developed of stock raising on the uplands and wheat farming in the valleys, both mainly supplying neighboring mining communities.[24]

The advent of railroads in the region in the late 1870s changed both the settlement pattern and marketing possibilities. By the early 1880s, wheat cultivation had been successfully extended to the benchlands, and farmers flocked to the basin. Desiring denser settlement to maximize land sales and haulage, the railroads, including the Northern Pacific, promoted irrigation in some of the valleys along their lines, hoping to spur the growth of higher-income crops such as fruit and hops. Intensive agriculture generally proved less attractive to the farmer than to the railroad corporations, as it inevitably required far more labor than extensive wheat farming. In spite of this, falling wheat prices did attract some to the much higher profits to be had from fruit crops. Overall, although the railroads made some advances in boosting irrigated farming and were aided by local speculators and businessmen, progress was slow, with farmers preferring to make their money from holding more land and doing less work.[25]

As early as 1890 the Northern Pacific hired engineers to investigate the potential for irrigable agriculture along the western reaches of the line. Of especial interest was the Yakima Valley, as the federal government had given the railroad about half of the land in the valley. Attempts at irrigation under the auspices of the Northern Pacific, the Yakima and Kittitas Irrigation Company, and others met with mixed success. The largest system in the valley, the Sunnyside Canal, reached approximately 64,000 acres by 1904, but only half of the acres were under cultivation. Valley farmers used the water to produce a variety of crops, including apples, which were carried to market on the railroad. The Northern Pacific had already established the precedent of using railroad funds to improve land in order to attract more settlers and to enable them to produce higher-value produce. The improvements in the Yakima Valley did attract increased settlement and promote town growth. However, the construction of irrigation systems consistently proved more expensive than expected, and the costs were not covered by returns. Consequently, most of the privately funded irrigation works were sold to the federal government in the years following the passage of the Newlands Reclamation Act in 1902, an act that placed much of the responsibility for irrigation on the federal administration.[26]

The Great Northern was also involved in irrigation projects in the northern part of the Columbia Basin, notably in the Wenatchee Valley and around Adrian, Washington, east of Wenatchee, to try and maximize settlement and railroad profit. Fruit growing was an especially attractive proposition to Hill, since he had always favored intensive rather than extensive agriculture. Additionally, Hill had a vested interest in the Wenatchee area. In 1888 attorney Thomas Burke and a group of other speculators from Seattle had purchased land on the Wenatchee Flats. They offered Hill a quarter of their holdings if he would route the Great Northern through the area. Hill accepted and therefore established a personal and commercial landed interest in the area.[27]

The Wenatchee River Basin, in the northwestern corner of the plateau, offered the potential for irrigated horticulture. The basin drains 1,350 square miles in central Washington. The river flows southeast forty-seven miles from the Wenatchee Lake to join the Columbia River. The town of Wenatchee is at the confluence of the two rivers. The subsoils of the valleys consist of gravel and sand deposited by glaciers and floods. Overlaying this is one to three feet of fertile, pervious, sedimentary topsoil. The land was conducive to irrigation, and water projects started in the valley shortly after the passage of the Desert Land Act in 1877, which allowed cheap purchase of public domain on the condition that the land be irrigated. That year Philip Miller hired Jacob A. Shotwell to build some ditches on his land. By 1881 Miller had established a "very promising orchard." Other settlers followed suit over the next decade, but it soon became apparent that the valley needed large-scale irrigation works, for which capital was not available. Irrigation generally proved successful when completed, providing water for bountiful crop yields and the establishment of orchards.[28]

From November 1891, a year before the Great Northern reached the valley on its way to Puget Sound, the railroad started investigating ways to translate the ecology of the region into profit through haulage. Thomas Burke, by then a representative for the railroad, incorporated the Wenatchee Development Company, which aimed to increase settlement by building up industry. The company's first interest was the construction of sawmills, with the intention of profiting from the necessary forest clearance. Concurrently, it wanted to extend irrigation works in the valley, with a view to replacing the existing forestation with orchards. Burke held the majority of the stock in the development company, but in 1892 the Great Northern purchased five hundred shares, thus assuming considerable power within the organization as well as a more direct interest in its success. The Wenatchee Development Company investigated the possibilities of irrigation around 1894. Burke had approached two private companies and planned, if that failed, "to see what can be done under the irrigation law of the state."[29]

Corporate promotion of irrigation next merged with local boosterism when an itinerant newspaperman named Arthur Gunn assumed the post of local agent for the Great Northern. Gunn borrowed enough money from Hill to help Jacob Shotwell, who had bought and irrigated his own land by 1891, to enlarge his ditch and draw up plans to irrigate the entire valley. As in the Red River Valley with Valentine, Hill promoted agricultural development in Wenatchee from behind the scenes, using Gunn as his front man. The Panic of 1893 and the subsequent depression delayed work in the valley, but in 1896 independent entrepreneurs and the Wenatchee Development Company united to form the Wenatchee Waterpower Company, with Gunn as president.[30]

This company was effectively a Great Northern subsidiary. Increasing national opposition to monopolies, and other business mergers that hampered free trade, had culminated in the passage of the Sherman Anti-Trust

Act of 1890. To avoid prosecution under this law, railroads and other large corporations hid their involvement in the development of businesses integral to their success. Thus, instead of running coal operations directly or arranging for special rates connected to bulk purchase, railroads created subsidiary firms, such as the Great Northern's Sand Coulee Coal Company. These businesses, independent on paper, were under the de facto control of the parent organization. The Great Northern applied this tactic to various development operations, including the Great Falls Development Company and the Wenatchee Waterpower Company. The latter not only received a loan of thirteen thousand dollars from the Great Northern to complete all the proposed irrigation systems, but in April 1897 the railroad bought the complete issue of bonds, totaling fifteen thousand dollars.[31]

The Wenatchee Waterpower Company's paper independence from the railroad also protected Hill and the Great Northern from farmer accusations of arbitrary corporate action, further reflecting lessons learned in the Red River Valley. By concealing the Great Northern's direct involvement and potential for profit from land sales, Hill hoped that the irrigation endeavors would seem to stem from grassroots action and be more palatable. Arthur Gunn worked on the continued construction of canals and also busied himself inducing settlers to move to the valley. He completed the ditch extension in 1898 and, the next year, persuaded a Dunkard Brethren congregation from North Dakota to move to the area. Sale of irrigated land started in 1899 with parcels of five to ten acres fetching $140 per acre, including perpetual water rights.[32]

This success was only achieved at high financial cost. By mid-1898 Gunn wrote to Hill that the bondholders should take possession of the company, which was on the verge of financial failure. The Great Northern did take over and assumed responsibility for the company's liabilities, pushing through the completion of a gravity irrigation system by December 1898. Although in the end the scheme did increase the valley's production, especially of fruit, it cost far more than anticipated, and Hill's secretary wrote that his employer was "not overly pleased with the result of our irrigation matters."[33]

Despite the achievements of the project, the valley still needed more irrigation. Local residents decided to hire W. T. Clark, who had recently built a successful irrigation system in the Yakima Valley, to build the Highline Canal. Clark funded the project initially with a loan from Robert Livingstone, president of the Oregon Mortgage Company based in Portland, and used farmers' land in the valley as collateral. Clark and his associates, as Burke informed Hill, acquired "$150,000 for the work from Scottish capital represented in Portland and other interests," which they used to found the Wenatchee Canal Company.[34]

This new company entangled itself with the Great Northern in May 1902 by entering into an agreement with the Wenatchee Development Company. The contract specified that Clark would irrigate the Development Company's land for $6,000, some land, and a fee of $1.50 per annum per acre for the rest, and that the work would be completed by May 1904.[35]

Clark's work progressed well but, once again, cost more than anticipated, and he continually searched for funding to avert bankruptcy. Once water flow started in September 1903, farmers in the valley complained of its high cost and often failed to take full advantage of the work done. Although the farmers set out new fruit trees, Thomas Burke complained that they "don't seem to carry on farming or horticulture according to modern methods. They do not seem to realize the importance of care and judgment in the selection of fruit trees or in their proper care afterwards." Therefore, Burke suggested to Hill that the railroad company might send out a horticulturist to the valley to instruct farmers. This small episode mirrored the awkward progression of the project as a whole. By 1902, although considerable irrigation work had taken place in the Wenatchee Valley, it had all been characterized by high costs to the railroad and railroad personnel. Moreover, these irrigation projects had yet to produce the substantial income for the farmers or the railroad that materialized in later decades.[36]

In 1896 the Great Northern embarked on a second irrigation project, this time on Crab Creek in Adrian, Washington. Crab Creek rises in the interior of the basin, southwest of Spokane. The stream drains more than five thousand square miles while describing a large "S" shape over the northern plateau, flowing through Soap Lake and Moses Lake before debouching into the Columbia near Beverly, downstream of Wenatchee. The town of Adrian, situated to the east of Soap Lake, marked a junction of the Northern Pacific and the Great Northern, making town promotion beneficial to both corporations. Working with J. D. McIntyre, who founded the Cooperative Irrigation Company, Hill agreed that the Great Northern would transport the equipment necessary for the construction of irrigation works and, upon their completion, buy the irrigated land at ten dollars an acre. Hill chose the parcels of land that the company would purchase before the Cooperative Irrigation Company began work. He also added a proviso to

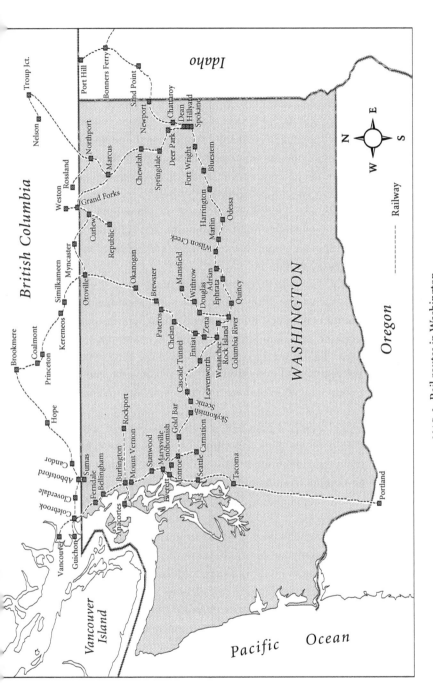

MAP 2. Rail routes in Washington

the contract that said "If there are any of these lands that the water cannot reach by gravity, your Company [the Cooperative Irrigation Company] will be required to put in the necessary pumping works and to put the water on the ground."[37]

Hill tried to protect his company's investment in Adrian. He ordered an independent survey of the land, which reported that the prospects were good. Construction began in 1896, and Hill kept a close eye on the project, receiving reports from various officials when they passed through the area. Little consensus existed on the advancement of the work, however, with disconcerting reports that the water flow would prove insufficient to irrigate the proposed area. A letter from Chief Engineer Jonathan Stevens followed, stating that "There is no doubt in my mind that there is plenty of water in Crab Creek one year and another to irrigate twenty to twenty-five thousand acres of land, possibly a good deal more."[38]

As in Wenatchee, the project cost the railroad much more than anticipated. McIntyre soon ran out of capital and asked the Great Northern for an advance to complete the work. Burke advised that to "prevent delay and possible abandonment" of the project, the Great Northern advance McIntyre $1,200 and pay his bills amounting to $3,800, which the corporation did, but McIntyre still fell short of expectations. The railroad soon found itself embroiled in a court case when various suppliers sued McIntyre for non-payment.[39]

Trying to cut his losses in Adrian, Hill utilized already tested pointmen. In August 1898, with the completion of work in the Wenatchee Valley, Hill had Arthur Gunn turn his attention to the problems around Adrian. Gunn's report bore little hope for the future of the project, pointing out three main problems. First, the Cooperative Irrigation Company had failed to establish legal rights to the water in the valley. Second, the creek had insufficient water to irrigate the intended land in the summer. And, finally, the ditch and its flumes were poorly constructed and would require considerable repairs to operate efficiently. Within a year, Hill had turned the work in Adrian over to Gunn, appointing him president of the Adrian Irrigation Company. Once again, the Great Northern found that irrigation through private companies proved difficult, if not impossible, to conduct successfully and extortionately expensive, generating little immediate profit.[40]

In promoting western development through irrigation, the Great Northern's president discovered a new flaw in his tactic of working through other institutions. As the University of Minnesota found with the Northwest experiment station, the price of altering the environment, whether through drainage or irrigation, was high. Like many others, Hill realized that private companies just could not float the necessary capital for successful irrigation. Faced with a practical rather than a strategic problem, Hill looked to ally with other institutions, notably the federal government, for future reclamation work.

Hill learned a similar lesson in pursuing irrigation in northern Montana on the Milk River. The river rises in the Rocky Mountains, close to the source of the St. Mary's River. Both streams then flow north, across the Canadian border. The St. Mary's finally empties into Hudson Bay, while the Milk flows east through the Canadian Plains, reentering the United States west of Havre. Continuing to flow east through northern Montana, the Milk River is one of the main tributaries of the Missouri River, joining it at the site of Fort Peck. The river meanders slowly through a wide flat plain of fertile alluvium. Both the main valley and those of the river's tributaries have sloping, grass-covered sides, conducive to farming. The land, therefore, was suitable for agriculture, except that the rainfall was insufficient for most crops. Many settlers and politicians saw the river's water as the solution, ignoring the disproportion between the light annual flows and the enormous area of land to be irrigated.[41]

Irrigation started in the Milk River Valley in 1889 when one T. B. Burns moved north from the irrigated Gallatin Valley and acquired water rights to land recently ceded by the Gros Ventre and Assiniboine Indians. The next year he constructed a dam on the river. Burns wanted to grow hay on the irrigated land. This would tie him into the main industry of northern Montana, which was still stock raising. The flow of the Milk River in the summer proved insufficient for irrigation on a substantial level, but a survey in 1891 by E. S. Nettleton of the USDA concluded that it would be feasible to divert water from the St. Mary's River to the Milk.[42]

Hill's interest in the project emerged in the late 1890s. In September 1897, J. D. McIntyre wrote to Hill detailing a survey he had completed of the irrigation potential of the Milk River Valley. Although the survey seems to have been commissioned by Hill, he took no action. Unlike in the Wenatchee Valley, large-scale irrigation in northern Montana continued to be complicated by the presence of several Indian reservations, notably the Fort Belknap Reservation, south of Harlem and Dodson. In the late 1890s the superintendents of this reservation started leasing its lands to non-Indian stockmen. The presence of reservation lands along the Milk River, with the added complication of leases to non-Indians, necessarily added a level of federal involvement across several departments to any irrigation plans.[43]

Unlike in Washington, Hill refused to do more than investigate irrigation possibilities in northern Montana. In 1898, after the Canadian government had started an irrigation project on the St. Mary's River, irrigation promoter W. M. Wooldridge, of Chinook, Montana, pressured Hill through letters to become involved in work on the Milk River. Wooldridge wanted to position the money and political influence of the Great Northern firmly behind any attempts at irrigation. This pressure continued for a year and met with categorical refusal. Hill stated that Montana seemed very disinterested in the railroad, charging high taxes and failing to protect railroad property. In addition to lacking philanthropic feelings toward the state of Montana, Hill pointed out that "The Company owns no lands there and does not intend to buy any. . . . It does not now or at any time hereafter, expect to spend any money in internal improvements in Montana."[44]

Hill's reasons were strong; unlike in the Wenatchee Valley, neither he nor his company could profit directly from land sales along the Milk River. However, despite what he wrote to Wooldridge, he recognized the need for irrigation in the area and worked quietly behind the scenes to involve the federal government in such a project. In late 1899 he and Senator R. F. Pettigrew, chairman of the Senate Committee on Indian Affairs, tossed around the idea of the government donating land to the state of Montana for the purpose of irrigation, but nothing came of it.[45]

Hill's experiences in Washington and Montana convinced him that irrigation could not be completed through private individuals or corporations. The financial costs were prohibitive and the need for engineering excellence high. At the end of the 1890s Hill remained convinced that irrigation was necessary to make the land along his line fruitful. His faith in promoting agricultural development through other institutions had in this instance, however, been considerably refined. By 1898 the financial failure of irrigation in eastern Washington persuaded Hill that only the federal government had the resources necessary to undertake reclamation projects.

Others also preached the necessity of federal involvement in irrigation. Attempts at irrigation throughout the West during the 1870s and 1880s, both by private and state organizations, had consistently fallen short or failed altogether because of the high costs of construction. In addition, states contested jurisdiction over water, which failed to conform to political boundaries. Increasingly, proponents of irrigation looked to the federal government to provide the necessary funding, if not to actually conduct the work. From the late 1880s congressmen drafted numerous bills proposing national involvement in western irrigation. In 1891 Salt Lake City hosted the first of many irrigation congresses to agitate for federal irrigation. These efforts proved fruitless, partly because of eastern and midwestern opposition to government expenditure on the West, and partly due to conflicts among the westerners themselves as to how the irrigation should be implemented. Some, such as Senator Francis E. Warren and Elwood Mead, both of Wyoming, advocated government surveys and construction of dams and reservoirs, yet they wanted land distribution and water allocation left to the states. This would necessarily favor the controlling powers in each state, which, in Wyoming, remained the cattle interests. Others, such as Senator Paris Gibson from Montana, who was Hill's pointman in that new state and trying to promote more intensive settlement, preferred the government to control land sales as well as construction.[46]

In 1897 Hill became actively involved in pressuring the federal government. At an irrigation congress that year in Wichita, Kansas, he worked with George Hebard Maxwell to form the National Irrigation Association. This organization ostensibly aimed at educating American citizens to the need for irrigation and the vital role that the federal government had to play. Although the association did perform this work through its publications, lectures, and Farmers' Institutes, its more important role was lobbying for irrigation legislation in Washington, D.C.[47]

Hill's initial contribution to the National Irrigation Association was financial. He persuaded two, and later four, other railroads to join with the Great Northern in contributing five thousand dollars per annum to the organization. By 1899 the Great Northern, Southern Pacific, Santa Fe, Union Pacific, and Northern Pacific each contributed five hundred dollars a month to maintain operations at the association's headquarters in Chicago.[48]

Maxwell headed the organization. He had been interested in irrigation for the small-scale farmer throughout his career. Observation of private and state attempts to irrigate land in California led him to realize the necessity for federal intervention. A dynamic, forceful publicist, Maxwell launched the magazine *Maxwell's Talisman* after the formation of the National Irrigation Association to promote irrigation, and he undertook the new art of political lobbying with zeal.[49]

Hill's involvement did not end with financial support, but extended to lobbying, as he saw federal irrigation as vital to the economic integrity of his corporation. During the first few years of the twentieth century, he worked hard in supporting Maxwell's maneuvers in Washington and exerting his own influence with congressmen. By late 1901 the sides in the debate had been clearly defined. On one side stood the supporters of total federal control of irrigation, including Hill. Generally, these men were not acting from a belief in big government, but because state control over irrigation would favor their economic opponents. On the other side stood westerners who supported the transferal of irrigated lands to the states, usually because this would give them and their business interests control over the disposition of the water. Elwood Mead, who was then head of the Office of Irrigation Investigations in the USDA, led the latter group. Mead's history as the territorial and state engineer for Wyoming linked him closely to the grazing interests of the West, for which control over land distribution was a vital issue.[50]

Despite his earlier interest in stock raising as a part of diversified farming, Hill had always opposed cattle ranching because it was an example of the extensive monocultivation that discouraged the dense settlement patterns he desired. Part of his opposition was ideological. Hill propounded a waning Jeffersonian ideology that promoted farming as the best occupation for man and that believed farmers made the best citizens for a democracy. This idea, which farming audiences found attractive, was a common theme in his speeches, such as the one to the Minnesota State Agricultural Society in 1904, where he stated that "Better men and better women live in the country."[51]

With the completion of the Great Northern in the 1890s and the need to maximize haulage from the railroad's territory, Hill came into direct conflict with stockmen for the first time. Less money could be made from hauling stock and supplying a few ranchers than could be generated from a well-settled agrarian hinterland. Hill opposed continuing the practice of cattlemen accumulating vast tracts of public domain, which precluded farmers from acquiring good land. Ranchers achieved this through buying up scrip and taking advantage of the Desert Land Act, the Timber and Stone Act, and the commutation clause of the Homestead Act, as well as by other nefarious practices. Finally, the increase in emigration to Canada worried those interested in the settlement and expansion of the American West. Thus Hill's support of federally sponsored irrigation reinforced his desire to undermine cattle interests and their political control in the West and to foster increased farm settlement.[52]

A federal irrigation bill drafted in early 1901 by George Maxwell, Senator Francis Newlands, and Frederick Haynes Newell, the chief hydrographer of the United States Geological Survey, met many of Hill's aims. The bill proved radical in two important ways. Unlike earlier bills proposing federal irrigation, this one did not finance irrigation from the Rivers and Harbor Fund or from taxation. Rather, it proffered a revolving fund wherein government sale of irrigated land would create the monies for subsequent works. This provision eliminated the main bone of contention among eastern politicians: cost. The bill also assigned the distribution of irrigated land to the General Land Office rather than to the states, thus effectively removing control from the cattlemen.[53]

The debate in the Senate centered on two different sets of western developers, with both sides trying to commandeer eastern support. Hill's main supporters were Montana's Paris Gibson and North Dakota's Henry C. Hansbrough, and they identified their main opponents as "the covert opposition of representatives from the Rocky Mountain states who are evidently under the influence of speculators and large cattle men." Hansbrough, acting as the senatorial sponsor of the Newlands Reclamation Act, saw danger lying in the West: "The South and East are willing that we should have what we want. The trouble, I fear, is in the Southwest with an occasional kicker from the Northwest." Hansbrough advised Hill, who spent half his time in New York at this point on business, to help the bill by "bring[ing] the eastern members of the House to a complete understanding of the question." He also persuaded the officials of the Chicago, Burlington & Quincy, a line that was controlled by the Great Northern by this point, to support the legislation, thus gaining a "powerful influence over the Wyoming delegation, in who we [the bill's sponsors] have but very little confidence."[54]

In lobbying for reclamation legislation, Hill consistently followed Maxwell's lead. When various changes removed the teeth from the bill, giving more control to the states, Maxwell reneged on his support in February 1902. Consequently, Hill reversed his position, understanding the bill to be "totally impracticable." Maxwell and Gibson believed that the bill would fail and hoped that they would at least be able to force legislation for federal irrigation in a couple of "special localities, which had been recommended by the Geological Survey." By April, however, Gibson gave Hill the go-ahead to resume lobbying, stating that the bill had "recently been so amended as to give very general satisfaction, and is now endorsed by Maxwell who will work for it with all his ability." In preparation for passage of the bill, Paris

Gibson persuaded the secretary of the interior to withdraw 1,700,000 acres from homestead access in Montana to await irrigation. Once again, Maxwell and Gibson exhorted Hill to use his influence in Congress, and in June 1902 the Newlands Reclamation Act passed. At least initially, this act represented a victory for businessmen like Hill, who had found their attempts to develop and profit from the West hampered by the predominant economic and political groups in some states.[55]

Although the passage of the act represented the fulfillment of the main aim of the National Irrigation Association, the organization did not disband nor did its funding cease. Rather, Maxwell embarked on a campaign to repeal the Desert Land Act and the commutation clause of the Homestead Act, both of which he saw as encouraging speculation rather than small-scale settlement. Additionally, the organization desired a forestry bill that could protect water supplies, and it wanted to ensure that federal monies appropriated for irrigation did not become a lever in interregional squabbles.

Overall, though, James Hill's involvement in irrigation reached its zenith of optimism in 1902 with the passage of the Newlands Act. This legislation brought with it the anticipation of federally sponsored irrigation throughout the West, but especially in northern Montana, which had sparked Hill's interest initially and promised to be one of the first areas developed. Certainly in the case of irrigation, Hill, in 1902 at least, could claim his policy of promoting agricultural development through other institutions had triumphed.[56]

Thus, by 1902 the Great Northern's involvement in agriculture had changed direction in a seemingly very successful way. Moving away from unilateral action as a eighteenth-century gentleman farmer, Hill had started to develop links between the corporation he headed and other institutions to further agricultural development. In his drainage endeavors, he worked through the state of Minnesota; in irrigation he first utilized subsidiary companies and later lobbied for federal involvement.

This change reflected Hill's acquiescence to the increased professionalization of agriculture in the late nineteenth century as well as changes in education. No longer did wealth itself indicate knowledge and expertise. Increasingly, these were displayed through formal education and institutionalization. Indeed, Hill retreated into his position as business expert and used his expertise and the power of his corporation to mobilize others. By employing engineers and publicists and lobbying politicians on the state and federal level, he had, by 1902, achieved more agriculturally in the previous nine years than in the entire fifteen years that preceded completion of the Great Northern.

Despite these successes, Hill's adoption of modern, narrow definitions of agricultural expertise was evidently more pragmatic than theoretical. Utilizing professionals toward his own ends, he never questioned his own claim to expertise, colored by the needs of his railway. Using the organizational genius with which he had built the Great Northern, he maneuvered people and opinions, and rejected ideas, however scientifically sound, when they did not promise direct benefit to his corporation or territory.

4 / "The Nation's Future," 1902–1907

Having weathered the economic and labor crises of the 1890s, the Great Northern Railway's personnel in the early twentieth century turned their attention to increasing traffic from all the environments along its roads, thus increasing its overall profitability. More ore and lumber haulage required more freight cars; the number increased from 13,818 in 1895 to 34,954 in 1906. These extra cars also reflected the continued expansion of wheat production in North Dakota, which surpassed Kansas in 1890 as the nation's leading wheat state. Unfortunately for James J. Hill, his political influence did not mirror his railroad's economic successes.[1]

Hill's financial and tactical support of William McKinley's 1896 and 1900 campaigns enabled him to maintain the leverage and lobbying power he had enjoyed at the federal level under Grover Cleveland. Like many contemporary business moguls, however, Hill had little faith in Theodore Roosevelt. As a New York City police commissioner, governor of New York, and in a variety of other political posts, young Roosevelt had demonstrated his interest in Progressive reform, which was often viewed as antithetical to business. His popularity following the charge of San Juan Hill in 1898 made him contemplate running for the presidency in 1904. The Republican Party decided to control what Marcus Hanna called this "damned cowboy," while capitalizing on Roosevelt's popularity by burying him in the vice-presidential slot in the 1900 election. McKinley's assassination in 1901 thus caused great consternation among the political and business elite, placing Hanna's "madman" in the White House.[2]

Roosevelt quickly justified Hill's concerns. As president, he continued his support of Progressive regulation of business. His chosen tool was the Sherman Anti-Trust Act of 1890, which forbade "combinations in restraint of trade." The legislation was vague enough to avoid successful enforcement during the 1890s except against unions, but in the new century, Roosevelt decided to see if it could be used against trusts. He chose Hill's Northern Securities Company—the holding company that brought the Great Northern and the Northern Pacific under one corporate umbrella—as the test case, and in February 1902 Attorney General Philander Knox filed suit.[3]

The Supreme Court did not return its verdict dissolving the Northern Securities Company until 1904. In the interim, Hill and his associates invested considerable energy attempting to mend fences between the Northern Securities conglomerate and Roosevelt. At a 1903 meeting between Howard Elliott, president of the Northern Pacific, and Roosevelt, the president assured Elliott that the law would be enforced, although he was glad to have a "Harvard man" in charge of the railroad. Elliott happily reported this implicit assurance of "old boy" support, failing to note the indirect attack on Hill, a self-made man who left school at fourteen. Hill, perhaps less naive than Elliott, railed against Roosevelt and invested considerable time and energy in defending the corporation, which he viewed as his personal property.[4]

The ripples from the Northern Securities case washed over all areas of Hill's life. The time and energy he invested in defending the holding company affected his health, and his family rallied around as he self-pityingly saw himself, in his mid-sixties, "growing old and helpless." He was amazed, as the case unraveled, that the court admitted no benefit in trusts or security companies. Attacks on combinations had been growing for more than a decade, but Hill failed to understand the extent to which many politicians had embraced the question of regulation for both pragmatic and ideological reasons.[5]

Fighting the case, he found himself defending an increasingly unpopular ideology in every possible way, including contributing an essay to a book in defense of trusts. Hill's quixotic position in *Northern Securities v. U.S.* reflected his earlier adoption of the obsolescent gentleman farmer image and foreshadowed his growing alienation from the mainstream of agricultural thought during the last fifteen years of his life. The case had more immediate consequences on Hill's agricultural success, reducing his political influence and exacerbating his antagonism to the federal agencies that were involved in western development.[6]

The Great Northern's loss of power on a national level had a detrimental effect on Hill's efforts to strengthen the agricultural infrastructure of his railroad through institutional cooperation. When federal irrigation programs failed to meet Hill's expectations, his only recourse was to complain bitterly about the inefficiency of the Reclamation Service, the federal agency established by the Newlands Act in 1902, and continue to try to foster irrigation by working through other institutions, such as universities and regional irrigation associations. As these efforts, too, proved ineffective, Hill began to invest more energy in dryland farming and crop diversification. Concerned about falling agricultural prices as well as agricultural production, Hill turned his attention to expanding American exports, especially with Asia, thus reducing dependence on European markets. As well as broadening the scope of his agricultural endeavors, Hill also returned increasingly to independent action in an attempt to regain the control he had forfeited to other institutions.[7]

Hill continued to promote irrigation after the passage of the Newlands Reclamation Act, initially by displaying support for the Reclamation Service. He firmly believed that in irrigation he had found a salvation for the nation as well as a meal ticket for his line. "No agency at work," he insisted of the Reclamation Service, "does so much to ameliorate, to elevate, to raise the general level of comfort and intelligence and even of character as the reclamation of our desert lands." Hill's moral slant on irrigation and rural life reflected the central precepts of groups such as the Country Life Commission, appointed by Theodore Roosevelt. Hill hoped that irrigation would replenish the yeoman farmer in the West, creating a place where "the small farm, thoroughly tilled, [replaced] the large farm, with its weeds, its neglected corners, its abused soil and its thin product." He also thought it would encourage dense settlement along his line, where a "spirit of associative enterprise" could be cultivated. These intrinsic benefits would counter the negative trends of industrialization, which Hill saw as "immense population centers, surrounded by a country sparsely settled, imperfectly cultivated, and looking to the metropolis for the realization of dreams." Hill's ideals were, as ever, inseparable from the needs of his line, which would profit from the high haulage generated by the creation of his envisioned agrarian Eden, and this led him to support the Reclamation Service wholeheartedly in the first years after the Newlands Act.[8]

Three weeks after the passage of the Newlands Act, Congress created the Reclamation Service within the United States Geological Survey, headed by Frederick Haynes Newell. Newell embodied the Progressive ideal of formally trained experts, a growing influence in America at the end of the nineteenth century. An engineering graduate of the Massachusetts Institute of Technology, he had led the hydrological studies of the Geological Survey from 1890. He saw the Newlands Act as the opportunity to centralize and rationalize issues of water throughout the West under the guidance of well-trained, professional engineers, rather than farmers or politicians. His perspective, which promoted scientific federal control, found no place for alternate viewpoints, whether embodied in state water laws or dictated by farmer incomes, and it propelled Newell into conflict on many fronts.[9]

The Reclamation Service proved slow and expensive in fulfilling Hill's visions. The Service took on too many projects in order to maximize its political support, and costs proved much higher than estimated. The requirements of the Newlands Act added further delays. Before a project received federal funding, the Reclamation Service's engineers had to establish the practicality of irrigating the region, and a grassroots interest had to be demonstrated. The latter requirement placed the onus for advancement once more on the same farmers whom Hill had always found so conservative. Along with this problem of popular support, irrigation projects in the two areas Hill was most concerned about, North Dakota and Montana, also floundered because of environmental limitations, political conflict on state, national, and even international levels, and, in North Dakota, a lack of academic backing.

In North Dakota, environmental conditions helped prevent substantial farmer support of irrigation. State politicians had displayed some interest in irrigation as early as 1889, with plans to irrigate the western reaches of the state using canals tapping into the Missouri River. These men viewed population growth as both the key to, and proof of, the state's success, and so they wanted to make some of the drier regions of the state more viable for settlement. The farmers who had already settled in North Dakota, however, had chosen the relatively well-watered lands still available and were farming at a time of generally adequate rainfall. They did not need the irrigation at that point and showed little interest in irrigating land for others.[10]

To generate farmer support and satisfy the conditions of the Newlands Act, state advocates of irrigation, backed by Hill, formed the North Dakota Irrigation Association in October 1903. Through this association, Hill aimed to keep irrigation in North Dakota at the forefront of federal and state minds. The group paid for a state engineer to assess irrigation potential independent of the federal government. It then mobilized bipartisan support for irrigation on a state level through newspaper campaigns and annual congresses. Most importantly, the organization developed an educational component to generate the support needed to obtain federal involvement by making "the value of irrigation . . . a permanent part of the common stock of knowledge; not the possession of a band of enthusiasts or a picked body of scientists and specialists."[11]

Although relatively successful in gaining political support, the North Dakota Irrigation Association had much less success in convincing farmers of the importance of irrigation. Part of their opposition was politically based. The association's president, Erastus Appleman Williams, had close affiliations with Alexander McKenzie. McKenzie, a railroad man by trade, had acquired considerable political power in North Dakota as a Republican national committeeman. He had always represented the interests of the railroads and other Twin Cities businesses, helping to make North Dakota, politically as well as economically, a colonial extension of St. Paul/Minneapolis. Farmers in North Dakota continually resisted McKenzie's politics and the state's colonial status, and they attempted, largely unsuccessfully, to control the railroads through legislation and taxes as early as 1890. Consequently, the North Dakota Irrigation Association, with its overriding political affiliations, faced considerable farmer skepticism.[12]

North Dakota farmers also opposed irrigation under the Newlands Reclamation Act on the basis of economics. They were wary of plans that would commit them to indeterminate costs. The structure of the Newlands Act made them responsible for repaying the expense of irrigation in annual increments, yet the Reclamation Service only provided them with an estimate of the final charges. Hill denied the farmers had any rational foundation for their opposition, dismissing their lack of enthusiasm as ignorance: "Work in North Dakota has been delayed by the slowness of the people, owing to a lack of appreciation of the great benefits accruing, to co-operate."[13]

Despite Hill's accusations of slowness, the farmers were not operating from a position of ignorance. Farmers in North Dakota, especially the eastern portion of the state, began during this period to pay more attention to advice disseminated by local scientists. The North Dakota Agricultural College had started Farmers' Institutes, and they were growing in popularity. Thus, agricultural academics did play some part in shaping farmer opinions. But the college experts did not support irrigation for the state. Their work, done in Fargo and at various statewide experiment stations, focused on farming adaptation to the North Dakota environment through crop rotation and diversification rather than by alterations of that environment via irrigation. Therefore, farmer disinterest in irrigation reflected, rather than rejected, the local academic position.[14]

Hill and other irrigation promoters in North Dakota tried to overcome this lack of interest in irrigation among local academics by using professors from Montana. With a history of successful irrigation in areas such as the Gallatin Valley, Montanans, as a whole, were more enthusiastic about reclamation. The Montana Agricultural Association, headed by W.M. Wooldridge of Hinsdale, who had corresponded with Hill in the 1890s regarding irrigation in Montana, promoted reclamation relentlessly. Moreover, unlike in North Dakota, the Montana Agricultural College's Experiment Station in Bozeman under Frederick B. Linfield also displayed an active interest. Consequently, Williams, as head of the North Dakota Irrigation Association, persuaded Wooldridge and Linfield to attend various congresses and the North Dakota State Fair, where Wooldridge exhibited crops grown under irrigation shipped gratis on Hill's Northern Pacific. Wooldridge acknowledged the importance of Farmers' Institutes in conveying information on irrigation in Montana and suggested attempting something similar in North Dakota.[15]

Despite these obstacles to grassroots support, irrigation promoters did achieve some progress in North Dakota. Some farmers in the Buford-Trenton region on the Missouri River and the Little Muddy River, which feeds into the Missouri just below Williston, agreed to comply with the requirements of the Newlands Reclamation Act. They formed water associations and contracted to pay back the cost of irrigation over the course of twelve years. Both valleys are composed of rich alluvial soil, and the interested farmers aimed to grow potatoes, sugar beets, and alfalfa on the irrigated land. The valleys were on the main line of the Great Northern, where farmers had a greater assurance of being able to market their crops. The area also had the advantage of being near a large deposit of lignite coal. This coal, while useless for railroads because of its tendency to spontaneously combust if stored, could generate electricity at the new power plant, which one booster described as being "practically as solid and substantial as the pyramids themselves." The electricity generated ran a main barge-pumping unit on the Missouri River and other, smaller pumps that distributed the water. The Reclamation Service completed construction in June 1907 and intended that the project should ultimately irrigate 52,000 acres.[16]

These irrigation schemes proved problematic from the start, despite attempts to boost their popularity. Secretary of the Interior James Garfield formally opened the Buford-Trenton and Williston projects in 1907. The

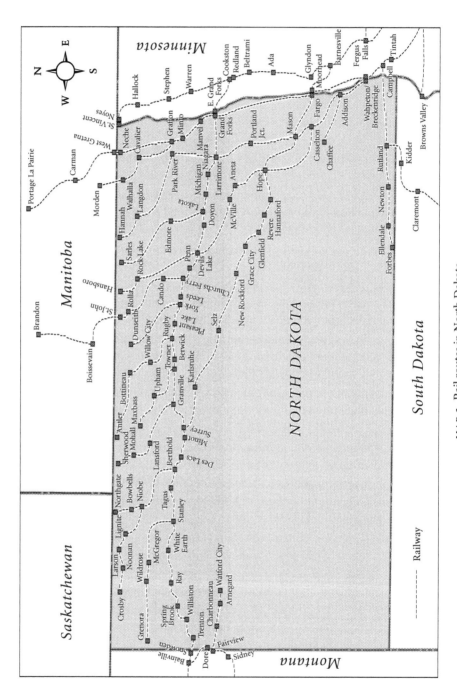

MAP 3. Rail routes in North Dakota

consequent publicity did not solve the inherent problems of cost and farmer resistance to irrigation. The majority of farmers holding land in the irrigation districts refused to join the water users' association and assume the costs, and so they were blocked from access to the water when it started pumping in 1908. Irrigation promoters believed that high yields on the irrigated lands would soon persuade reluctant farmers of the project's benefits.[17]

Hill's experiences with irrigation in North Dakota demonstrated continued problems with realizing his agricultural vision. Having lobbied and advertised on a national level for five years, in 1902 he faced the same problem of garnering grassroot farmer support that had plagued him since his earliest years as an agricultural promoter. Continuing to operate through other institutions, he had helped to found the North Dakota Irrigation Association, lending the organization his stature and agricultural expertise. As with his distribution of cattle and his attempts to drain the lands of the Red River Valley, however, Hill found his credentials insufficient to influence agriculture. When contemplating changing their practices, farmers relied on a more complex network of information than that provided by one railroad man backing a group of unpopular politicians. In North Dakota, regardless of the efforts of Hill, boosters, and politicians, only a few farmers with direct access to railroads showed any interest in irrigation.

Unlike in North Dakota, the problems faced by irrigation promoters in Montana in the early years of federal reclamation tended to be more political and environmental rather than social or economic. Irrigation in the state had begun as early as 1865 along the river valleys. By 1880, 350,000 acres of the state were, according to the director of the Montana Agricultural College's Experiment Station from 1904 to 1937, Frederick B. Linfield, "under the ditch." Irrigated lands had increased to nearly one million acres by the passage of the Newlands Act. Hence, Montanans, both farmers and academics, were well aware of the benefits of irrigation.[18]

Political factionalism, on the other hand, prevented much irrigation in Montana in the early twentieth century and embroiled George Maxwell, Hill, and their colleagues in a contest for dominance within the state. The problem originated in Washington, D.C. Elwood Mead, as head of the USDA's Office of Irrigation Investigations, favored greater state control over water issues in all western states, including Montana. Mead had been both the state and territorial irrigation engineer in Wyoming, where he helped create the water policy of the state constitution in 1889. The Wyoming law extended the Colorado system of placing unappropriated water under state ownership by claiming that all water in the state was state property for which people could apply for a right of use. This creation of a powerful bureaucracy worked fairly effectively in states such as Wyoming, which operated essentially as oligarchies, but it portended conflict in states like Montana, where a variety of vested interests contended for available resources. Mead supported federal involvement in irrigation because only the national government had the resources for the extensive surveys necessary, but he remained a strong advocate of a decentralized program that would allocate substantial power to individual states.[19]

Due to their different approaches to federal irrigation, Mead had always been in conflict with Frederick Newell of the Geological Survey, who favored federal control and rationalization. Their conflict expanded in 1898, when Mead was appointed head of the newly created Office of Irrigation Investigations in the USDA. With the triumph of centralized control and the appointment of Newell in 1902, Mead lost the battle in Washington. He now moved the struggle to the state level, where he encouraged disgruntled western politicians to pass laws similar to those established in Wyoming, intended to reassert as much state control over water as possible. This, according to George Maxwell, an avid proponent of federal centralization, would hamper the Reclamation Service's ability to work in the state that offered "greater possibilities than any other state for development under the national irrigation policy."[20]

In Montana the sides for this debate lined up as they had over the Newlands Act. Maxwell anticipated that the livestock interests would favor greater state control over water, while the mining interests would be disinterested and thus open to persuasion by ranchers. The stockmen had little interest in agricultural irrigation and, once they gained power over water issues, could stymie federal irrigation projects in the state. Maxwell strategized by calling in political favors and persuading his allies, such as Hill, to do the same. In addition, Maxwell sent a lengthy press release to all Montana editors, legislators, and members of the National Irrigation Association, detailing the problems inherent in the idea of state control of water. These efforts proved successful, indefinitely postponing or derailing in the state senate all four bills introduced into Montana's lower house. The energy invested in this debate, however, prevented much action being taken on launching state irrigation projects.[21]

Although political conflict delayed extensive irrigation in much of Montana, the Milk River project was halted by geographical issues. The federal government approved the valley for irrigation in 1903 and ordered a survey by district engineer Cyrus C. Babb. In hearings before the House Committee on Irrigation of Arid Lands in 1904, Babb reported that irrigation in the lower valley between Chinook and Glasgow was eminently feasible. He advocated a storage reservoir on the St. Mary's River, in what is now Glacier National Park, which would channel additional water into the lower Milk River.[22]

Unfortunately, a variety of problems rooted in the immediate economic environment confronted construction of the irrigation system. A cattle company owned the proposed reservoir site, and the irrigation works would result in the flooding of some Great Northern tracks. Railroad engineers had estimated that the necessary modifications would cost four hundred thousand dollars, and it was unclear how the burden of this cost would be divided between the government and the railroad.[23]

A more significant dilemma facing the proposed irrigation came from the political environment, both national and international. The Fort Belknap Reservation was situated on the Milk River south of the towns of Harlem and Dodson. In 1905 the federal government took settlers in the upper valley to court for irrigating crops. The government claimed that these settlers, upstream of the reservation, had failed to leave sufficient water in the river for the reserved lands. Subsequent appeals upheld this ruling, establishing the *Winters* doctrine of reservation water rights in 1908. The legal process temporarily slowed federal irrigation activity in the valley. It also meant that the Reclamation Service had to ensure sufficient water in the Milk River to irrigate the upper valley and still supply the reservation.[24]

To increase the water supply in the Milk River, the Reclamation Service advocated diverting water from the St. Mary's River, but this brought political and natural environments into conflict. After rising in western Montana, the Milk River first flows northeasterly into Canada for over a hundred miles before recrossing the international border into the eastern part of the state. The St. Mary's River also flows north into Canada and stays there. By 1904 an irrigation company backed by the Canadian government, the Canadian Northwest Irrigation Company, had established a canal network that watered thirty thousand Canadian acres from the St. Mary's River. The Canadians objected to the idea of diverting water from the St. Mary's into the Milk River before the former crossed the border. This international political conflict considerably complicated matters and forced district engineer Cyrus Babb to involve the state department in negotiations over water rights. Frederick Newell, also present at the hearings as the head of the Reclamation

Service, pointed out that, although initially appearing most favorable, the problems encountered on the Milk River suggested that reclamation monies in Montana could be better used elsewhere in the state, namely in the southern portion.[25]

This diversion of attention from the Milk River Valley did not endear the Reclamation Service or Newell to Hill. It demonstrated that the problem of relying on other agencies for agricultural change lay in the potential for diverging agendas. The political, environmental, and bureaucratic complications that delayed federal irrigation in the Milk River Valley forced Hill to consider other options for making the railroad's territory in Montana profitable.[26]

While working in North Dakota and Montana to encourage irrigation under the Newlands Reclamation Act, Hill continued to lobby for more federal control over western land use through George Maxwell and the National Irrigation Association. With federal irrigation legislation now in place, Hill, Maxwell, and their congressional allies turned their attention to what Hill described as "the insane policy of land laws which tend toward the exhaustion of the public domain by the land monopolist and speculator." These various loopholes in the homesteading and other land laws allowed ranchers, miners, and speculators to appropriate large acreages at the expense of the small-scale settler. Mine and cattle companies encouraged their employees to register claims, which the companies later purchased.[27]

Cattle owners were particularly motivated to exercise control over the western environment. Like other westerners, they depended on water for their business interests, especially after the blizzards of 1886 and 1887 forced them away from free range grazing. The dramatic losses of cattle in the storms had convinced many cattlemen to provide winter shelter and fodder for their stock. They needed regular access to water to raise forage and water their herds while in confined winter quarters. Thus, they frequently abused the land laws to gain control of streams in the public domain, making the adjacent land useless for farming or for other ranchers.[28]

The National Irrigation Association began a push to repeal laws which facilitated such land fraud. The commutation clause of the Homestead Act allowed settlers to buy title to their land after only six months at $1.25 to $2.50 per acre, based on a preemption right. This clause had been in the Homestead Act since its inception, but major abuse did not start until the late nineteenth century. Although stockmen did take advantage of commutation throughout the West, fraud actually peaked in North Dakota during the first decade of the twentieth century. The wheat boom encouraged speculators to homestead land, commute their claim, and sell the land for a huge profit to large-scale farmers. The Timber and Stone Act of 1878 allowed the low-priced sale of timberlands to prospective settlers. By the 1880s, this act was being used to transfer public timberlands almost directly to lumber corporations. The Desert Land Act of 1877 sold a settler a section of land for twenty-five cents per acre on the condition that they irrigate it within three years. Stockmen used this law to acquire large acreages of grazing land, making only nominal attempts at irrigation. Joseph Quarles of Wisconsin introduced a bill to repeal these three land laws in November 1903, and the Senate referred it to the Committee on Public Lands.[29]

The composition of the opposing forces in the conflict over the Quarles bill resembled the struggle over state or federal water control in Montana. On the one side, according to George Maxwell, were the "Elwood Mead-Wyoming coterie," who wanted to protect their interest in "speculative land grabbing or the building up of great stock ranches to the exclusion of settlers." Mead, so dependent on ranching support, could not afford to back actions so obviously designed to undermine his constituency. On the other side were aligned Maxwell, Hill, the members of the National Irrigation Association, as well as men such as Chief Forester Gifford Pinchot. These public figures hoped that reform of land policy would result in greater federal control over western resources, thus fostering a West that was "one continuous village, with . . . no incentive for the creation of vast centers that breed evils." They couched this view in the most ideological terms. They opposed "speculating interests" who were "grabbing" land intended "for the benefit of the people." Only true settlers could utilize land "which is now idle or waste," and the nation depended on the association, which faced "a very hard fight, for personal interests [the opposition] will get up and work in the night while patriotism is asleep." These repealers did not deny their self-interests in the matter, but they insisted that the "development of the west" was vital, "especially to the commercial interests . . . who must have population to create trade."[30]

Concurrent with the promotion of the Quarles bill, the National Irrigation Association was busy trying to squash a bill proposed by a former ally, Senator Henry C. Hansbrough of North Dakota. Hansbrough, a McKenzie man, had consistently supported the Hill faction with respect to reclamation and settlement in lobbying for the Newlands Act. However, his reelection in the winter of 1902 had been contingent on his appeasing "the cattle and land speculating interests in his State." Hansbrough recognized the difficulty of his position, caught between two opposing groups: the railroads and the ranchers.[31]

Consequently, Hansbrough tried to walk a tightrope between the two factions in 1903 by introducing a bill that made land fraud more difficult. He proposed amendments to the Desert Land Act and outright repeal of the Timber and Stone Act. He advocated leaving the commutation clause of the Homestead Act alone, arguing that fraud occurred less than "the yellow journals would make us believe" and that the clause provided an important benefit to genuine homesteaders. To ameliorate matters further, Hansbrough argued that the repeal of the Desert Land Act would hinder public land sales and thus prevent the construction of a sizable fund for reclamation.[32]

Unfortunately for Hansbrough, this bill did not appease the leaders of the National Irrigation Association who opposed him. The association denied claims that little fraud was committed under the Desert Land Act and the commutation clause of the Homestead Act. Instead, Montana Senator Paris Gibson, a close friend, business partner, and political ally of Hill's, saw Hansbrough's actions as "just what the stock-men and speculators want, and . . . simply designed to give them more time in which to gobble up the remaining agricultural land." Gibson also dismissed as ridiculous the idea that repeal should be delayed in order to fund reclamation, writing, "How absurd that we should permit the wholesale stealing of the public land, for the sake of creating a reclamation fund!"[33]

Hill worked to publicize the salient issues, too, as for him, at least, the ideological stance of the supporters of the Quarles Bill was not assumed. Despite his holdings of western lands, such as those given to him by the Wenatchee Development Company for routing his railroad through the valley, he did not see himself as a "speculator" (a negatively charged term), but as a "developer." That those supporting the Quarles bill stood to gain financially from the repeals did not make their contention that the legislation represented the best for America any less sincere. Self-interest compounded rather than contradicted their position, and they stood firm, backed by a legacy of over a century of Jeffersonian agrarianism.

To boost the act, Hill integrated the complex issues of land laws into his public addresses, telling audiences to demand the "repeal of vicious and fraudulent land laws still in force, by which all our lands are being dissipated." Influencing public opinion was all Hill could hope for, as his political clout had diminished with the advent of Roosevelt's administration. Hansbrough's appointment as chairman of the Senate Committee on Public Lands further compounded the problems confronting the National Irrigation Association, despite the fact that the committee also held powerful pro-Hill forces, such as Knute Nelson, Paris Gibson, and, to a lesser extent, Francis Newlands. Political deadlock resulted, and in the spring of 1904 the U.S. Congress "indefinitely postponed" the bills proposed by Hansbrough and Quarles.[34]

After 1902 Hill's hopes for an irrigated West were increasingly frustrated by political opposition and bureaucratic complexities. Environmental realities and farmer lassitude delayed projects on the ground, while the National Irrigation Association failed to maintain its influence on federal policy. The lack of further legislation favoring small-scale settlement, combined with the slowness of the Reclamation Service's work to irrigate Montana, forced Hill to consider alternative ways to encourage a more populated, agrarian West than through irrigation. Thus, in 1905 he belatedly followed the lead of the Great Northern's sister railroad, the Northern Pacific, by becoming involved in the dryland farming movement.[35]

Dryland farming used water-conserving cultivable techniques to make more of the plains suitable for small-scale grain farming. The idea was largely initiated by a Vermont native, Hardy Webster Campbell. In 1879 he entered a homestead claim in Brown County, Dakota Territory. He began to experiment with various types of cultivation techniques aimed at conserving the moisture in the soil, and in 1890 he invented the sub-surface packer. This machine was comprised of a series of wedge-shaped wheels, which revolved around an axle that cut deep into the soil, tamping it at the bottom of the cut while mulching the topsoil. It provided the basis for the Campbell System of cultivation, which Hardy Webster Campbell sought to publicize through the Western Agricultural Improvement Society, founded in 1895.[36]

The basic premise behind the sub-surface packer centered around the capillary moisture in the soil. This is the small amount of water that surrounds each soil particle and moves through the soil as water moves through a sponge. Campbell and others argued that to maximize the retention and use this water, two things must be done. First, the subsoil, from two to sixteen inches below the surface, had to be packed down to encourage capillary action upward through the soil. Second, the top layer of soil had to be carefully and repeatedly cultivated in order to decrease its capillary action, thus hindering evaporation on the soil surface.[37]

Campbell gradually developed more concepts related to dryland farming. By 1902, when he published his first *Soil Culture Manual*, the Campbell System advocated 160-acre farms. On these farms he recommended deep fall plowing, cultivation before and after seeding, and alternating summer fallow with tillage of the soil during fallow as well as crop years. Campbell's success lay partially in his ability to tie his work closely to scientific experiments being done at various experiment stations. He frequently quoted F. H. King of the University of Wisconsin's Experiment Station and Willet Hays of the University of Minnesota's Experiment Station, among others. Most importantly, though, Campbell was an effective publicist. He incorporated a number of dry farming organizations, including The Campbell System of Farming Association. He also published many dry farming journals and magazines, such as the monthly *Dry Farming Magazine*, and proselytized his ideas to the railways, which happily financed and promoted his work.[38]

As early as 1895, two regional railroads, the Northern Pacific and the Burlington, financed dry farming promotion through Campbell. In that year Campbell ran five experiment stations for the Northern Pacific in North Dakota and gave lectures on dry farming along the Burlington. Campbell did approach the Great Northern, writing to Hill in 1895 to request a meeting to discuss the viability of dry farming. He wanted Hill's help in proving "to our people and outside parties that we have a country actually superior to the Eastern humid districts." Hill was disinterested, and Campbell received no funding from the Great Northern.[39]

Other Great Northern personnel, however, did show interest in dry farming. In early 1897 B. S. Rufsell of the Great Northern drafted an agreement with Campbell regarding dry farming experiment stations in North Dakota. The agreement stated that the Great Northern would give Campbell $3,300, free transportation, and supplies for maintaining seven 40-acre farms for three years. In return, Campbell would supply a thousand copies of *Campbell Soil Culture and Farm Journal* throughout the region and instruct local farmers on the methods and benefits of dry farming. This agreement, however, was never put into practice. With Hill firmly in charge of the Great Northern's agricultural policies in the 1890s, the line followed his lead and channeled its agricultural efforts into irrigation promotion.[40]

Hill's disinterest in dryland farming was directly linked to the needs of his railroad. Although the Great Northern profited from transporting wheat from the plains, and Hill advocated increased wheat production to match anticipated population growth, he initially had reservations about the dry farming movement. Needing stable, productive agriculture, not just land sales, to make profit on his railroad, he hesitated to invest in a potential dryland farming economy that might bust as quickly as it had boomed. Additionally, dry farming tended toward extensive monocropping, which rested uneasily with Hill, a man devoted to intensive diversification. But, after 1905, stalled federal irrigation combined with other railroads' successful boosting of dryland farming to alter Hill's perspective.[41]

Hill's increased interest in dryland farming resulted from a pragmatic reassessment of irrigation potential, but his strategies of promotion remained consistent. As with irrigation, Hill utilized the expertise of others to enhance his own standing. The involvement of state experiment stations in dryland farming lent scientific validity to the movement. While continuing to believe in his own claim to expertise through practical experience and business acumen, Hill valued the professionalization of farming by university personnel. This endorsement by academic experts gave dryland farming additional credibility that Hill recognized he could not provide alone. Although he based his agricultural authority in the obsolete notion of the gentleman farmer, he nevertheless thought that Progressive notions of scientific research and farming would uphold, not undermine, his ideologies and prominence. He was wrong.

The Great Northern's first venture into practical dry farming experimentation came through its sister railroad, the Montana experiment station, and the USDA. In the fall of 1904, Thomas Cooper, land commissioner of the Northern Pacific, wrote to the agricultural college at Bozeman, noting that successful wheat growing in eastern Washington took place in an area with less rainfall than eastern Montana. Cooper also approached the USDA and asked for cooperation in the investigation of dry farming. In February 1905, Cooper met with Elwood Mead, head of the USDA's Office of Irrigation Investigations, and Professor Frederick B. Linfield, director of the Montana Agricultural College's Experiment Station. They decided to establish four demonstration farms in Montana at Helena, Dillon, Miles City, and the station north of Glendive. The Northern Pacific contributed the most support, providing twenty-five hundred dollars to the work, while the USDA and Montana Agricultural College's Experiment Station gave a thousand dollars each.[42]

This cooperation between corporate and governmental organizations gave way to contests over jurisdiction after 1906, when the USDA ceased its involvement, having established its own Office of Dry Land Agriculture under Ellery Channing Chilcott. Initially the problems remained limited to Utah. The Office of Dry Land Agriculture enabled the USDA to fully control, or at least to try to control, all dryland farming investigations that received federal funding. At the Agricultural College of Utah, the college president, Walter Jasper Kerr, had obtained a ten-thousand-dollar state appropriation in 1905 for irrigation and dryland farming investigations, subject to a like appropriation from the federal government. Mead at the USDA insisted that all work, except at the agricultural station itself at Logan, be under his control through Chilcott. Kerr fought for equal jurisdiction for the college. Frederick Linfield, who had taught in Utah for nine years, was avidly tracking this debate. He decided to avoid similar problems in Montana by circumventing the federal government altogether, approaching the railroads directly and arranging for financing for continuing research.[43]

Initially the partnership between the agricultural college and the Hill railroads was smooth. In 1906 the Montana Agricultural College and the Northern Pacific discontinued the stations at Helena and Dillon because they were too far from the railroad. Work at Miles City also stopped as the expert in charge, W. W. McLaughin, originally of the Agricultural College of Utah's Experiment Station, judged it to "be a waste of time." Instead, the Northern Pacific sponsored three stations in Montana: north of Glendive; near Forsyth; and north of Billings. The same year the Great Northern, at the instigation of Linfield, committed two thousand dollars to maintain three dry farming stations along its lines: 640 acres north of Harlem, 100 acres near Shelby, and 40 acres near Great Falls. Results were promising. The first year of Great Northern involvement saw some successful grain production, and samples of grain from all three sponsored plots were exhibited at the Montana State Fair.[44]

Despite this apparent initial success, the Great Northern plots soon floundered. The Harlem station, an exercise in cooperation, was undermined by its environment. Congress authorized the use of a section of land for ten years, and the Great Northern donated transportation for the university men and equipment. No agency, however, could overcome some of the inherent difficulties of the site. The land was at a considerable distance both from the town and from water, which exacerbated the problems of dryland farming. The isolation of the site allowed range cattle and horses to damage the crops before fencing could be constructed. Grassroots support ultimately proved vital in establishing this station as local townspeople did what they could to help. During the first season, they built a house on the farm, fenced the land, and drilled a well.[45]

In addition to problems on the sponsored plots, the Great Northern also became embroiled in conflict with the USDA. The 1906 decision of the USDA to end its involvement in dryland farming investigations in Montana created a gulf between its personnel and those of the experiment station and railroad. Collaboration had hidden conflicts over authority and expertise that, now exposed, added to the confusion surrounding the viability of dryland farming. Aware of the problems in Utah, Linfield had been careful to prevent the USDA from trespassing on his authority. However, the Montana Agricultural College was largely financed by the state. College personnel were aware of the tremendous political power of the railroads and knew the college had to please its constituents. Therefore, college representatives generally showed determined optimism when discussing the prospects of dryland farming. On the other hand, representatives of the USDA, which had a broader audience and a wider financial base, could afford to be more outspoken in this matter.

Not dependent on railroads or other interests for funding, USDA personnel voiced their reservations regarding dryland farming promotion and research with impunity. In response to inquiries about dryland farming statistics from a Great Northern immigration agent, Ellery Channing Chilcott expressed many of his nascent concerns. He believed that the Great Plains had undergone a period of "abnormal rainfall for the last three years," and that this, rather than any "so-called methods or systems of dry land farming," had spurred the crop improvement. Chilcott criticized the promotion of dryland farming being undertaken by the railroads. "I would say that many of the articles that have appeared in magazines and other publications concerning the possibilities of dry land agriculture are wildly exaggerated."[46]

While the responsibilities of the federal government led Chilcott to assume a conservative position regarding dryland farming, the Montana Agricultural College's railroad funding colored its scientific assessments. The college publications of this time optimistically advocated dryland farming techniques. Financial need, as well as determination to assert his independence from federal overseeing, temporarily trapped Linfield and his staff in subordination to the railroad's research agenda, blurring the objectivity of their science.[47]

From the railroad's perspective, dryland farming always ran a poor second to irrigation. Hill's dedication to irrigation remained strong as late as 1904, when he stated that all the land in Montana that was cultivable without irrigation had been claimed. His caution with respect to dryland farming was linked to the needs of the Great Northern. Because the railroad lacked land grants, it required successful long-term development of land and not just the initial attraction of settlement and land sales to make a profit. In addition, incorporating dryland farming, with its emphasis on large-scale monocropping, into Hill's "gospel of the small farm" proved difficult.[48]

The Great Northern did not limit its cooperation with academic institutions during these years to dryland farming and the Montana Agricultural College. The railroad also helped the North Dakota Agricultural College reach the farmers of its state and transmit the foundations of scientific agriculture. Throughout the early years of the twentieth century, the railroad transported groups of farmers gratis to visit the college in Fargo. Unlike the Montana school, however, the North Dakota Agricultural College refused to actively investigate either dryland farming or irrigation for arable production, preferring to focus on identifying suitable crops and crop rotations for the state. This academic alienation from one of the prime interests of the Great Northern strained relations between the two organizations.[49]

Divergent experimental interests aside, the North Dakota Agricultural College personnel generally assumed a more suspicious approach toward the railroad than their peers in Montana. Much of this caution stemmed from the different perceptions of the leaders of the two institutions. Frederick Linfield in Montana had trained in Guelph, Canada, under Thomas Shaw at the Ontario Agricultural College. Linfield was thus part of the same socio-intellectual network that included Hill, and the later involvement of Shaw in dryland promotion of the Great Northern helped make it more accessible and acceptable to him. President John H. Worst of the North Dakota Agricultural College, on the other hand, proved perennially suspicious of railroads. Early on he assumed an activist stance, trying to break the railroads' hold on farmers by recasting the oft-touted cry of interdependence. At a speech at the college in 1907 he stated, "We owe much to the railroads and to other forms of corporate wealth, but they owe more to us. We could live without them, but they cannot do business without us. Our interests at least should be mutual and not one sided, and not on their side at that." This pro-farmer political activism, which often manifested itself as anti-railroad, continued throughout his life. Worst participated fully in the farmer-driven Nonpartisan League uprising in North Dakota starting in 1915 and advocated state-owned terminal elevators. He later became commissioner of immigration under the new state government.[50]

Although inherent antagonism existed between the North Dakota Agricultural College and the railroad, they did embark on some collaborative work. In 1906 the Great Northern and the Northern Pacific financed work on six demonstration farms in North Dakota. The railroad paid farmers to cultivate five four-acre plots on their farms in accordance with directions from E. G. Schollander of the agricultural college. Although similar in method to the dry farming work in Montana, the focus was somewhat different. The objectives, according to the college, were "to determine, what method of crop rotation is best adapted for that particular neighborhood, to introduce field corn and clover into the fields, to build up the fertility of the soil, instead of summer fallowing, and by extra tillage preserve the moisture and clean the land." This tied in with Hill's agricultural aims, as feed for livestock, crop rotation, and fertility were some of his prime concerns.[51]

Despite this cooperation, relations between the Great Northern and the college were never close. President Worst resisted corporate dominance, and his antagonism would become even more pronounced over time. In 1905 Louis Hill, James Hill's second son, and by then a vice president of the Great Northern, became concerned when he discovered that the North Dakota Agricultural College had run an agricultural train in conjunction with the rival Minneapolis, St. Paul & Sault Ste. Marie Railroad, also known as the Soo Line. President Worst justified the action as a response to crop failures along the line the previous year. He pointed out that similar failures had not occurred along the Hill lines, and so farmers along those railroads were less in need of the expert aid provided by the agricultural trains. Louis did not believe this explanation, perceiving instead a conspiracy to decrease the Great Northern's power in the state. "I am more inclined to think that Pennington [president of the Soo line] is trying to get a foot-hold in North Dakota politics and has been cultivating the Deputy Commissioner of Labor and Agriculture, Kaufman, of Bismarck, and that Worst is very willing to fall in line."[52]

Louis Hill thought Worst nursed a grievance against the Great Northern because of the railroad's continual delay in building a promised spur to the college heating plant. The supposition proved insightful. When accused of favoritism, Worst expressed surprise, suggested that the Great Northern run an agricultural train in conjunction with the college, but then raised the issue of the spur. After the railroad completed the spur in 1906, the agricultural college cooperated with the Great Northern in its "Good Seed Specials," which toured Minnesota and both Dakotas. Thus Worst successfully played one line against its competitor to benefit his school's infrastructure. Additionally, he gained support from both the Hill lines and the Soo lines in his agricultural outreach programs.[53]

The Good Seed Specials ran along the Great Northern lines in the spring of 1906, covering nearly two thousand miles. The trains carried academic agricultural experts selected by James J. Hill from various universities around the region, such as the University of Minnesota and Iowa State College. These scientists gave talks on how to select good seed grain, how to treat the grain to prevent smut and other diseases, and the importance of rotating crops and maintaining soil fertility. Over ten thousand farmers attended the trains' presentations, which compared favorably to similar trains run by the Canadian Pacific and Northern Pacific. The total cost of the enterprise was approximately $1,900.[54]

A pivotal voice among the scientists on the trains, at least from Hill's perspective, was the agricultural agent of the Great Northern and the Northern Pacific, Thomas Shaw. Born in Woodburn, Ontario, of Scottish parents, Shaw spent his early career at Ontario Agricultural College at Guelph before accepting the chair of animal husbandry at the University of Minnesota. Here his interest in cattle feeding led him to investigate potential forage crops and drought resistant plants, and he published three works on forage crops in the late 1890s. Forage research drew Shaw into dryland farming investigations, where he gained a considerable reputation. In 1899 scientists in South Dakota wrote that "it is our judgement that no one in the West is better fitted to supervise such . . . [dryland] experiments [than Shaw]." In 1902 Shaw resigned from the University of Minnesota to assume the editorship of *The Farmer* in St. Paul before moving to *The Dakota Farmer*. He then became employed by the Great Northern Railway. The Great Northern, however, did not put Shaw to work directly on the question of dry farming. His first official involvement with the line was on the demonstration trains in 1906.[55]

Shaw proved vital to the Great Northern's corporate, and Hill's private, agricultural programs during the subsequent decade. Meeting each other first in Minnesota around the turn of the century, Hill and Shaw developed a friendship based on their common heritage and interest in agriculture. Long before Hill officially employed Shaw, the latter's ideas reinforced Hill's own, and he acted, according to his son, as "a sort of agricultural explorer to report on the future development of agriculture in the undeveloped regions." The respect Shaw commanded in academic circles reflected on the Great Northern and lent Hill's ideas scientific credibility.[56]

Despite Shaw's employment by the company, the Great Northern's relationship with educational institutions, notably the University of Minnesota and the North Dakota Agricultural College, deteriorated still further in 1906 and 1907. Hill, working from his position as gentleman farmer, used the agricultural trains to publicize a new breed of corn that he believed was especially suited for northern climates. Anxious to promote his vision of the small-scale family farm and diversified agriculture, Hill had taken on one of the problems facing stock farmers in the northern Great Plains: winter feed. In more temperate regions such as Iowa, corn worked very well as a high calorie, nutritious feed, but in the early years of the twentieth century corn remained a risky crop in colder regions of the Dakotas and Montana, often failing to ripen.[57]

In 1905 Hill started pursuing the problem of feed on a personal level, working with another private expert, his friend Frank Sturgis of Round Hill Farm, Fairfield, Connecticut. Sturgis wrote to Hill about his "flint corn," which he claimed matured in nine weeks at forty to fifty bushels per acre, or 50 percent more than the average yield for Iowa farmers at the time. Hill acquired some seed for his North Oaks and Humboldt farms and, following his speech about the corn at the North Dakota State Fair in 1905, he received letters from various educational institutions requesting some of the corn.[58]

Good publicity attracted considerable interest, both grassroots and academic, and Hill distributed the corn throughout Minnesota and North Dakota from the Good Seed Specials. In addition, Shaw took the corn and growing information out to the farmers. The corn had been named "Jim Hill corn" to associate it with the virile western agricultural image the railroad man had engineered for himself. The St. Paul Experiment Station was willing to help with the research by distributing ten bushels to farmers for experimentation, while keeping enough at the station to maintain a pure genetic stock. Even John Worst at the North Dakota Agricultural College agreed to mount trials of the corn.[59]

The corn was a disaster, not only failing to mature earlier than other types of corn, but often much later. Letters from the farmers who received the corn, either from the university or from the Good Seed Specials, stated that it matured late (if at all, frost ruined some crops), that it was too hard for cattle or horses to eat, and that even Dent corn matured earlier. At the North Dakota Agricultural College "six varieties of corn . . . were planted. . . . When the first freezing weather came in the fall from 90 to 95 percent of all the corn had fully ripened with the exception of the Hill corn." The failure of "Jim Hill corn" epitomized for university agriculturists Hill's shortcomings as a scientific farmer.[60]

At this time agricultural scientists had not yet solidified their legitimacy and authority to dictate the future of American agriculture or land use development in the West. Their expertise remained contested by many, including small-scale farmers who, consciously or otherwise, recognized the inherent threat to their livelihood embodied in the promulgation of a capital- and technology-intensive agriculture. Attempting to assert their dominance, these university experts opposed all other forms of agricultural knowledge, including Hill's. Jealously guarding their newly won professional provenance, academics were wary of Hill's claim to expertise. Based solely on experience and money rather than objective experiment, scientists perceived Hill's authority as an antiquated, and therefore unreliable, approach to improving agriculture.[61]

Thus professors viewed Hill's expertise askance. At the University of Minnesota this distrust, theoretically rooted, had been reinforced earlier through embarrassment over the waterlogged Northwest Experiment Station, and by their rejection of Hill's advocacy of dual-purpose cattle during the last decades of the nineteenth century. Now the debacle of "Jim Hill corn" further alienated collegiate institutions from Hill and his agricultural plans, but this break was far from complete. The Montana Agricultural College still cooperated with the railway in its dry farming demonstrations, and no university within the northern tier of states could afford to completely antagonize the president of the Great Northern Railway.

The increasing suspicion with which academics viewed Hill mirrored his growing disillusionment with them and with institutional agricultural development. Dissatisfaction with the Reclamation Service shook Hill's conviction that institutional cooperation would advance farm improvements. Although not completely abandoning cooperative ventures, Hill became more circumspect in his choice of partners and once more launched some independent programs.

One such independent program was a good farming competition Hill mounted in 1906. In late 1905 Thomas Shaw, then northwestern editor for *The Farmer,* wrote to Hill about an agricultural contest that the paper

The Great Northern Railway, pictured here in 1895, traversed huge areas of farmlands. To increase profit from the line, company president James J. Hill tried to manipulate the environment to maximize agricultural production. (Courtesy Minnesota Historical Society, HE6.2G/r3)

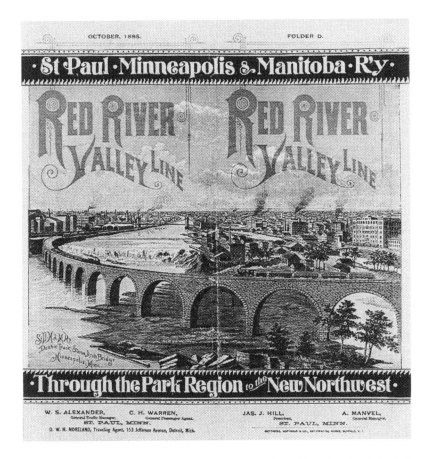

OCTOBER, 1885.   FOLDER D.

·St Paul ·Minneapolis &.Manitoba·R'y·

RED RIVER VALLEY LINE   RED RIVER VALLEY LINE

S.D.M&M.
Double Track Stone Arch Bridge
Minneapolis Minn.

·Through the Park Region to the New Northwest·

W. S. ALEXANDER,   C. H. WARREN,   JAS. J. HILL,   A. MANVEL,
General Traffic Manager,   General Passenger Agent,   President,   General Manager.
          ST. PAUL, MINN.   ST. PAUL, MINN.
D. W. H. MORELAND, Traveling Agent, 153 Jefferson Avenue, Detroit, Mich.

The personnel of the St. Paul, Minneapolis & Manitoba Railway interlaced the Red River Valley with branch lines to maximize profits from bonanza farming, 1884. The haulage generated was used to float loans to extend the railroad to the West Coast. (Photograph 1884; courtesy Minnesota Historical Society, HE6.6/p10)

(Facing page, top) At his farm, North Oaks, James J. Hill experimented with cross-breeding cattle, 1900. He wanted to develop dual-purpose stock that produced quality milk and meat and were also hardy enough to survive winters on the northern Great Plains. (Photograph 1900; courtesy James J. Hill library, JH549jpg)

(Facing page, bottom) Bonanza farms, which were often owned by corporations, were enormous, with fields commonly a mile square. The wheat grown on these farms was taken by train to Minneapolis, where it fed the burgeoning flour industry. (Photograph by the Northwestern Photographic Studios, Great Northern Rwy. Collection, Minnesota Historical Society)

James J. Hill bought his own bonanza farm in the Red River Valley close to the Canadian border. In the 1910s, Walter Hill, James's youngest son, took up residence and tried unsuccessfully to turn it into a stock farm. (Photograph 1915; courtesy James J. Hill Library, JH70.jpg)

Although Hill's bonanza farm encompassed some 45,000 acres, his employees and later his son, Walter, cultivated only about 3,000 acres. The rest were drained and sold in small lots of 80 to 160 acres to encourage settlement in the valley. (Photograph ca. 1900 by Simmer Studio, Great Northern Rwy. Collection, Minnesota Historical Society, SA4.6/p112)

In the mid-1890s, Hill gave Great Northern land in the Red River Valley to the University of Minnesota for the establishment of the Northwest Experiment Station at Crookston. This land proved problematic as it flooded easily. (Photograph 1911; courtesy University of Minnesota at Crookston)

The Great Northern Railway's Elevator Company in Minneapolis, c. 1905. (Courtesy Minnesota Historical Society, MH5.9/MP3.1G/p26)

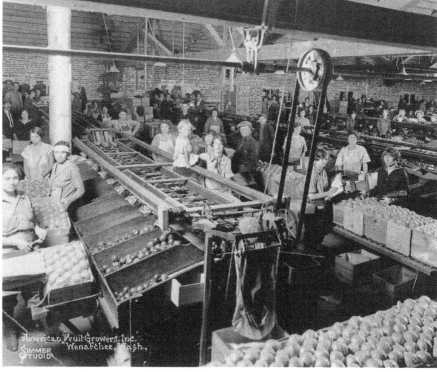

American Fruit Growers, Inc.
Wenatchee, Wash.
Simmer Studio

The Great Northern Company hoped that irrigation in the Wenatchee region would change the environment sufficiently to permit apple growing. This did happen, as seen in these three publicity shots. However, the irrigation process cost the railroad considerably more than anticipated, while profits remained slim during Hill's lifetime. (Undated photograph; Kiser Photograph Company, Great Northern Rwy. Collection, Minnesota Historical Society)

(Facing page, top) Other institutions were interested in the development of the fruit industry on the Columbia plateau. This photograph of Wenatchee from 1912 comes from the Seattle Chamber of Commerce photo album. (Courtesy MSCUA, University of Washington Libraries, UW25041)

(Facing page, bottom) Although apple production did increase, the need for expensive refrigerated cars to ship the fruit decreased the potential profit margin. (Undated photograph; Simmer Studio, Great Northern Rwy. Collection, Minnesota Historical Society)

Although the Milk River in Montana was one of the first areas targeted by the Reclamation Service, work was considerably delayed. Some canals, like this one, were built, but they were useless without the necessary pumps and water. (Undated photograph from the Great Northern Rwy. Collection, Minnesota Historical Society)

(Facing page, top) Along the western reaches of the Great Northern, the problem confronting agriculture was irrigation not drainage. The Columbia plateau has plenty of rivers, such as the Wenatchee River seen here, but the benchlands in between are semiarid. (Photograph c. 1912; courtesy MSCUA, University of Washington Libraries, UW 21915)

(Facing page, botttom) In 1903, Wenatchee Canal Company workers constructed irrigation pipes near Wenatchee. The company was indirectly financed by the Great Northern, which hoped to gain from increased agricultural production in the valley. (Courtesy James J. Hill library, JH 477.jpg)

This pumping barge, part of a Reclamation Service project in North Dakota, moved water from the Missouri River to the fields. Most farmers found, however, that water costs were higher than increased profits from the irrigated lands. (Undated photograph; courtesy Institute for Regional Studies, North Dakota State University Libraries, 162.3.12)

Frederick Haynes Newell had spent his entire career as a hydraulic engineer for the United States Geological Survey and so was well placed to serve as the first head of the Reclamation Service. (Courtesy National Archives and Records Administration, 115–P-130)

Another way to profit from the harsh lands of the northern Great Plains was through dry farming. This plowing technique was used by William Schroeder, a German immigrant, on his farm twenty miles northeast of Chinook, Montana. (Photograph 1914; Great Northern Rwy. Collection, Minnesota Historical Society)

Frederick Linfield, director of the Montana Agricultural College Experiment Station in Bozeman, Montana, was a proponent of dry-land farming. Under his direction, several cooperative ventures were launched to investigate the process. (Photograph 1902; courtesy Montana State University Archives)

James Hill and his son Louis often attended public events that promoted the northern Great Plains. Here they are at the American Land and Irrigation Exposition in New York City in 1911. (Photograph by Bostwich of Omaha, Minnesota Historical Society, por/8540/p10)

In North Dakota, university personnel were less favorable toward the railroad than in Montana. Led by John H. Worst, president of the North Dakota Agricultural College, they supported farmers in their view of railroads as extortionate. (Undated photograph; courtesy Institute for Regional Studies, North Dakota State University Archives, FW077.5)

To encourage farmers to embrace practices such as dryland farming, organizations held special events. This picnic day was sponsored by the Montana Agricultural College Experiment Station at one of their demonstration farms in 1911. (Courtesy Montana State University Archives)

Thomas Shaw was hired by the Great Northern to promote dryland farming throughout the railroad's territory. Coming from the same area of Ontario as Hill, he shared a common background and understanding of agriculture as his boss. (Courtesy Minnesota Historical Society, por/14882/Lee 1)

THE MODERN NEPTUNE.

James Hill also wanted to expand the profit of his railroad by tapping into Asian markets. To do this he built two ships, the S.S. Dakota and the S.S. Minnesota. The venture was not successful. (*Great Falls Daily Tribune,* April 19, 1903)

(*Facing page, top*) As well as supporting private farm exhibits, the Great Northern also sponsored corporate displays from the lands along their line. These exhibits were characterized by a tremendous bounty of grains, fruits, and photographs. (Photograph 1915; courtesy Minnesota Historical Society, E300/p15)

(*Facing page, bottom*) Taking a more academic approach to teaching, the Great Northern, like other railroads, sent out educational trains. In 1923, these farmers gathered at the train depot to learn about summer tillage. (Courtesy Montana State University Archives)

In 1912, the city of St. Paul gave a banquet in honor of James Hill's birthday. At this event, the aging Hill launched a virulent attack on the University of Minnesota's track record of teaching farmers. (Photograph 1912; courtesy James J. Hill Library)

By the end of his life, Hill's agricultural opinions were basically ignored. In this photograph, taken in Havre, Montana, in 1913, few people seem to be listening to the old man, and his grandson Cortlandt appears bored. (Courtesy James J. Hill Library)

intended to run. Shaw wanted to offer prizes for five consecutive years, aiming to improve cultivation techniques and wheat production. Hill expressed interest in this plan, seeing it as an opportunity to improve farming practices and increase diversification using a monetary incentive. Consequently, by early 1906, he had agreed to provide the prize money. The competition covered the congressional districts of Minnesota and the Dakotas, and first prize in each district was three hundred dollars.[62]

Using his financial backing as leverage, Hill demanded certain changes in the contest to bring it more in line with his vision of agricultural development. New rules were introduced, making livestock ownership an integral part of the competition. As he said two years after the competition, "I stipulated that a man, in order to be entitled to compete, should have twenty head of live stock for breeding purposes." By the time the paper published the criteria for the contest, they looked like a list of Hill's personal concerns for agriculture. In addition to number and quality of livestock, the judges considered rotation of crops for soil fertility and good yields, drainage, and fertilizing techniques. Along with tailoring the competition's criteria to meet his views, Hill also took control of its process. The Good Seed Specials and *The Farmer* publicized the contest, and the latter also did the paperwork. The judges were Shaw and Torger Hoverstad, both supporters of Hill. Thus, although the contest originated with *The Farmer,* Hill used his financial strength to commandeer it to meet his needs.[63]

The competition had only limited success. Out of five hundred farms that entered, only a hundred had sufficient livestock to be considered eligible, reflecting poorly on Hill's chances of achieving agricultural diversification along his line. Ultimately, the contest affected only the few farmers already practicing scientific agriculture. It was a case of Hill preaching to the choir. One of the winners, D. Tallman, of Willmar, Minnesota, exposed this dilemma in a letter to Hill thanking him for a first prize. The award, he said, "compensates one for the work they have been doing along lines in an agricultural way so different—in this instance—from my neighbors." Once again Hill's personal attempts to change farming practices fell flat, and the contest was not repeated.[64]

The failure of the good farming contest characterized the Great Northern's and Hill's agricultural endeavors after 1902. Hill's reaction was to adopt an overall pessimism regarding the future of agriculture that was to last the rest of his life. In part he expressed his concern by stressing the need to broaden the export markets for America's agricultural products. He wanted production levels to remain high through exports to prepare for the massive American population boom he foresaw. Hill was not alone in his dire predictions. Many economists saw an increasing population not matched by expanding farm acreage and predicted disaster.[65]

International developments heightened Hill's gloomy view of his nation's population growth in relation to its productivity. Early-twentieth-century America sold much of its surplus wheat to the British Empire. In 1902 Joseph Chamberlain, England's colonial secretary, sought to revive his own political fortunes, as well as an empire struggling from the effects of the Boer War, by advocating tariff reform. The reform he proposed centered around reciprocal imperial preference, whereby a protective tariff wall would foster inter-empire trade by placing taxes on goods from other nations. This would make American grain less competitive on the English market in comparison with that of Canada. Launching his proposal in a speech in Birmingham in May 1903, Chamberlain plunged England, where many had long favored free trade, into political turmoil and created fears for international markets around the world. These concerns did not abate until the dramatic end to Chamberlain's political career following a stroke in July 1906.[66]

Hill, very aware of Chamberlain's push to institute a protective tariff on non-imperial goods coming into England, saw that the best way to maintain American exports was through expanding trade with Asia. In 1904 he gave a speech at the Minnesota State Fair which illustrated his concerns. If instituted, Hill claimed, this English tax would cost Minnesota and the Dakotas twenty to thirty million dollars a year. By increasing Asiatic trade, especially with China, America would maintain its export market for wheat regardless of the actions taken by the British Empire. Hill believed "that every nation, including India, once they get wheat flour, prefer it to all other food."[67]

Corporate profit also factored into Hill's desire to tap Eastern markets. An Asian trade network would benefit the Great Northern enormously, allowing it to haul grain and other products in both directions along the line. The Canadian Pacific had established a shipping network to the Far East in 1886. In 1892 Hill, dismayed that this foreign line should profit from carrying American products, sent employee Herman Rosenthal to Japan, China, and Korea to investigate potential trade. Rosenthal's report was favorable, and Hill explored the possibilities of starting transoceanic trade using Japanese steamships. He had found no vessels suitable for Pacific crossings when his attention was distracted by the 1893 crash.[68]

The Great Northern's need for trans-Pacific commerce increased proportionally to its growing eastbound haulage. Working with his neighbor in St. Paul, Frederick Weyerhaeuser, Hill and the railroad greatly fostered the development of the lumber industry in the Pacific Northwest. By 1896 the Great Northern Railway carried so much timber from the West that cars consistently returned empty from the East, and Hill considered an empty car to be a "thief." The problem of what to send West undergirded the notion of trade with the Far East. In 1896 Hill sent more agents to Japan, and Japanese vessels started shipping goods from the Great Northern railhead in Seattle across the Pacific.[69]

Unsatisfied with foreign ships that would remove much profit from the country, Hill lobbied for more American shipbuilding. With the advent of the Spanish-American War, he joined the campaign to secure federal subsidies for building merchant marine ships. Frustrated by congressional delays, Hill capitalized the Great Northern Steamship Company in 1900 and started to build his own ships, launching the first one in 1903. He planned to ship lumber east and cotton (from the South by way of the Burlington, with which the Great Northern had established a working affiliation in 1886) west and then across the Pacific. Hill's promotion of Asiatic trade mirrored his earlier attempts at sponsoring agricultural education, as he worked in isolation. He organized and financed the development of a trans-Pacific network independent of governmental institutions.[70]

Hill's eagerness to establish this trade with Asia extended beyond speeches and promoting westward freight on his lines. He commissioned the construction of two oceangoing liners, built at Groton, Connecticut. The S. S. *Dakota* was launched in February 1903, and her sister ship, the S. S. *Minnesota,* in April. Within two years, both ships regularly traded with Japan and Hong Kong. In their day they were the largest ships ever built in America, the largest under the United States flag, and the largest trading in the Pacific. Despite their monopoly on size, the vessels failed to be profitable. Underpowered and difficult to handle, they lost money on every voyage. In March 1907 the S. S. *Dakota* sunk, with no lives lost, one mile out of Yokohama on a well-charted reef. Hill tried to sell the S. S. *Minnesota* in 1908, but did not find a buyer until 1915, when World War I increased the demand for shipping.[71]

Again, Hill proved unable to independently launch an agricultural development program. Despite his fervent belief in the necessity of Asiatic trade, his shipbuilding ability fell far short of his talent for railroad construction.

Part of the problem lay in federal reluctance to encourage American ship-building. In the late nineteenth century, America turned its attention toward internal improvements, investing in railroads and industrial developments. Although he had built his railroad without government land grants, Hill could not rescue American shipbuilding from its postbellum decline, which many recognized but did little to resolve until the impetus of world wars.[72]

By 1907 Hill's attitude toward agriculture reflected the failures of the previous five years. The Newlands Reclamation Act, which had been such a triumph in 1902, proved to be slow, ineffective, and overly bureaucratic. Problems with international water rights and Indian reservations delayed construction in the Milk River Valley, and farmers in North Dakota did not display the necessary interest to encourage federal spending. Frustrated, Hill launched a program of investigation into dryland farming in conjunction with the Montana Agricultural College. By 1907 this, too, became problematic, with its very optimistic results being questioned by USDA officials.

Other agricultural efforts that Hill ran personally or through the railroad were no more successful. The Good Seed Specials attracted attention, but were not repeated until the 1920s, while his best farm contest reached only those farmers already practicing diversified agriculture. Consequently, Hill became increasingly pessimistic. With few available alternatives, Hill displayed his fears for "the Nation's Future" in foreboding neo-Malthusian speeches, predicting America's inability to feed its citizens. "Within twenty years under the present conditions our wheat crop will not be sufficient for home consumption," and then "how are we to provide our own children with . . . their daily bread. . . . What must be the end?"[73]

5 / Conflict and Disillusion, 1907–1912

The more the Great Northern corporation tried to influence western development using federal agencies, the more frustrated the railroad management became. Continued exposure to governmental action and expertise during the five years from 1907 to 1912 increased corporate annoyance with bureaucratic inertia and highlighted the gulf between governmental and railroad perceptions of western agricultural needs. As federal bureaucrats and experts solidified their control over public land management and consistently ignored criticisms from Great Northern personnel, the corporation shifted its tactics. Returning to political lobbying, the Hills, both James and his second son, Louis, favored state rather than federal control of western resources, hoping that state control would foster railroad influence over resource use and conservation.

Despite a financial panic in 1907, the nation generally enjoyed a period of prosperity during these years. Internal political unrest had been largely left behind with the old century; agricultural prices were high and crops bountiful. Internationally, Theodore Roosevelt launched his corollary to the Monroe Doctrine, which, for many, asserted America's rightful place in international affairs. Faith in human abilities and the potential of reason to cure all ills reached center stage as the federal government embraced Progressivism.[1]

In keeping with the times, the Great Northern flourished. By 1907 it had purchased the assets of all fifteen of its affiliated railroad companies. Thus it avoided the creation of an illegal holding company, forming instead a corporate giant. The railroads operated efficiently and effectively, increasing haulage capacity and lacing the Northwest with new spur lines. Railroad promotion of settlement in Montana began in earnest in 1908. Remarkably successful, the number of farms in that state nearly doubled between 1900 and 1910. Having established a prosperous corporation, Hill increasingly invested his time in other ventures.[2]

In 1907 James Hill resigned as president of the Great Northern in favor of his son, Louis. Although still chairman of the board and still maintaining a close watch on operations, Hill removed himself from much of the day-to-day running of the railroad. He devoted much of his newfound free time to promoting agricultural development in the Northwest. Now in his early seventies, Hill expended considerable energy on his vision of a settled, agrarian Eden in the northern tier of states through continued emphasis on irrigation and dryland farming. His concern for soil fertility involved him in federal conservation efforts.[3]

Louis Hill aided and abetted his father in all of these activities mainly because, at this stage, the older Hill still dominated Louis. Louis would have preferred the life of leisure his father's fortune afforded him, but his father insisted on his employment in the Great Northern Railway corporation. Louis's inclination toward self-gratification was reflected in his corporate stress on railroad tourism, especially the development of Glacier National Park. Hill failed to interest his son in agriculture or soil conservation but, at least in the years 1907 to 1912, he managed to dictate Louis's actions and decisions from behind the scenes. Thus, for five years, Louis basically followed his father's lead, although he added a polished style to his actions that reflected his more elite educational background.[4]

With more time to spend on his interests, Hill played the role of agricultural expert with renewed zeal. The prominence of his line in the northern Great Plains and Pacific Northwest, combined with Hill's carefully crafted public image, had elevated him to celebrity status. In his quasi-retirement, he expanded his public visibility, accepting a larger proportion of speaking invitations. He spoke at most of the county fairs along his line and at many others. His arguments did not change. He believed "that the tillage of the soil is the natural and most desirable occupation for man" and pushed for a national recognition of the importance of agriculture. Along with this he advocated improved farming practices, especially soil conservation, to maintain American production levels. Only through "high grade farming," increased governmental involvement, and expenditure in agriculture could farmers hope to feed the growing American population.[5]

Hill's agricultural interests during these years continued to affect the Great Northern's western development schemes, despite his retirement. He agitated for effective irrigation by the federal government to encourage intensively farmed smallholdings in the arid West. He also advocated the need for soil conservation through fertilization. By 1908 he found a new forum for these long-held beliefs in the conservation movement, ironically led by his old foe, Theodore Roosevelt, and Roosevelt's friend, Gifford Pinchot.

Although his railroad continued to fare well, Hill's agricultural enterprises did not. Already somewhat disillusioned with federal and university experts, his lack of faith grew from 1907 to 1912. Distrust became antagonism and even outright opposition. Concurrently, Hill found himself implicitly thrust in the position of having to justify his right to criticize these experts. Borrowing much from his earlier experience as a gentleman farmer, Hill refined his notion of personal expertise, using the railroad and a group of sympathetic college men to expand and solidify his position.

Hill's relationship with mainstream conservation broke down in 1908 as he discovered that, as with irrigation, federal control of land policy undermined the power of his corporation to steer development. This schism mirrored the national fracture between President William Howard Taft's new secretary of the interior, Richard Ballinger, and Pinchot, who remained chief forester in the Department of Agriculture. Hill had peripheral importance in this swirling political and ideological controversy, eventually finding himself on the losing side of a battle not of his own making.

Pinchot, who had largely dominated all of the Roosevelt administration's public land policy from his position in the Bureau of Forestry, enjoyed strong federal bureaucratic control over natural resources in the West. Seeing resources as assets to be rationally harvested, Pinchot believed federal management was necessary for the nation to garner the greatest good for the greatest number. Consequently, he proposed legislative changes that increased the federal government's power in determining and policing the use of the public domain. Simultaneously, he promoted the higher education of conservationists, starting with the establishment of the Cornell Forestry School in 1898, to facilitate the creation of an elite body of federal experts. Pinchot's vision of Progressive conservation had been augmented by the unswerving support of President Roosevelt, which gave Pinchot almost dictatorial powers, and the presence of many like-minded men in other branches of the bureaucracy, notably Frederick Newell of the Reclamation Service in the Department of the Interior.[6]

The election of Taft in 1908 undermined Pinchot's dominance. Taft appointed Richard Ballinger, a Seattle lawyer and one-time commissioner of the General Land Office, as secretary of the interior. Ballinger disagreed with Pinchot's land policy, not so much on ideological grounds as on practical issues of management. Ballinger wanted a lessening of federal control in the West and an increase in private enterprise. Pinchot, who had been used to his vision dictating the actions of the Department of the Interior as well as the USDA, saw in Ballinger the undoing of the Reclamation Service.[7]

The political squabble that followed muddied everyone involved. Ballinger and Pinchot both fielded an army of subordinate spies. Taft vacillated, failing to offer clear support to either party or to discipline anyone. In 1909 Pinchot stepped outside bureaucratic channels and used the media to accuse Ballinger of illegal mismanagement of Alaskan coal lands to benefit several business interests. This obvious breach of policy forced Taft to action, and he fired Pinchot in January 1910, but the storm continued. Congress, upset earlier by Pinchot's and Roosevelt's highhanded executive style, held hearings to investigate the actions of both Pinchot and Ballinger and their respective bailiwicks. Although the commission formally exonerated Ballinger of all charges, he resigned the following year due to Taft's refusal to allow him to move the Department of the Interior fully away from Pinchot's concepts of strict federal resource management.[8]

This national debate on western asset management engulfed the Great Northern and both Hills, pivoting, as it did, around irrigation and conservation. Issues directly involving the railroad played a part in the conflict, such as the irrigation of the Milk River Valley and a scandalous fair exhibit that promoted only irrigation projects on southern railroad lines. These issues drew the Great Northern personnel deeply into party politics and national contests over resource control. Having initially pushed for federal involvement in irrigation, Hill increasingly found his own power undermined by federal experts. In response, Hill tried to backtrack and supported Ballinger's advocacy of a larger degree of state and private control in developing western lands. Hill hoped, of course, that this would restore his influence, and that of the Great Northern, over irrigation policy.

Having unambiguously supported the lobby for federal irrigation, Hill discovered that the Reclamation Service had completely eclipsed the Great Northern's power to affect change in the West. As the Newlands Reclamation Act approached its tenth anniversary, James and Louis Hill's dissatisfaction with the Reclamation Service increased, and they were not alone. Federal reclamation progressed slowly and often stalled altogether, largely due to unpredicted costs. This heightened local frustration with the Reclamation Service, as it sometimes withdrew land indefinitely from the public domain for reclamation. With the delay of irrigation plans, the land often became unobtainable and unusable, while remaining unirrigated. At other times public domain was accessible, and homesteaders staked claims with an anticipation of irrigation, which remained unfulfilled.[9]

In addition to western discontent, some government officials complained about the cost of the projects, which federal personnel often underestimated. The Ballinger-Pinchot senatorial hearings of 1910 revealed that the Reclamation Service had completed only two out of thirty projects started. One official of the Reclamation Service judged this "an inordinate and unjustifiable failure to produce results." The majority of the congressional committee ruled that "It would have been better if a less number of projects had been in process of construction at the same time, as more funds, more energy, and more speed could have been obtained in such case."[10]

Along the Great Northern line in North Dakota, the Buford-Trenton and Williston projects continued to be underused as settlers proved reluctant to pay for water. Those who used the water complained that the charges were excessively high. By early 1910 settlers at Williston had organized a Water Users' Association, which issued a statement listing grievances and proposed solutions. The cost of irrigation, farmers asserted, was "excessive and . . . extravagant," being at least twice the estimate they had been given. They wanted the years 1908 and 1909 to be considered experimental, with little or no payment required for the water "on account of the inability [of the Reclamation Service] to furnish water when necessary." The association also recommended that all construction charges be postponed until 1913, by which time the settlers hoped to be benefiting financially from the irrigation. In addition they contended that, even if forced to sell their land, they would not realize enough money to pay the current debts to the Reclamation Service. Their petition failed, however, and the Service refused to turn the water on until farmers had paid all back debts.[11]

The Water Users' Association judged the ensuing crop a "fiasco" and turned to the Hills and Congress for help. Louis Hill assured the settlers that their only hope lay in the Curtiss bill, then before Congress, which authorized the secretary of the interior to negotiate new contracts, and he urged the association members to write to their congressmen. Louis Hill also wrote his own letters to Congress and to Newell of the Reclamation Service, persuading Northern Pacific personnel to do the same. Congress passed the

Curtiss bill in 1911, and the Reclamation Service negotiated new contracts with the settlers. Although not exactly what they wanted, farmers did receive water for the 1911 crop year.[12]

Unfortunately, federal irrigation in North Dakota compared favorably to the Reclamation Service's progress on James Hill's pet project, the Milk River Valley in Montana. The Reclamation Service had withdrawn land from settlement and water rights from Montanans shortly after the passage of the Newlands Act in order to irrigate the valley. However, the Service became bogged down in negotiating international rights with Canada. To pacify the settlers, the Service did construct the Dodson dam and canal between Havre and Malta, but these were useless without water. Aside from badgering the Service and congressmen, the Great Northern could do little to rectify the situation. Negotiations with Canada continued, and a treaty was reached in 1909 apportioning the river water between the two nations. This was finally signed into law in May 1910. However, the problem of reserved water for the Fort Belknap Reservation remained, and citizens of the valley, among others, such as Montana Senator Thomas Carter, invested much energy in contesting the *Winters* doctrine in court or trying to circumvent it by the allotment of reservation lands. Therefore, ten years after the passage of the Newlands Act, no part of the Milk River Valley had yet been irrigated by the Reclamation Service.[13]

During the late summer of 1909, Louis Hill took a trip along the Great Northern line in the company of the Senate irrigation committee and reclamation engineers, both to assess the progress of irrigation and to conduct some grassroots publicity. During this journey he attended some local meetings held by the Reclamation Service. At these he "was greatly impressed with the fact that the people are very critical about and generally displeased with the reclamation service."[14]

In fact, settlers complained so vociferously, especially regarding the delays in implementing projected schemes, that Louis proposed subcontracting several of the projects from the Reclamation Service and having Great Northern engineers complete them. He collected cost/acreage statistics for a variety of northern Great Plains' projects and corresponded with W. M. Wooldridge, who was still promoting irrigation in Montana. His proposal received endorsement from "settlers [who] think we [the Great Northern] could do it in one-half the time and at one-third of the cost." Several newspapers also promoted this idea of corporate intervention.[15]

By March 1910 Reclamation Service officials were responding to the idea of corporate involvement in the Milk River irrigation scheme. Arthur P. Davis, chief engineer of the Service and a friend of Newell, wrote to Louis explaining the problems with international water rights and stating "It is questionable whether any new work should be undertaken until . . . arrangements [are] made for securing additional waters from St. Mary [sic] River." At the same time, Davis encouraged the railroad to construct canals so as to "expedite the ultimate irrigation of the valley." Alerted to potential diplomatic problems, Louis quickly backed out, stating that the responsibility for irrigation lay with the federal government and that Great Northern personnel had merely been encouraging settlers in their territory to keep "alive to the situation . . . and keep after this subject until they get what is properly coming to them."[16]

The Great Northern's frustration with the Reclamation Service escalated in 1909 with an unfortunate exhibit at the Minnesota State Fair. Edmund Taylor Perkins—engineer-in-charge, head of the Chicago office of the Reclamation Service, and a strong ally of Ballinger—planned a publicity campaign to highlight Service activity and attract settlers to irrigated areas. The campaign took the form of an exhibit named the "Black Tent Show," which toured various state fairs in the fall. In the tent, officials displayed illustrations of irrigation projects, gave lectures, and provided literature.[17]

Perkins had approached a number of railroads, including the Hill lines, for help in financing the campaign, expressing concern that "all Reclamation Service projects be covered." The publicity issued by the Reclamation Service included railroad advertising. One of the Hill lines, the Chicago, Burlington & Quincy, declined the opportunity to participate, believing they "could get better results from newspaper advertising." Perkins took this rejection to include all the Hill lines, despite the assurance of the general traffic manager of the Great Northern, W. W. Broughton, that his line would participate. When the Black Tent Show started its circuit in the fall of 1909, the entire cost of Perkins's project had been assumed by the rival Union Pacific.[18]

This corporate dominance of a federal promotion project on the part of a competing transcontinental line upset Great Northern personnel. In September 1909 the Reclamation Service set up the Black Tent Show at the Minnesota State Fair, and Louis Hill stopped in to see the work. Furious to find only southwestern projects in Union Pacific territory advertised, he wrote a series of complaints to congressmen, such as Thomas Carter in Montana, and to Frederick Newell himself. Louis complained of Perkins's incompetence and ignorance in his belief that the Chicago, Burlington & Quincy could make decisions for the Great Northern. He suggested that advertising only those projects in the territory of an interested railroad was "illegal from the standpoint of discrimination," and he called for a complete reorganization of the Reclamation Service. Perhaps to add substance to his complaints, Louis expressed his father's concern over the matter and the elder Hill's demand that President Taft be informed. At Louis's instigation, the St. Paul Jobbers and Manufacturers' Association launched a simultaneous series of complaints about the geographical limitations of the Black Tent Show. The association complained directly, lobbying federal officials, and promoted a general regional grievance against the Reclamation Service through local Minnesota papers.[19]

Spurred by the fair exhibit and the problems along the Milk River, Louis Hill further investigated the actions of the Reclamation Service. He discovered that Perkins made a personal profit from the publicity venture of the Black Tent Shows. Louis asserted that this would not be tolerated in the railroad business and that "it appears an innovation that a salaried Government man should engage in outside matters in which the Government is involved securing profit to himself through the operation." Louis's accusation of vested interest struck at the ideal of civil service and impartial government, supposedly a hallmark of Progressive land management.[20]

Louis Hill also took the matter up with Frederick Newell, asking for Perkins's resignation or threatening to "put the whole matter before the Press." In their defense, Newell and Perkins claimed that the Service had not neglected northern irrigation projects but represented them with slides and pamphlets. Again they raised the fact that the Chicago, Burlington & Quincy had declined involvement on behalf of all the Hill lines.[21]

Louis Hill informed the Minnesota State Fair organization of the involvement of the Union Pacific in the exhibit. The fair association had waived the fees for Perkins's Black Tent space on the basis of federal involvement. On hearing of the corporate contributions to the show, the secretary of the fair's association, Mr. Beek, demanded the requisite one hundred and fifty dollars, payable by all private organizations. He also complained that the visitors had been misled and that they "had a right to know with whom they are dealing, whether the Government, in the exercise of a government function, or a private corporation promoting its own interests." In essence, Beek was attacking the federal government for failing to live up to its expressed Progressive ideals of objectivity.[22]

Louis Hill coordinated many of these attacks, making sure that appropriate letters circulated among interested parties. With a view to generating public sympathy to his cause, he ensured that Beek billed the Chicago, Burlington & Quincy for the Black Tent space first, so that the railroad could publicly deny involvement, pointing the finger at the Union Pacific.[23]

Frederick Newell used the furor over the Black Tent Shows to his own political advantage. While defending the Reclamation Service's actions to outside critics, the attack gave him leverage in his internal war against Richard Ballinger. Newell denied personal involvement in the shows, stating that Perkins had ignored the official chain of command and worked directly with Ballinger. Newell also used Louis's complaints to justify two departmental investigations. These verified Louis's accusations that Perkins had profited personally from the Black Tent Shows, receiving five hundred dollars a month from the Union Pacific over and above his federal salary of two hundred and seventy-five dollars. Perkins had also agreed to route the tent shows on that line and its subsidiaries.[24]

The investigations and their findings reflected a broad problem within the Reclamation Service beyond graft. With the appointment of Ballinger in 1908, an ideological rift yawned between the Pinchot-ite Newell and his new boss. In the subsequent power struggle, Perkins sided with Ballinger, reporting that "The administration of F. H. Newell has been disastrous to the Reclamation Fund. . . . He is not a skilled or experienced engineer. . . . He is of a weak and vacillating nature." Perkins also provided Ballinger with details of the costs of the various projects undertaken and his opinion of their success. He believed that "neither foresight nor ordinary engineering or business ability were shown in undertaking the construction."[25]

Newell, on the other hand, received significant political support from Pinchot, who wrote to President Taft that "Under Mr. F. H. Newell, as Director, the U.S. Reclamation Service has become an organization of exceptional efficiency." Pinchot-ites opposed Ballinger as a puppet of western power trusts who would inevitably turn public resources over to greedy corporations. Pinchot saw Ballinger's aim as augmenting the influence of railroads and power and mining companies, which resulted in "his desire to cripple the reclamation service by ousting the man [Newell] who has built it from an iridescent dream to a great, practical, home-making, dollar-yielding reality."[26]

This internal division in the Reclamation Service supported Newell's claim that he knew nothing of the Black Tent Shows and that they had been arranged through Perkins and Ballinger. On the basis of the investigation, Newell then attempted to discipline Perkins. Newell first informed Perkins that he "should immediately cease all such connection by which you profit personally" and, five days later, suggested his resignation.[27]

In defense of his own actions and those of his subordinate, Ballinger launched his own inquiry into the events surrounding the Black Tent Shows and the efficacy of the Chicago office generally. Not surprisingly, his investigation reached markedly different conclusions than that conducted under Newell. This research exonerated Perkins from the charges of graft and, in fact, the report recommended that the Chicago office be reorganized by giving him more authority.[28]

Louis Hill and the Great Northern had hoped to use the Black Tent Show imbroglio to effect a complete reorganization of the Reclamation Service and its personnel. To this end, Louis Hill launched a lobbying campaign, buttressing letters to federal bureaucrats by sending copies of relevant reports and letters to politicians and press agents. Although believing he had successfully squashed the Black Tent Shows through a visit to Washington, D.C., Louis failed in the more important part of his corporation's agenda, instigating a reorganization of the Reclamation Service.[29]

In fact, the Great Northern faced a serious political dilemma as the investigations into the Black Tent Shows progressed. Despite the fact that Louis publicly claimed that "I have no interest for or against Mr. Pinchot or Mr. Ballinger," he, like many other power brokers in the West, heartily opposed Pinchot's conception of conservation. Privately, he asserted that Pinchot's "theories are not favorably accepted in the western states for the reason that they would seriously retard the development by withdrawing too great a portion of the public domain and closing forest reserves that should be partially open for settlement." Louis Hill realized that his railroad held a vested interest in exonerating Ballinger from Pinchot's charges, yet the trail of responsibility for the Black Tent graft led directly to Ballinger, not Newell. Realizing this, Louis settled for the end of the shows and resumed generic criticisms of the Reclamation Service that demanded its reorganization, while his specific attacks remained firmly focused on Frederick Newell.[30]

Louis Hill's campaign against the Reclamation Service in general, and Newell in particular, received a boost in 1910. In June a Chicago real estate businessman sent him a copy of an article supposedly written by Newell for the Canadian Pacific. In this article Newell compared the irrigation projects in Canada and the United States unfavorably to the latter, and also decried the possibilities inherent in dryland farming. The same source also supplied Louis with information regarding money the Reclamation Service had invested in projects that it later abandoned. Louis distributed this information to various editors and complained to Ballinger, who promised an investigation.[31]

Ballinger had already received a copy of the article from Perkins a few months prior to Louis Hill's complaint. Perkins claimed that it had been submitted to the *National Irrigation Journal*, but that the editor, noting the "fulsome...praise" given to Canadian projects, especially those in the Bow River Valley, had sent it to Perkins. Despite this agitation, Louis and others achieved nothing by their campaigning. Louis was unable to prove Newell's authorship of the article, and the personnel of the Reclamation Service remained in place.[32]

Ballinger, as determined as the Hills to dispose of Newell, tried to capitalize on his victory over Pinchot in the 1910 senatorial hearings by asking Taft to approve the dismissal of Newell and his chief engineer, Arthur Davis. Taft refused, fearing further public controversy. The hollowness of Ballinger's congressional triumph became clear in the fall of 1910, when Progressive, pro-Pinchot victories in the western states further undermined his authority. Having initially fostered the controversy through vacillation, Taft adopted a more active stance by firing Pinchot in 1910. Increasingly convinced that the factionalism in the conservation movement and, more importantly for Taft, in the Republican Party could only be healed by the removal of the other main antagonist, Ballinger, Taft forced him to resign in March 1911, replacing him with Pinchot-ite Walter L. Fisher.[33]

Toward the end of 1909, growing disillusionment of Great Northern personnel toward the Reclamation Service crystallized. The combination of the Black Tent Shows financed by the Union Pacific, continual complaints from settlers along the Great Northern line, and Newell's supposed authorship of an article promoting Canadian irrigation resulted in an all-out campaign against the Reclamation Service by Louis Hill. The campaign resurrected earlier political tactics, such as those used in the push for the Newlands Reclamation Act. Louis wooed editors, called in private markers with congressmen, and even contemplated taking over some reclamation projects. However, all his efforts accomplished little, and the political victory went indisputably to the opposition.

The failure to effect change in the Reclamation Service succeeded in nurturing Louis Hill's personal, and the Great Northern's corporate, animosity toward that federal agency. Despite both institutions' belief in the need for irrigation in the arid West, the gulf between them had only widened as the Reclamation Service actions became stalled in bureaucratic red tape. The corporate focus of the Great Northern prevented its personnel from recognizing support for irrigation projects outside the railroad's territory as anything other than favoritism.

The removal of Ballinger from the Department of the Interior and the triumph of the Pinchot-ites in federal land management constituted a serious blow to the Great Northern Railway. It represented the failure of the corporation, headed by Louis, to sustain the political influence that had proven so useful. Additionally, the loss of Ballinger resulted in the dominance of Pinchot's ideology of governmental management of the public domain, at least within the federal bureaucracy. Finally, the Pinchot-ite victory reflected a clear-cut move toward a narrower, Progressive definition of expertise, moving authority and power to academically qualified bureaucrats. Ballinger, with his deference to private as well as public interests, tacitly acknowledged that expertise in land management could reside in a multiplicity of places and persons. With Ballinger's resignation, Pinchot's vision of a public domain controlled by formally trained bureaucratic experts gained ascendancy.

At the same time as the Great Northern company fought and lost the battle over the Reclamation Service, many of the same characters contested many of the same issues through the forum of the national conservation movement. As with irrigation, Louis Hill marshaled much of the political struggle over conservation, but it was James Hill, with his cultivated image as a gentleman farmer and long-held concern for soil conservation, who moved to center stage.

James Hill had always asserted that wasteful farming lay at the root of many American agricultural problems. Despite the continued success of monocultures, Hill believed that American farmers needed to practice the intensive, diversified agriculture found in many European countries to maintain high production levels. Thus, as early as 1903, Hill became interested in the issues surrounding soil conservation and fertility, an interest which naturally sprung out of his push for diversification and his concern about the perceived decline in American productivity. His Malthusian vision of America's future centered around the waste of the soil, which he considered "the sole asset that does not perish," capable of "infinite renewal." Through poor farming practices, including monocropping and a failure to fertilize, the American farmer was destroying this perpetual resource. Using production statistics to prove his case, Hill claimed that bad farming practices had resulted in a decline of wheat production in the West from twenty to thirty bushels per acre to twelve. Hill's consistent use of numbers in his speeches reflected his commitment to Progressive notions of science, objectivity, and proof. Perhaps, more importantly, it reinforced his expertise. By employing a standardized and objective referent such as numbers, Hill removed his knowledge firmly from matters of personal interests and prejudices into an abstract, impersonal sphere.[34]

Hill's concern for soil conservation increased with the growing emigration of American farmers to Canada in the late nineteenth and early twentieth centuries. The falling number of farms on the Great Plains compounded the decline of wheat production in the United States. This necessitated a continuation of extensive farming practices, which, in turn, resulted in a draining of soil fertility and a reduction in productivity. As American farmers moved north across the international boundary, more immigrants flooded the nation's cities, which exacerbated Hill's Malthusian predictions. Thus Hill foresaw that "within twenty years under present conditions our wheat crop will not be sufficient for home consumption."[35]

Hill proffered a complex solution in which the conservation of farming resources, especially the soil, played a vital part. In his public addresses at the end of the first decade of the twentieth century, Hill consistently stressed the need for farmers to be more conservative in their methods, especially with respect to soils. He had long preached that "what you take from the soil you must put back." Indeed, the production of manure for fertilizer had always been one of his key arguments for diversification. Hill's advocacy and the visibility of his ideas grew as an academic discussion propelled the issue of soil fertility into the public eye. As soil conservation became an issue of national debate, so Hill, temporarily, found a forum for his concerns in the early national conservation movement.[36]

Soil fertility and conservation gained public prominence in 1903 when Head of the Bureau of Soils Milton Whitney issued a *Farmers' Bulletin* disclaiming the need to fertilize soil. Whitney argued that "practically all soils contain sufficient plant food for good crop yields, [and] that this supply will be indefinitely maintained." He claimed that experiments at the Rothamsted station in England, based on the work of eighteenth-century agriculturist Jethro Tull, demonstrated that farmers could maintain soil fertility solely by appropriate crop rotation and careful tillage.[37]

Whitney based his argument on the belief that the soil contained all necessary chemicals, which could be continuously replenished by water movement. Using the research of the Bureau of Soils, he concluded that soils differed little in their compositions and that the issue of maximizing production pivoted on soil physics rather than soil chemistry. Productivity rested on three factors: the "mechanical condition of the soil"; the ease with which water could permeate it; and the amount of moisture present in the soil or the climate. Whitney postulated that the only chemical problem inherent in cultivation centered on different plants excreting toxins, which proved deleterious to subsequent crops, the best solution to which was crop rotation.[38]

Whitney's claims caused an uproar among many university soil scientists. At a time when scientific agriculturists could still face powerful attacks on their claim to expertise and leadership, many believed in the necessity of presenting a united informational framework. Whitney's deviation from the mainstream of academic thought undermined the apparent objectivity and certainty of science. Additionally, a federal leader's propagation of incorrect information provided opponents of scientific agriculture with a formidable weapon. Whitney's academic opponents countered that crops did permanently deplete the soil and that scientifically designed, artificial fertilizers offered the only effective remedy. Concern for their tenuous ascendancy as objective experts, combined with a growing fear among agriculturists that American farm practices would lead to a food shortage if not unchecked, made responding to Whitney's bulletin imperative.[39]

Dr. Cyril Hopkins, a professor of agricultural chemistry at the University of Illinois, led the opposition. Hopkins cast Whitney's error in the most invidious terms, predicting that "the injury to American agriculture that may result from the wide dissemination and adoption into agricultural practice of erroneous teaching from one occupying a national position of high authority is too vast to justify agricultural scientists and investigators in the easier and more agreeable policy of ignoring these teachings." Hopkins rationalized the attack on Whitney as an unpleasant but necessary moral crusade. The ensuing conflict lasted much of the decade. Both sides published evidence supporting their theories, and both mobilized support from authorities as varied as the Association of Official Agricultural Chemists and the United States Congress.[40]

Despite the continuing controversy, Whitney remained in office and kept advancing his theories. In 1908 he presented a report to the National

Conservation Commission that offered a modified perspective. Whitney changed his main thrust, attacking "unscrupulous manufacturers" who sold farmers "worthless materials for exorbitant prices." He called for more investigation into the principles governing fertilizers and more legislation to control their manufacture. The next year he issued another *Farmers' Bulletin* that compared the mineral compositions of soils in America and Europe. The similarity of his findings, compounded by the high productivity of some European systems, led him to conclude once more that "there is [no] danger of permanent loss of fertility of our soils through loss of mineral plant-food constituents . . . through the removal of our very moderate crops."[41]

The emergence of this debate over soil science, synchronous with James Hill's growing concern with soil exhaustion throughout the nation, increased his visibility and the apparent respect for his agricultural knowledge. The director of the University of Illinois's Agricultural Experiment Station, Eugene Davenport, gave Hill's opinion considerable weight when referring to "warnings of soil depletion from men such as James J. Hill." As a result of this visibility, President Roosevelt invited Hill to be one of four guest speakers at the Governors' Conference on the Conservation of Natural Resources, held at the White House in May 1908. The official invitation cited his areas of expertise as being "transportation and . . . the commercial development of the country." Hill accepted with alacrity and highlighted his area of concern: "The greatest foundation of value and, I might say, of life itself, is in the fertility of the soil, and this is being wasted as recklessly and rapidly as any of the others."[42]

The conference, intended to promote conservation among the politically active elite, was well attended. Governors from forty states and territories came, along with members of the cabinet and the Supreme Court, representatives from various national organizations and periodicals, and special guests, including Milton Whitney. Hill and two other speakers, Andrew Carnegie and John Mitchell, arrived early on the first day and took front row seats in the East Room of the White House. Carnegie and Mitchell both spoke that first day, one about ores and minerals, the other briefly on the waste of coal. On the second day, Hill's lengthy address provided, according to a variety of newspapers from Chicago to Atlanta, the "stellar speaking attraction," which "won more attention to the 'conservation of resources' proposition than all other efforts in that direction." Although he touched on forests and coal, Hill spent most of his time detailing the declining productivity of American soils. With his usual extensive use of statistics, Hill demonstrated the diminishing returns of soils throughout the nation. The remedy he offered combined crop rotation with natural fertilizers to act as "tonics" for the soil, stressing manure as fertilizer.[43]

His speech was well received, making a "very deep impression" on Secretary of Agriculture James Wilson. William Jennings Bryan, who also attended, remarked that Hill had "rendered the Conference a real service." Professor Charles Van Hise of the University of Wisconsin and president of the National Association of State Universities upheld Hill's ideas about the importance of manure as a fertilizer in a later presentation. Accolades paid to Hill's speeches by federal and university experts, combined with favorable coverage in the newspapers, catapulted Hill to a position as an expert regarding soil conservation.[44]

The media's acknowledgment of Hill's expertise in soil conservation, seconded by the federal experts attending the conference, placed James Hill in a favorable position to exercise influence over national environmental development. Semi-retired from the railroad, Hill toured his territory in the fall of 1909, speaking at county fairs. His talks continually refined his arguments about soil conservation, and in 1910 he collected and published sixteen of his essays on favorite topics in a book, *Highways of Progress*. Five of these papers dealt directly with agriculture, all of which included Hill's views on soil conservation.[45]

News of the impending book alarmed Professor Cyril Hopkins in Illinois. He approached J. P. Morgan to arrange an interview with Hill. Hopkins was anxious to set Hill straight on several matters "in connection with the rotation of crops and the maintenance of the soil," especially because of "the tremendous influence [the] book will have." Hopkins's concern centered upon Hill's statement that "a proper three or five year rotation of crops actually enriches the soil." He feared that Hill's view trespassed on the errors enunciated by Whitney, whom Hill had met at the Governors' Conference. Hill reassured him in a well-cited letter that this was not the case and that he merely saw rotation as an intrinsic part of a three-part system that included fertilization and careful tillage.

Cyril Hopkins also stated that manure provided an insufficient fertilizer, questioning the work of Van Hise (also at the conference), who asserted that if a farmer applied all manure to the soil all the necessary elements would be returned. Hopkins pointed out that livestock utilized soil nutrients through feed for meat and milk production, and thus the chemicals ingested far exceeded those excreted. Even if farmers applied all barnyard manure to the soil, therefore, it would remain insufficient to maintain fertility. Hopkins's arguments proved persuasive enough that Hill began to embrace the importance of artificial fertilizers, although he never abandoned his stress on the ease and importance of manuring.[46]

The attention directed at soil science due to the Whitney-Hopkins controversy, in combination with Hill's longstanding interests in productive farming and the nascent conservation movement, temporarily validated Hill's claim to agricultural expertise on a national level. Recognition and deference from federal and academic experts ostensibly placed Hill in a position to influence national policy as well as farming practices. However, the larger political conflict surrounding the Ballinger-Pinchot controversy soon subsumed questions of Hill's expertise and soil conservation.

By the time of the first National Conservation Congress in Seattle in 1909, that controversy was in full spate. Although a congressional hearing had yet to be called, the main ideological and material issues had crystallized in the months following Ballinger's appointment. Both sides had spent the summer of 1909 publicizing their positions, but the Pinchot faction successfully dominated the Seattle meeting, receiving considerable support from westerners. This interregional backing of Pinchot undermined claims by the Ballinger-Hill group that the problem lay in sectional misunderstanding, with the East attempting to dominate and direct the West. The congress adjourned after deciding to hold the following meeting in St. Paul at the other end of the Great Northern.[47]

The St. Paul meeting offered the Hills another chance to promote their corporate perspective. In 1910 the Governors' Conservation Committee asked Louis Hill to help raise funds to defer expenses of the St. Paul meeting. Louis proved more than willing and petitioned various local railroad companies for a contribution of five hundred dollars. He also participated in the local committee to appoint the speakers, and he worried that Gifford Pinchot and "his crowd, who are all eastern theorists," would dominate the conference. Pinchot, although fired from federal office early in 1910, still held the position of chairman of the National Conservation Association, the sponsoring body for the conference. The men who dominated the association, Louis believed, "would seriously retard the development [of the West] by withdrawing too great a portion of the public domain." He feared that unless some effort was made to contain this eastern influence, many important westerners would boycott the St. Paul meeting. Consequently, he launched a lobbying campaign to ensure that men "who can speak in the interest of home settlement in the west" accepted invitations to speak at the conference.[48]

The invitations to speakers came from the National Conservation Association's national offices in Washington, D.C. and were, according to Louis Hill, dominated by Pinchot. Despite this, James J. Hill received an invitation to speak at the conference on soil conservation as, so the letter read, "No man in the United States is so well qualified to discuss this subject as yourself." When the association published the proposed list of speakers, Louis Hill objected to Taft's secretary, Charles Norton, that the list was "decidedly against the present administration," and that Pinchot's group refused to allow the conference to stage a Taft Day, recognizing presidential contributions to conservation. Minnesotan Knute Nelson, chairman of the Senate's committee on public lands and an old political ally of the Great Northern, concurred with Louis Hill. He believed that Pinchot and his allies intended to utilize the entire conference as "a drive at President Taft," especially by Pinchot's attorney in the congressional hearings, Louis Brandeis, who Louis Hill judged as "one of the worst and most unscrupulous pettifoggers I have ever seen."[49]

The proposed representation for the conference upset other politicians and businessmen who favored greater state control of western resources. Governor Marion Hay of Washington also favored the states' rights position. Having been asked to nominate delegates for the conference, his advocacy for at least one pro-state control representative met with outright refusal. This forced Hay into open opposition to the federal position on conservation, and he sent letters to western governors inviting them to a meeting in Salt Lake City to protect western interests.[50]

Despite considerable machinations and negotiations on the part of westerners such as Louis Hill and Marion Hay, including meetings in Chicago and Salt Lake, the program for the St. Paul conference remained little changed from Gifford Pinchot's original proposal. Taft had been invited, but "North and South Dakota, Montana, Washington, Oregon, Wyoming, Utah and Colorado are only represented on the program by Senator [Joseph M.] Dixon, of Montana." At this point, Louis changed his tactics, realizing that the program could not be altered in his favor. Instead, he started working to implement a boycott of the meeting. Leaking information on the program so that Montana's Governor Edwin Norris could take it to the meeting of western governors in Salt Lake City, Louis Hill noted that the western governors should not sanction the meeting by attending. In addition, he refused to offer reduced rates on the Great Northern if the governors boycotted the meeting, thus encouraging more absenteeism. This ploy worked, and many of the western governors stayed away, for which Louis publicly blamed Pinchot.[51]

The conference proved a triumph for the Pinchot-Roosevelt faction, favoring federal control of conservation. Governor Hay, who did attend, had little impact and later wrote of the conference as "The frameup at St. Paul [which] was so rank that it was really laughable." Overall the states' rights advocates were ignored and ridiculed. The speeches given by critics of federal conservation met with disinterest from the audience, showing, as in Seattle, that despite the attendants' claims, they did not represent a West unified against federal control. Many westerners, such as former federal attorney Francis Heney of California and representatives of Oregon, New Mexico, and Washington conservation commissions, stood solidly behind Pinchot, believing that only federal authority could undermine the region's industrial political machines and ensure more equitable land use and management.[52]

James J. Hill gave his speech during the afternoon of the third day. Despite the title of "Soils, Crops, Food and Clothing," Hill used the opportunity to attack federal control of national resources. Using irrigation as his example, he stated, "There are dangers inseparable from national control and conduct of affairs. The machine is too big and too distant; its operation is slow, cumbersome and costly. So slow is it that settlers are waiting in distress for water promised long ago." Roosevelt, Pinchot, and former secretary of the interior James Garfield, among others, vociferously opposed Hill's opinions, defending federal intervention in western development. The old railroad man was also subjected to direct personal attack for his speech. Two days after his presentation, Francis Heney, a San Francisco lawyer and avid Pinchot-ite, accused Hill of wasting national resources through the congressional land grant worth at least six hundred million dollars to the Great Northern. He also stated that Hill's annual salary was fifty thousand dollars. Despite the inaccuracy of his statements—the Great Northern received no land grant, although the St. Paul & Pacific Railroad had, and Hill had never drawn a salary, personally profiting from shares alone—the attack proved very popular with the audience. Hill received no opportunity to respond, and the conference ended the same day with considerable strife over its resolutions. Although the federal component won out, state advocates such as Governor Hay offered heated opposition.[53]

The outpouring of conflict and acrimony that marred the conference took some time to die down. *Leslie's Weekly*, a Chicago newspaper that favored the Hills, issued a lengthy description of Gifford Pinchot's manipulation of the program of the conference and of the fight launched to add some pro-western speakers. To refute Francis Heney's attack, James Hill issued a public statement that "The Great Northern did not receive a dollar in money or an acre of land from the federal government [and] . . . that I have never received . . . one dollar of salary from any railroad company."[54]

Despite these defenses, the pro-federal conservation movement remained dominant, receiving added strength from the victory of a number of Progressive, pro-federal governors in western states in the elections of 1910. Federal experts aggressively asserted their hegemony over public land management, assuming power previously distributed among states and corporations.

Hill, a victim of this centralization, removed himself from involvement in the growing national movement for conservation. Responding to a request from the new president of the National Conservation Congress, Henry C. Wallace, to pay for the printing of the proceedings of the St. Paul meeting, Hill wrote, "While I have for a long time, and am now, deeply interested in conservation of our natural resources, I have not forgotten the unfair and shabby manner in which many of its friends were treated in Saint Paul." Wallace also invited Hill to address the third National Conservation Congress in Kansas City. Hill refused and remained adamant despite Wallace's repeated requests. Hill did include in his letter a five-page statement on conservation, which could be read at the conference if desired, a strategy he repeated in 1912.[55]

James Hill remained, however, avidly interested in conservation. He involved himself in local groups, which he could more easily dominate, using their meetings as a forum for propounding ideas and attacking national trends. In November 1912 Hill delivered a speech at the Second Minnesota Conservation and Agricultural Development Congress in Minneapolis. "The first business of real conservation," he insisted, "is to lift agriculture to the rank of a science well understood and practically applied. . . . This is real Conservation. It is not a temporary fad, not a method of serving personal ambition or local interest, but a system of harmonious co-operation between the laws of man's environment and his liveliest anticipation and most joyous activity." Thus he simultaneously vindicated his interest in conservation as altruistic, while condemning his opponents as self-aggrandizing and unnatural.[56]

Hence, by 1912, Hill found that his earlier use of federal expertise to promote agricultural change had backfired. The creation of the Reclamation Service enabled federal experts to refine their conception of expertise and ensure its dominance at the expense of amateurs like Hill. Government officials such as Pinchot and Newell, who had received Hill's support as late as 1904 when they joined together to fight land fraud through the Quarles bill, inaugurated policies of which he disapproved and about which he could do little. Former governmental allies undermined Hill's position as an agricultural expert.[57]

Gifford Pinchot's professionalization of federal land management and his success in the struggle with Richard Ballinger heightened Hill's isolation. Roosevelt and Pinchot used Hill's prominence to launch a national awareness of conservation, but they had no intention of deferring to Hill's ideas at the White House's Governors' Conference on the Conservation of Natural Resources. Thus, while they achieved some validation as agricultural experts, James and Louis Hill remained paper tigers when it came to national policy.

Loss of the federal political clout he had enjoyed before William McKinley's 1901 assassination effectively hamstrung Hill and his railroad in policy areas other than transportation. The Hills' continued attempts to influence agricultural development in the northern tier of states by political lobbying, direct media attack, and appeals to presidents consistently failed. The ghettoization of Hill's agricultural interests resulted in his removing himself and his railroad from the agricultural institutional involvement that he had cultivated for two decades. The increasing national emphasis on professional expertise compounded this isolation. As civil engineers dominated the Reclamation Service and professional foresters assumed control of the public domain, amateurs such as Hill and Ballinger were marginalized in policymaking and their claims to expertise refuted.

While this process played out on a federal level, a similar pattern unfolded between the railroad and local institutions. Embarking on a series of dryland farming ventures to compensate for the lack of irrigation taking place in his territory, James Hill found his expertise as contested by state and regional institutions as it was on a national level by federal authorities.

6 / Isolation and Expertise, 1907–1912

The five years from 1907 to 1912 saw the Great Northern Railway losing its power to influence environmental change at state and local levels, as well as at a national level. At the same time as the Hills and their railroad fought for recognition and influence in national decisions concerning irrigation and conservation, they continued their struggle for dominance in the advancement of dryland farming, with no more success. To shape western development, the company gradually resorted to corporate-driven initiatives in which railroad personnel could retain control. As with federal conflicts, differing visions of western development shaped the battles with state and local institutions. Internal corporate disagreements about profit, goals, and the nature of expertise added nuance to these struggles.

With governmental irrigation stalled in the northern tier states and interaction between the railroad and federal agencies degenerating into acrimony, James J. Hill and the Great Northern explored new ways of increasing agricultural productivity along the line. By the early 1900s the obvious alternative to irrigation, at least on the northern plains, had become dryland farming. The federal government recognized this by creating the Office of Dry Land Agriculture in 1905 and then passing the Enlarged Homestead Act in 1909, which allowed homesteading grants of up to 320 acres of nonirrigable land. The Great Northern's interest in dryland experimentation and promotion began as early as 1906 and, as conflicts with the Reclamation Service grew, so did the railroad's financial commitment to dry farming. Attempts to coordinate research, development, and promotion with the Montana Agricultural College and the Dry Farming Congresses proved as frustrating as alliances with the Reclamation Service and conservationists.

The Great Northern once more found itself at loggerheads with institutions and agencies at local and state levels.[1]

The Great Northern started financing dryland farming experimentation in 1906 through a regional cooperative agreement with the Northern Pacific, the state of Montana, and the Montana Agricultural College. The Great Northern continued to fund experiment substations along its line in Montana for three years. In 1909 the railroad cut back support, limiting its expenditure to $1,700 for a new station at Chester and fifty dollars a month toward the salary of supervisor M. L. Frang of the Montana Agricultural College's Experiment Station. The line also furnished transportation for Frang and for Professors Frederick Linfield and Alfred Atkinson to visit the stations at Harlem, Havre, Chester, Fort Benton, Great Falls, and Moccasin.[2]

The Great Northern's decision to discontinue its support of the Montana Agricultural College's Experiment Station's dryland farming program was intimately connected with the requirements of the railroad. While all parties involved hoped that dryland farming would boost settlement and the productive development of Montana, the Great Northern's aims were more specific. The corporation helped fund the program to encourage settlement and agriculture along their line, thus increasing the railroad's grain and freight haulage. Louis Hill deemed the results insufficient to justify further expenditure, although some of stations had successfully promoted settlement. In October 1909, Thomas Shaw, an avid supporter of the program and his position in it, reported to Louis Hill that 250 homestead claims had been filed around the recently established station at Chester. He also reported that land prices at Moccasin had doubled since the experiment station had opened eighteen months previously. Despite these successes and Shaw's pressure to continue the experiments, Louis judged the program as unworthy of further financing, writing in February 1910, "At present I feel that we should not donate anything for Montana experimental stations for the reason that in the past we have not obtained satisfactory results." Louis's refusal reflected the corporation's need for production. Despite an understandable interest in settlement, the main concern of the Great Northern was generating haulage through crop production, especially wheat. In 1908, the last year that the Great Northern funded the stations at Harlem and Great Falls, the substations' production proved abysmally small compared to yields at the University of Minnesota's Experiment Station (see Table 6.1). Even allowing for climatic differences, the Hills decided that funding the Montana Agricultural College's program was a poor investment.[3]

Conflicting goals led to tension between the railroad and university academics over the future of dryland farming. The Great Northern wanted to promote dry farming settlement faster than the experiment stations believed justifiable so as to spur production and haulage. The Montana Agricultural College also wanted increased settlement, but not at the expense of its scientific reputation. In early 1910 the director of the Montana Agricultural College's Experiment Station, Frederick B. Linfield, expressed his concern that settlement was proceeding too swiftly and would lead to farm failure. He worried that boosterism had overtaken agricultural science, resulting in farmer reliance on unproven techniques. Linfield's reservations came to the attention of Louis Hill, who responded with a letter of complaint to Montana's Governor Edwin Norris. The letter testified to Louis's interest in settlement and his inherent Social Darwinism: "I do not feel that anyone can take the responsibility of educating all the people who came to Montana to make a living for themselves. We can only handle this matter by selecting the best people we can allowing the theory of survival of the fittest to provide the final outcome." Thus Louis disavowed responsibility for potential farm failure, placing it squarely on the inadequacy of settlers, while, at the same time, sidestepping the concept of scientific proof.[4]

Therefore, the Great Northern's dual focus on relatively fast environmental development to spur production and settlement led its officials to terminate their involvement with the Montana Agricultural College in 1909. As a corporation independent in many ways of the Great Northern, the Northern Pacific continued its funding because of greater concern with land sales. Additionally, the yields on the experiment farms it sponsored, such as Forsyth, proved much better than those along the Great Northern (see Table 6.1).[5]

However, the Great Northern's interest in and promotion of dryland farming did not end when it severed relations with the Montana Agricultural College. In 1909 the Great Northern gave considerable financial support to another dry farming organization: the Dry Farming Congress. Initially called the Trans-Missouri Dry Farming Congress, this paternalistic organization had started two years earlier in Denver and included representatives from almost everywhere except the farm. Governors of states and territories could appoint delegates, as could mayors, county commissioners, national and state agricultural associations, railroads, and chambers of commerce. The congress also encouraged the attendance of senators, congressmen, officers of the agricultural colleges and the USDA, as well as state engineers and members of state land boards.[6]

The 1907 meeting, like subsequent Dry Farming Congress meetings, combined boosterism and scientific presentation. Ellery Channing Chilcott, head of the USDA's new Office of Dry Land Agriculture, gave a paper on crop rotation; William M. Jardine of the Agricultural College of Utah's Experiment Station and Robert Gauss, editorial writer of the *Denver Republican,* talked on breeding drought resistant strains of plants; and others, such as Governor Bryant R. Brooks of Wyoming and a certain Mr. Adams, a minister from Arizona, testified to the beauty and potential of their regions, the energy and industry of the American people, and the belief that science would find an answer, even if the question often remained ill-defined.[7]

The Dry Farming Congress continued until 1915, the scope of its work broadening to promote national and, by 1911, international development. The annual congresses made no attempt to affect the farmers directly or to encourage their participation at conferences, but they considerably increased dryland boosterism. By the time of the Fourth Dry Farming Congress at Billings in the fall of 1909, the organization published a hundred-plus page booklet detailing the attractions of Montana and the opportunities for settling and establishing profitable farming.[8]

These congresses were testaments to the Progressive belief in the efficacy of science. For many Americans, science offered an objective, nonreligious cure to social problems. The image of science in the early twentieth century was that of an industrial process of cogs and gears rather than a negotiated, organic interaction between man and nature. Hence, the issues confronting society generally, and agriculture specifically, in the arid West could be dismantled into discrete, solvable problems and then reassembled to create a newly invigorated rural society.[9]

The Great Northern corporation agreed with Dry Farming Congress members about the utility of science in agricultural improvement. However, James Hill found himself at odds with the majority of the congresses' participants regarding the nature of expertise. As with irrigation and land management, dryland farming researchers and federal bureaucrats successfully established a narrow, credential-based criteria for agricultural expertise, heavily reliant on formal training. Hill, on the other hand, continued to subscribe to an organic view of farm development based on a symbiotic relationship between man and land. Although he supported scientific farming and looked to educational institutions to disseminate ideas and methods, Hill firmly believed that "what has to be taught is not abstruse." The growing dominance of professional agricultural experts undermined Hill's position, making expertise dependent on quantifiable credentials.[10]

The conflict between experience- and education-based knowledge was apparent as early as the 1907 Dry Farming Congress, when Progressive scientists challenged Hardy Webster Campbell's authority on dry farming. Campbell, a self-created agricultural expert like Hill, advocated intensive wheat culture with alternating summer fallow in conjunction with subsoil packing as the basis for dryland farming. At the meeting, held in Denver, Campbell's work received two direct attacks from the new experts. First, federal official Ellery Channing Chilcott's paper opposed the notion of summer fallow, instead proposing crop rotation to replenish the soil. Second, scientist William Jardine stressed the need to develop drought resistant strains of plants to complement water-conserving tillage methods, offering plant genetics as an important component, which was neglected by Campbell. These two papers presented a scientific alternative to Campbell's amateurism. As the boom of dry farming spread and more scientists launched controlled, empirical experiments, many involved in the movement began to dismiss the Campbell System. Chilcott, Jardine, and others revealed through rational, scientific study the weakness of the Campbell System, especially its tendency to oversimplify the needs of arid agriculture. They stressed that tillage systems had to be adapted to particular soil types, that rotation and crop variety enhanced the chances of profitability, and that larger acreages proved more profitable than 160 acres. Overall, the scientists were wary of Campbell's extravagant claims for dryland farming, being reluctant to promote farming techniques that had not met their finely defined criteria of proof.[11]

Attacks on the Campbell System represented more than an increased understanding of the complexities of dryland farming. Campbell, a competent farmer turned publicist, symbolized an increasingly suspect type of expert in the eyes of the dominant Progressive culture: an uneducated one. Federal officials and academics aimed to undermine his position and assert their own dominance. Their ease in executing this coup demonstrated both the widespread acceptance of empirical proof by the 1910s and the consequent vulnerability of authorities like Campbell and, of course, Hill himself, who lay outside academe or government.[12]

The Great Northern did not have any official representatives at the Denver meeting, but by 1909 the corporation had demonstrated substantial interest in dry farming. Dry Farming Congress authorities approached the railroad to help organize their next meeting both administratively and financially. Max Bass, the line's immigration agent, represented the Great Northern on the board of directors and agreed to contribute $1,500 for advertising and miscellaneous costs. The line also offered special rates to people traveling to and from the congress. General Traffic Manager W. W. Broughton expressed the corporate position when he noted that it was in the line's interest "to stir the people up and get as many as possible to attend this dry farming congress. . . . There is nothing now going on in Montana that will do us more good than the proper advancement of this dry farming question."[13]

The same year, James Hill personally donated one thousand dollars in prize money to exhibits displayed at the International Dry Farming Exposition held in conjunction with the congress. The Hills wanted to promote interest in dry farming, but they specifically saw the donation as a way to publicize the farmlands along the railroad. Louis Hill, administering the gift, insisted on exhibits representing the railroad's territory: "It is easy enough to get a list of prizes, but it is also up to us to see that the people along our line make exhibits. If they do not, the effect of the prizes is lost, as it will be taken for granted that we have not any crops to exhibit."[14]

In addition to promoting settlement and production along the line, the management of the Great Northern saw the Fourth Dry Farming Congress in Billings as a way to increase haulage along the railroad by attracting the attention of eastern terminal buyers. Louis Hill organized a large party of business and press people to accompany him to the congress on his private train, in effect to view the wares of the West. In a letter to one of the businessmen from Duluth, he stated that "The real object of the trip is to identify our eastern terminal markets with the Montana territory."[15]

The Hills also wanted to popularize and promote the land along their railroad. They persuaded the exposition to offer special prizes for areas east of the Cascade Mountains in Oregon, to promote settlement in the Deschutes Valley. Their desire to make a good showing from the area was so great that they sent railroad agents to obtain display produce, paid farmers' entry fees, and subsidized traveling expenses. Great Northern officials viewed their involvement in the congress as a golden opportunity to effect changes that would boost the region's settlement. The company further hoped that the meeting's publicity would pressure federal officials to accelerate the surveying process, especially for townships within eight to ten miles of the railroad.[16]

The Hills and the Great Northern wanted the Dry Farming Congress to operate largely as a promotional tool, boosting the land along their line and its potential for agricultural development. This corporate emphasis led to

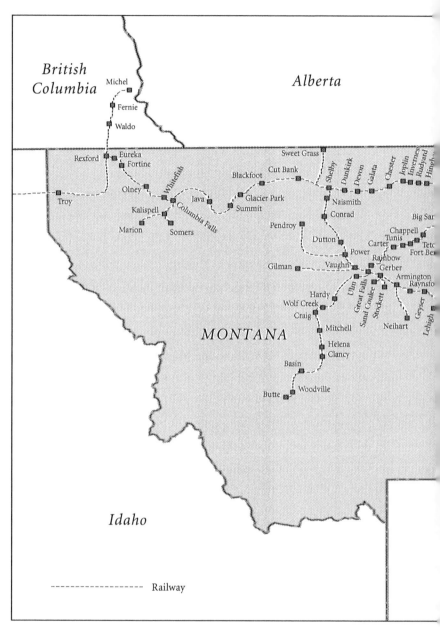

MAP 4. Rail routes in Montana

Saskatchewan

Scobey
Plentywood

Pacific Jc
Havre
Lohman
Chinook
ox Elder
Harlem
Coburg
Dodson
Malta
Bowdoin
Saco
Hinsdale
Tampico
Glasgow
Nashua
Frazer
Oswego
Wolf Point
Poplar
Brockton
Medicine Lake
Bainville
Snowden
Trenton
Williston

Dore

Culbertson
Fairview
Sidney
Charbonneau

Richey
Lambert
Jenks

occasin
Lewistown
Hanover
Judith Gap

MONTANA

North Dakota

Cushman
Broadview
Comanche
Rimrock
Billings
Mossmain

South Dakota

Wyoming

N
W ✦ E
S

a semantic debate with the more scientifically driven members of the organization. This conflict, begun in private, continued during the congress and became pivotal to the Great Northern's decision to disengage from future congresses.

The Hills believed that use of the terms "arid," "semi-arid," and "dry farming" ultimately deterred settlement, giving "a seriously erroneous impression to prospective settlers" that western lands were marginal and difficult to farm. James J. Hill, by now chairman of the board of the Great Northern Railway, gave one of the opening addresses at the congress in Billings in 1909, and he used the opportunity to make reference to the most contentious issue at the meeting: its name. He said, "dry farming will fail, but intelligent farming, intelligent cultivation of the land will not fail." The following day the congress discussed the name change. Louis Hill argued that the concept of dry farming discouraged settlement and investment by association with aridity. "We cannot get the co-operation of the railroads or expect to get people to come out here if we class this as a dry farming country."[17]

One group that opposed the corporate attempt to change terminology was the Progressive academics, who saw the extant wording as objective and descriptive. The main opponent in the initial debate was none other than Professor Frederick B. Linfield, head of the Montana Agricultural College's Experiment Station and long-time investigator of dry farming, who saw the term "dry farming" as merely semantic and not pejorative. Later, when the congress revisited the issue, the discussion was far more acrimonious. Ellery Channing Chilcott stated that "dry farming" represented a scientific term applying to agriculture in areas with less than twenty inches of rain per annum and that the focus of the congress should be on developing scientific methods to farm lands in these regions. He accused the Hills of trying to turn the congress into a colonization organization. Louis Hill did not rebut this charge. Instead, he pointed out that people intimately interested in development of the region, Great Northern representatives and delegates riding with them, had attended with the expectation that the name would be changed. Louis petulantly threatened to disassociate from the congress unless the name change occurred. He also criticized the federal government for the scarcity of land offices in Montana, accusing it of neglecting the state's interests.[18]

Louis Hill's threats mobilized another group of opponents in the form of anti-railroad members, who resented the Great Northern's attempts at dominance. The Hills had failed to assess the political temperament of the congress. Before the vote, an Oklahoma representative addressed the issue of railroad involvement and the name of the congress. "I know the sentiment among the farmers," he began, "They are not getting scared of this Dry Farming Congress. . . . If the railroads tell us they will not support us, let them go. We can get along without them." With general sentiment opposed to the Hills and their attempts to flex railroad power, the vote overwhelmingly reaffirmed the name "Dry Farming Congress."[19]

This defeat underscored the corporation's declining influence in agricultural issues. The Great Northern's subsequent financial and organizational disassociation from the Dry Farming Congress stemmed from the divergent environmental and economic aims of the many agencies involved. All parties understood that the seemingly insignificant debate over the name of the conference was really about the deeper purpose of the congress. As one Mr. Harcourt from Alberta noted, "this question [addresses] . . . whether this organization—this Congress—is to be an institution for the boosting of land or for the boosting of education." By making the decision to retain the terms "dry farming," the congress sided with the latter. Delegates remained committed to boosterism, but they would proceed cautiously and rely on the Progressive scientific information issuing from the USDA and experiment stations rather than simplistic propaganda.[20]

By the early twentieth century Progressive experts from universities and government had clearly gained national ascendancy, if not universal farmer trust. In view of their waning influence, the Great Northern's management withdrew the corporation from involvement in the Dry Farming Congress. The following year it offered one thousand dollars worth of prizes for exhibits at the exposition accompanying the Spokane meeting, but they offered to contribute no money for the congress itself. In light of this omission, the organization's officials refused the offer. The Hills' formal break with the conference did not, however, mean noninvolvement. Louis Hill still sent observers, although not as delegates who would "bring forth the fact that the railroads were trying to run the meeting, as they stated last year." In subsequent years the line focused solely on the congresses' exhibitions. The Great Northern, the Northern Pacific, and the Chicago, Burlington & Quincy sent produce display cars to Tulsa in 1913, and Louis Hill instructed Great Northern agents to encourage settlers along the road to submit exhibits at expositions. Although the Hills recognized that they could not control the Dry Farming Congress, they still hoped to attract settlers to the railroad's territory through exhibits while avoiding the detrimental attacks, which ensued from greater participation.[21]

Unlike the break over the experiment stations, which focused on production, the Hills' rift with the Dry Farming Congress was founded on a conventional emphasis on settlement promotion. Of course, this reflected the Hills' ownership of a number of different railroads. The work the Great Northern undertook with the Montana Agricultural College had been restricted to specific geographic locations, with the limited aim of persuading farmers and settlers along the Great Northern to adopt dry farming techniques to increase agricultural production. The Dry Farming Congress, however, with its greater national visibility, was a means to increase settlement throughout the Hill lines. The Hills desired to utilize these forums in a broader fashion to benefit all their railroad properties. They believed in scientific utility, but they wanted to channel scientific knowledge to aid their railroads. Working from the assumption that James Hill's expertise, resting on farming experience and business acumen, should predominate, the Hills abandoned the congress when the majority rejected their opinions.

By the start of 1910 the Great Northern had thus practically disassociated itself from all official scientific agencies dealing with dry farming in Montana. They had rescinded their support of the Montana Agricultural College's experiment stations, and the dispute over terminology effectively ended their involvement with the Dry Farming Congress. Both squabbles also exacerbated the existing rift between the railroad and the USDA. Arguments over conservation and western development had soured relations with Milton Whitney of the Bureau of Soils and Chief Forester Gifford Pinchot, and the breach with the Office of Dry Land Agriculture and the federally supported Dry Farming Congress simply compounded the antagonism between the railroad and relevant federal agencies.

Despite rifts with dryland farming institutions, the corporation still recognized the economic importance of dry farming along its lines. But, because the railroad had failed to control other agencies, its personnel decided to launch their own program of demonstration farms, revisiting private action. However, aware of the problems inherent in James Hill's earlier image of the gentleman farmer, the company carefully established a more professional basis for expertise, working through extant corporate offices and hiring established agricultural authorities.[22]

In 1910 the Great Northern management instructed Thomas Shaw of its Industrial Department, established to promote industrial development in the communities along the line, to supervise five-acre plots on forty private farms. The plan involved farmers cultivating a five- to six-acre plot of their land under the direction of Thomas Shaw and maintaining accurate records of the results. In return for this, the Great Northern supplied the seed and paid the farmers ten dollars an acre.

The selection of Shaw represented an amalgam of the two models of agricultural expertise. Shaw was, in many ways, a self-made, hands-on expert, but he also represented the Progressive scientific expert whom Hill both utilized and feared. Shaw, an academic professor before coming to work for the railroad, collaborated with grassroots agricultural organizations. He was a recognized authority on dryland farming in Montana, often appearing as a guest speaker for Fred S. Cooley, superintendent of the state's Farmers' Institutes. In the winter of 1909 he lectured in thirty-five locations in forty days. He also wrote a regular "On the Farm" column which many Montana papers carried.[23]

Shaw shared many of Hardy Webster Campbell's ideas, but he approached dryland farming in a more sophisticated, scientific manner. Like Campbell, Shaw recognized the importance of subsoil packing and regular cultivation, but he believed that the details of soil cultivation depended on the needs of each particular soil type. Similar to Campbell and Hill, and in opposition to some mainstream academics, Shaw advocated the settlement of small-scale farms. Shaw's thought deviated most from Campbell, however, in his emphasis on crop rotation to supplement, and even replace, summer fallow and the use of drought-resistant strains of plants. Shaw also stressed the need for diversification through livestock to provide food and fertilizer for the farmer.[24]

Shaw launched the Great Northern's private dryland farming experiment program by visiting a number of farms in the fall of 1909 to assess their potential as demonstration plots. In his report he highlighted the railroad's aims: "this land should be amply advertised to induce speedy settlement, and that means [it] should be adopted to instruct the settlers in the principles and methods that underlie the successful handling of land with a light rainfall." To determine which farms would be useful for the Great Northern, Shaw applied five criteria: the current effectiveness of the farming; the sparcity of local settlement; the proximity of the farm to a railroad station; the proximity of crops to the track for observation by passing trains; and the representativeness of the terrain. Once again, the needs of the railroad shaped the Great Northern's desire to improve agriculture through dry farming techniques. In locating the demonstration plots, Shaw understood the need for visibility, both to encourage a change in production techniques and to promote settlement. In addition to Shaw's recommendations, the railroad also

TABLE 6.1. Production Figures for Experiment Stations
in Montana and Minnesota, 1908

	Great Falls	Harlem	Forsyth	St. Paul
Spring wheat	12.77*	4.33	17.34	32.6
Sixty-day oats	18.25	27.06	32.92	44.0
White barley	12.73	8.00	29.90	44.0
Turkey Red wheat	10.40	16.63	45.31	32.6
Fall rye	8.71	——	32.46	39.8

Source: Alfred Atkinson and J. B. Nelson, "Dry Farming Investigations in Montana," Montana Agricultural College Experiment Station, Bulletin 74 (December 1908): 74–75; Andrew Boss et al., "Seed Grain; Selection, Treatment, Varieties, Distribution," Agricultural Experiment Station, University of Minnesota, Bulletin 115 (April 1909): 376–83; L. W. Hill to Broughton, 21 February 1910, Great Northern Railway Papers, Minnesota Historical Society, St. Paul, Minn.

*All figures given represent bushels per acre.

contacted commercial clubs for names of suitable farmers. In this way, the Great Northern further linked itself to the boosterish rather than to the scientific side of dry farming.[25]

For many residents of Montana and North Dakota, the appeal of the Great Northern demonstration farms was their practical orientation. O. P. N. Anderson of the North Dakota Railroad Commission remarked to Louis Hill in 1910, "Certain classes of our very good farmers . . . look with certain suspicion on almost anything proposed by a college professor. . . . The very fact that your people are suggesting certain things in the way of farming is to most . . . evidence that it is practical and will pay." For some farmers, who saw academics as otherworldly and divorced from the financial realities of farming, the business success of the railroad offered reassurance that the corporate proposals for agriculture would be economically viable.[26]

Yet, the railroad's break with academia was more apparent than real, and the corporation continued to fully utilize university resources. It obtained seed for its demonstration farms from the University of Minnesota and the University of Wisconsin, and it employed Professor M. L. Wilson of the experiment station at Bozeman to work under Shaw. The Great Northern's demonstration farm program ultimately reflected Hill's desire to balance the practical and scientific in his definition of expertise.[27]

The demonstration program started in 1910 and continually struggled

TABLE 6.2. Averaged Production
on the Great Northern Demonstration Farms, 1912

Crop	Yield in bushels per acre
Winter wheat	30.00
Durum wheat	19.14
Winter rye	22.00
Oats	72.14
White barley	30.00
Flax	13.83

Source: Thomas Shaw to L. W. Hill, 31 December 1912, Great Northern Railway Papers, Minnesota Historical Society, St. Paul, Minn.

against Louis Hill's attempts to cut costs. The first year Shaw worked with over forty farms in Montana. The next year the program extended geographically into North Dakota, but the overall number of farms enrolled remained fairly constant. Louis was anxious to maintain the benefits of the program in the most economical manner and suggested that farmers be persuaded to follow Shaw's direction without being paid. Louis's obvious lack of interest in the program reduced it quickly and significantly. By 1912 only twenty-five farms remained involved in Montana. After this, the program ceased in Montana but continued in North Dakota under the auspices of another Great Northern agricultural expert, A. E. Chamberlain. Chamberlain came from the South Dakota Experiment Station but had been born and trained in Ontario.[28]

Despite the short-lived nature of this program, the demonstration plots met the needs of the railroad in promoting profitable land use, both through agricultural production and stimulating settlement. In the fall of 1912 Shaw reported average crop figures for twenty-five farms involved in the program. The totals compared favorably to production levels of the experiment station in St. Paul four years earlier (see Tables 6.1 and 6.2). In addition to small grains, the plots produced considerable amounts of hay (2.75 tons per acre), fodder corn (2.14 tons per acre), and alfalfa (1.62 tons per acre). Settlement, too, increased under the influence of many dry farming boosters, including the Great Northern program. Homestead acreage quadrupled in one year from about a million acres in 1909 to 4,732,807 acres in 1910, and remained over three million acres annually until 1917. In 1912 James Hill tried to foster this settlement boom by announcing during a speech in Havre, Montana, that family-sized farms could prosper in northern Montana.[29]

Hill's speech reinforced the flood of literature that heralded the efficacy of dryland farming in conquering the semiarid West. In fact, the claims of some boosters offered unlimited promise as they asserted that "Dry-Farming methods can be utilized with profit upon every acre in every district of the world." Through all of this optimistic promotion, a few hesitant voices could be heard, usually those of academics, who suggested that more research was necessary and that recent rainfall had been abnormally high. Most parties ignored these words of caution, though, and immigration to the Plains surged in the early twentieth century. By 1922, 42 percent of the region had been homesteaded, and most farmers followed the tillage and rotation practices advocated by Campbell, Shaw, and Hill.[30]

By 1912, therefore, the Great Northern corporation had progressed through several distinct phases in its attitude toward dryland farming, with mixed results. Its initial response, reflecting the ambivalence of Hill, mutated into endorsement as the railroad cooperated with various institutions promoting the movement. The corporation's desire to develop a system geared to the line's specific needs of production and settlement fuelled growing opposition to the Montana Agricultural College's scientific caution and to the low production on cooperative experimental plots. Consequently, the line eventually severed connection with that institution in 1909. The same year James and Louis found themselves unable to manipulate the ideology and direction of the Dry Farming Congress and, in response, ended all official involvement. By 1910 the hierarchy of the Great Northern had decided that the optimum way to promote dry farming in Montana was to launch their own demonstration farm program. This met with considerable short-term success.[31]

In response to the growing antipathy between the railroad and institutional agricultural promotion on a federal and academic level, the Great Northern increasingly developed its own independent development program. In addition to the dryland farm plots, Louis Hill decided to increase corporate sponsorship of local fairs. Involvement in such a relatively small organization gave the railroad and the Hills considerable potential for control.

The National Apple Show in Spokane, Washington, was an obvious choice for support, as the competition had close links with Hill's promotion of irrigation and intensive agriculture on the Columbia Plateau. In 1908 both the

Northern Pacific and the Great Northern contributed one thousand dollars, and James Hill personally gave one thousand dollars for the show's operating expenses and another one thousand as prize money for the best one hundred boxes of apples from the Wenatchee district. Louis also contributed five hundred dollars of prize money for the best fifty boxes of apples from along the Great Northern. This corporate sponsorship lasted for six problematic years. The first year Louis acted as president of the show, but farmers from the Yakima Valley in the Northern Pacific territory claimed he had shown favoritism to Wenatchee entries. Accusations of bias were valid. Louis had, indeed, issued detailed instructions concerning which areas along the Great Northern he wanted represented in James Hill's contest of the best one hundred boxes of apples. Trying to quell the attacks, Louis suggested that Howard Elliott, head of the Northern Pacific, serve as the next president, thus maintaining a strong railroad presence.[32]

The Great Northern also sponsored local fairs, hoping that their financial backing would leverage support at a grassroots level for the type of scientific agriculture and environmental development the corporation wanted. In addition to the National Apple Show, it offered "a silver plated cup and several hundred ribbons to any county [fair] that asks for them." This policy proved considerably cheaper than financing large specialized shows and was intended to stimulate farmer interest in scientific agriculture. According to Louis, "there is nothing better than carrying on well arranged county fairs to encourage agriculture in these states." The Hills donated more elaborate prizes to state fairs along the line and to the corn show at Omaha. The Great Northern exercised considerable control in such endeavors, specifying the categories for awards and expending considerable energy collecting champion specimens from their territory.[33]

Although appearing as grassroots phenomena, such fairs were usually the product of powerful boosters trying to attract local settlement and link regional production with international markets. Viewed in this context, the Great Northern's participation was an attempt to coordinate its corporate interests with local institutions. Two factors made this strategy more attractive than other forms of institutional involvement. First, fair associations were usually weak and thus easily dominated by wealthy benefactors. Second, fairs did not present a single ideological front. Because of their spatial and conceptual designs, they were modular events where a variety of potentially conflicting ideas could be expressed simultaneously. Money donated by Hill and the railroad could target specific purposes, promotions, or prizes. Yet, at the same time, funding from other sources could potentially further contradictory perspectives. Consensus and discussion were not required or encouraged. For all these reasons, the Hills tried to maintain complete control over fair prizes and their inherent messages. This resulted in a degree of success that mostly eluded them with other institutional cooperation.[34]

In addition to expanding their sponsorship of agricultural fairs, shows, and organizations, the Great Northern also extended corporate agricultural experimentation. Partly as a result of Thomas Shaw's successful work on dry farming, the company decided to create a separate Agricultural Extension Department that would continue the work previously done under the auspices of the Industrial Department and also be responsible for experimentation and promotion. In 1912 the department was founded and staffed with professional agriculturists who supported Hill's views. Unlike later railroad agricultural departments that functioned solely as a means of disseminating university information, the Great Northern's department in the early years clearly had its own agenda and conducted its own research.[35]

The department's initial research looked at the maintenance of soil fertility rather than dryland farming. Intent on establishing demonstration farms along the Great Northern, James Hill hired Professor F. R. Crane from the Special Agricultural School in Menominee, Wisconsin. Crane selected five-acre plots on farms beside the Great Northern. The owners agreed to farm according to Crane's instructions, and Crane provided seed, fertilizer, smut treatment, and paid eight dollars per acre. Farmers retained their rights to the produce. The program aimed to demonstrate how scientific agriculture increased production.[36]

This program was an apparent success. Good seed and careful farming improved the first year's crop 40 percent over previous yields, according to Hill. He then approached Dean Albert Woods, head of the University of Minnesota's College of Agriculture, and asked him for the use of the university facilities for soil analysis to determine fertilizer needs. When Woods declined, Hill converted the greenhouses at his St. Paul mansion into soil laboratories and prepared for the 1912 growing season. In 1913 the Great Northern shipped 150 to 200 pounds of soil to Hill's mansion from each of the 361 farms. By 1915 farmers had enrolled 987 plots in the program. Inside the converted greenhouses, Crane and his assistant conducted a variety of tests to determine the best fertilizers for specific soils. Based on Crane's reports, farmers in 1914 and 1915 purchased four hundred tons of fertilizer, all shipped via the Great Northern.[37]

Dean Woods's refusal to involve the University of Minnesota with this demonstration farm project had stung Hill deeply, and he eventually expressed his discontent at a public banquet in honor of his seventy-fourth birthday. Held at the St. Paul Auditorium in September 1912, the occasion was splendid. Banners draped the walls of the hall, while electric lights emblazoned the dates "1838" and "1912." The 1,200 men and one woman (Mary Hill concealed in an alcove near her husband) enjoyed a sumptuous meal, while an orchestra and bagpipes provided entertainment. After the feast, encomium followed encomium as business leaders arose to praise the man as much responsible for their prosperity as any. In the midst of this festive and self-congratulatory atmosphere, Pierce Butler called on Hill to make a speech. The short, stocky, grizzled-haired veteran of the commercial world stood up.

Hill's presentation was one of aggression rather than gratitude. As expected, the speech took listeners back to the early days of the Twin Cities, to a frontier town and a small village at the falls of St. Anthony. As Hill spoke, however, his themes took an unexpected turn. He started to address the issues of soil conservation and the laws of nature, but, before his audience had a chance to catch their breath, Hill's frustration boiled over, and he launched into a virulent attack of the University of Minnesota's agricultural school. He vilified their education program, claiming that "in the last twenty five years, the school has not been worth 25 cents to the state."[38]

Hill's speech generated much debate about the agricultural education responsibilities of the university. In the following days, newspapers reported on the banquet, Hill's attack, and a subsequent letter war between Hill and Woods. Hill argued that the university had done nothing to benefit the farmers of Minnesota. He gave statistics showing the increased yield on the Great Northern's demonstration plots and concluded: "Somebody ought to have taught the farmer to do this long ago. It does not seem unreasonable to assign the duty to the state agricultural college." In Hill's mind, the university had failed to benefit farmers, which was, after all, its primary job as a land-grant college. Hill's attacks were not new. In fact, criticism of university-based agricultural education had a long history. From the early 1870s, farmer groups expressed their concerns about the state of rural America by criticizing various educational institutions for not providing effective education for young farmers. The grounds for attack varied: too theoretical syllabi; undersubscribed courses; and encouraging farm boys to leave the farm.[39]

The University of Minnesota had not escaped these attacks in the nineteenth century. In 1887 the Grange and the Farmers' Alliance claimed that "snobs and theorists" had diverted college funds for a theoretical and experimental program that offered no practical help to farmers. They demanded that the legislature institute a separate agricultural college where practical farming could be taught via demonstration and hands-on experience. Cyrus Northrop, president of the University of Minnesota, prevented the establishment of a separate institution by founding the agricultural school on the St. Paul campus and providing a practical education in basic agriculture and domestic science for farmers' children.[40]

Thus Hill's critique of the university and his stress on demonstration farms paralleled the views of many farmers' organizations. Despite fundamental differences over issues concerning railroad regulation, Hill, the Grange, and other farm groups shared a deep suspicion of book learning. In each case, suspicion stemmed directly from an unwillingness among many farmers to relinquish their claims to agricultural expertise to academicians.

By the time of Hill's attack in 1912, however, most of the antagonism between farmers and universities had subsided into an uneasy truce. Although still suspicious of academics, farmers had forced universities to embrace practical agricultural education. This compromise appeared on the national level with the Hatch Act of 1887, which had established federal funding for experiment stations, and on the regional level when state institutions implemented their own extension programs. While farmers remained skeptical of scientists' claims of expertise, they did manage to at least partially manipulate university education toward their own ends. Consequently, Hill's attack on the agricultural school was, like many of his development strategies, outdated.[41]

Dean Woods highlighted Hill's anachronistic position by countering Hill's vituperation with charges of amateurism. Woods claimed that the railroad magnate had failed to understand anything about agriculture or the university's mission. He stressed Hill's dependence on experts, including those from the university, and emphasized Hill's agricultural incompetence by citing the problems of drainage at Crookston and the failure of "Jim Hill Corn." He also suggested that the high yields from the Great Northern's demonstration farms resulted more from Hill's largesse rather than from improved farming: "Whether or not it is practicable for the average farmer to produce in his farm what Mr. Hill is able to produce on five acres . . . is a question that would have to be settled after knowing the amount of money and labor expended by Mr. Hill in securing the results." By stressing Hill's wealth, Woods undermined Hill's position as an agricultural expert by reclassifying him as a rich amateur, unacceptable in a world driven by empirical, rational science.[42]

Indeed, James Hill's establishment of the largest private demonstration farm scheme in the United States, which supposedly promoted modern scientific methods by quantifying fertilizer needs, was antiquated. Farm organizations had largely ceased their attacks on formal agricultural education by the turn of the century. Although they did not relinquish their claims of expertise to academics, farmers and their organizations, such as the Grange, increasingly adopted a utilitarian approach toward science. They incorporated information from agricultural scientists as part of their data for decision-making, often weighing it on subjective criteria, such as the personalities of extension agents.[43]

While relations with the University of Minnesota degenerated to public mudslinging, problems still existed between the corporation and other land-grant schools, such as the North Dakota Agricultural College. The Hills sponsored the Better Farming Association in North Dakota, both privately and corporately. This association, financed by banks and railroads, aimed to improve farming practices through an extension program at the college. As an organization funded by businesses, it upheld Hill's longstanding belief that the interests of corporations and farmers were complimentary, not contradictory, although many farmers disagreed. Many believed that their problems stemmed from corporate greed rather than from agricultural methods.

One measure of this skepticism was the creation of the American Society of Equity. This North Dakota grassroots farmer organization opposed the Better Farming Association, its business sponsors, and its links with the North Dakota Agricultural Experiment Station. Many farmers throughout the nation had consistently pointed to railroads and other agricultural businesses as primary sources of their financial difficulties rather than to their own inefficiency. The farmers in North Dakota were especially extreme in this respect and would eventually take control of businesses that affected them through the Nonpartisan League. But even in the early 1910s, they resented the development of alliances between their perceived enemies and the land-grant institution ostensibly founded for their benefit.[44]

The president of the North Dakota Agricultural College, John H. Worst, found himself caught in a struggle between businessmen, who often provided much-needed funds to the college, and farmers, the college's constituency. The conflict continued to fester until after James Hill's death, when the Nonpartisan League gained control of North Dakota in November 1916, giving farmers a temporary ascendancy over business. Once again, the conflict surrounding the Better Farming Association saw Hill's agricultural expertise questioned, by farmers as well as academics.[45]

The continued antagonism between James Hill and educational institutions and the development of independent corporate agricultural programs highlighted the corporation's alienation from farming and educational trends of the time. The last years of James J. Hill's official involvement with the Great Northern Railway marked the culmination of his dissatisfaction with institutional agricultural development. During these years, national movements to promote irrigation, conservation, and dryland farming developed. These organizations marginalized Great Northern personnel, undermined their ability to promote corporate-specific regional development, and disputed their expertise.

Consequently, the railroad gravitated toward independent agricultural programs. With the hiring of Professor F. R. Crane, the Great Northern inaugurated its own agricultural department and pursued Hill's vision of effective agriculture. In many ways this department reflected Hill's earlier endeavors as a gentleman farmer, being closely guided by the needs of the Great Northern. That the department operated as part of a corporate entity was also significant. Even Hill realized the uselessness of promoting agriculture on the basis of his personal expertise, so he sought professional validation by allying academics with the railroad's corporate success. Thus, Hill hoped to meld business and academic expertise. Although the department enjoyed some success in promoting fertilizers, the program floundered with Dean Woods's damning attack on Hill's amateurism.

By 1912, when James Hill retired from the Great Northern's board of directors, his agricultural policies and those of the railroad had almost come full circle. His family and his railroad backed no agricultural ventures on a federal level, and very few institutional enterprises on any level at all. Increasingly, the railroad developed internal corporate mechanisms to stimulate agricultural improvement. Still, much had changed. This professionalized agricultural department, staffed by scientists with the same credentials as those at universities, demonstrated at least a tacit acquiescence to academic standards of expertise. Although refusing to remove himself from direct involvement or to admit academic superiority, Hill continued his attempts to use the department to affirm his claims to expertise. Instead, his very presence continually challenged and contested the information that the department tried to disseminate.[46]

7 / Retirement and Retreat, 1912–1916

The pattern of failure James J. Hill had established in influencing agricultural western development continued to his death. During his last four years, the federal government solidified its control over regulating western resources, including land. Concurrently, Hill's own railroad abandoned attempts at innovative western development. A growing professionalism in the corporation isolated Louis Hill and his father, creating rifts between them and company management. Louis was increasingly seen as a liability by the company, while his father chose more and more to retreat to his own farms, adopting the mantle of an archaic gentleman farmer.

The election of Woodrow Wilson in 1912 heralded the ascension of corporate Progressive ideology to the federal level. Little interested in social reform, Wilson and Louis Brandeis, Gifford Pinchot's attorney, gravitated toward a system of pro-business regulation. The creation of the Federal Reserve in 1913 and the Federal Trade Commission in 1915 exemplified Wilson's belief in using government intervention to secure economic opportunity. In the years before American involvement in World War I, the nation witnessed a florescence of corporate efficiency, reform, and regulation. These trends moved America away from the laissez-faire economic climate that had allowed the rise of industrial barons such as James J. Hill. Additionally, Wilson's increased emphasis on regulation solidified federal involvement in western development.[1]

Hill increasingly resembled a cultural dinosaur. The triumph of the federal bureaucracy in the struggle to control western resources had firmly undermined those advocating states' rights. Hill's agricultural ideas, too, were out of sync with general trends. Mechanization encouraged the development of large-scale, monocrop farms, but most farmers could not afford to purchase steam tractors, popular between 1908 and 1915, or gasoline engines. The farmers who could buy the new machines tended to be wealthier and possess greater acreage. They benefited from the heavy, unwieldy machines in ways small-scale farmers could not. Consequently, federal policies and mechanization nurtured agricultural economies of scale and the decline of smallholder opportunity, especially on the open western Plains. The dryland farming wheat boom on the northern Great Plains flourished, especially as international demands grew during World War I. Profit and technology had undermined the relevance of Jeffersonian ideals, and farmers, politicians, and businessmen alike fostered nascent agribusinesses. Ironically, the robber baron and railroad consolidator, Hill, remained among the last defenders of the small-scale, commercial farmer.[2]

The Great Northern corporation's activities contributed to Hill's ideological isolation in the face of national agricultural trends. In 1912, at seventy-four, Hill resigned his position as chairman of the board of the Great Northern Railway. Although this marked the end of his official involvement with the line, he maintained an office in the railroad's headquarters, which he utilized regularly until just before his death in 1916. He remained unofficially active in railroad business during his retirement, but day-to-day operations increasingly devolved on the new president, Carl R. Gray, and on Louis Hill, who replaced his father as chairman of the board. Moving out from his father's shadow, Louis developed his own style. He still paid attention to his father's areas of interest, such as agriculture, but increasingly acted independently and with growing self-assurance. Although the railroad management continued to make some concessions to the antiquated views of the railroad's founder, they nevertheless modernized the line and its outlook, including the agricultural sphere.

In James Hill's absence and under the auspices of Louis Hill, and especially under the professional management of Carl Gray, the Great Northern's interest in agriculture both diminished and conformed more to Progressive norms. The railroad abandoned much of its demonstration and experimental work. Although the agricultural extension department continued, it mutated into a publicity department, employing academics to disseminate ideas developed elsewhere. Such a change represented an essential abandonment of the railroad's claim to agricultural expertise.

Redefining the role of the agricultural extension department in promoting western development involved relinquishing much of the department's independent research. Despite the apparent success of the Great Northern's private dryland experiment program, Louis Hill wrote to Thomas Shaw in 1913 that they should see if they had "reached a stage where the farmers will do the work themselves along the lines suggested by you without being paid to do so." Shaw opposed this suggestion. He said more work was necessary to determine relative returns of winter wheat on corn land and summer fallow, the best method for growing alfalfa, and the best way to increase moisture-retention of vegetable matter in the soil. He explained this to Louis Hill, but Louis rejected Shaw's advice and terminated the demonstration farms, although the railroad continued to encourage farmers, through local booster groups, to grow and exhibit dryland crops. Louis did not necessarily disagree with Shaw on the need for more experimental work, but he believed that neither Shaw nor the railroad commanded enough attention to make their agricultural endeavors significant.[3]

While Louis Hill and Carl Gray tried to align corporate ideology with early-twentieth-century professional views of agriculture, James Hill remained a vocal and formidable obstacle. Consequently, the company kept some remnants of the older programs instituted by Hill in deference to the "Empire Builder." Professor F. R. Crane's soil experiments continued with some success until 1915, at least if judged by the amount of fertilizer shipped by the railroad. Dean Woods at the University of Minnesota, however, continued to attack Crane's program as amateurish. By the scientific standards of the early twentieth century, Crane did, indeed, conduct experiments in a highly subjective manner. He failed to establish controls, and it remained unclear whether improved yields resulted from increased care in cultivation, good seed, or fertilizers. Crane also had highly unrealistic expectations of farmers' abilities and time for crop care. He gave detailed instructions on how to grow, cut, store, and thresh grain, including cleaning the thresher out before and after threshing and admonishing farmers not to thresh into the wind. In addition, Crane carefully instructed farmers on how to report yields. They were to estimate ideal production from any swampy land or areas of damaged crops and add those estimates to the total. As a result, farmers invested three to six times more labor to produce crops from experimental plots than for regular fieldwork.[4]

By the 1910s Crane's scientific methodology was outmoded. Increasingly, scientists designed experiments that could be quantified by standard numerical measurements. By making their work reproducible, scientists upheld claims to objectivity; by using statistics, they communicated in a language that the ever-increasing scientific community could understand and uphold.

Crane and Hill's work, falling into an older scientific tradition of observation and multiple variables, offered an easy target for professional scientists, who intellectually disagreed with their conclusions and professionally were intent on defending their own status.[5]

This policy shift by the Great Northern away from experimental agriculture had much to do with the shift in power to new personalities, and was as well an acknowledgment that the onus for agricultural development lay outside the railroad's bailiwick. Neither Louis Hill nor Gray showed much interest in agriculture, and the direction of the development department (which encompassed agriculture by this time) from the company's hierarchs dwindled. Once his father retired, Louis also lost interest in funding farmer organizations, fairs, and shows. Instead, the railroad utilized its business and marketing expertise to expand extant markets and develop more efficient ways of shipping produce.[6]

This change in emphasis was reflected in new personnel and personnel management and in very different corporate plans for development. In October 1911 the Great Northern had hired A. E. Chamberlain, former superintendent of the Farmers' Institutes in South Dakota for the South Dakota Agricultural Experiment Station and a writer for *The Dakota Farmer,* as the commissioner for its development department. Although Thomas Shaw continued to work for the railroad, Chamberlain's hire signaled a more institutional approach to agricultural development. Unlike Shaw, Chamberlain had little contact with James Hill beyond sending him copies of reports. Most of his orders came from his immediate superior, General Manager W. P. Kenney. Chamberlain also displayed a level of business professionalism that Shaw lacked. He neatly typed reports with clear subheadings, unlike Shaw's scrawled and rambling handwritten letters. As the department professionalized, the direction of corporate agricultural work grew increasingly removed from James Hill's control and ideological influence.[7]

Chamberlain directed his major efforts to ways that haulage could be increased, not by the farmers, but by the railroad. He showed special interest in increasing express shipments of fruit from the Pacific Northwest to the East. He believed that by constructing cooling plants in western Washington and Oregon, fruits "that are now being canned or evaporated and shipped by freight, could and would be shipped by express." He also suggested that the railroad provide more cars for fruit shipment to silence complaints about insufficient numbers of cars and their "filthy and unfit condition." In 1912 the Great Northern lagged behind the Northern Pacific in its number of icing cars, and the problems of fruit car scarcity and poor maintenance continued.[8]

Rather than trying to engineer further environmental change in the West, Chamberlain accepted the extant land use and emphasized marketability of produce and methods for the line to maximize profits from perishable goods. This thrust marked a distinct break with the past. Abandoning Hill's conceptualization of the best type of land use, the focus now remained solely on maximizing corporate profit. In addition, the shift demonstrated a growing affinity between railroad personnel and prevailing notions of professionalism. Deferring to university and governmental expertise in the matter of agriculture, Chamberlain and others concentrated on issues of shipment, marketing, and business, areas of corporate expertise. This change of emphasis meant that the development department worked with agricultural business organizations as much as with farmers. In keeping with Chamberlain's geographical interest in the Pacific Northwest, much of this interaction was with fruit organizations. The railroad aided the Commercial Club of Wenatchee by donating land for a booth to exhibit local fruits and produce. In addition, the line constantly attempted to maintain the number of refrigerator cars necessary to ship fruit and fish east.[9]

Unlike Shaw, and indeed unlike James Hill himself, Chamberlain deferred to established expertise in matters of agricultural experimentation and development. Most notably, he turned to the federal government for aid, acknowledging bureaucratic scientific authority as well as the Wilsonian consolidation of federal power to direct environmental change and development. In early 1912 Chamberlain wrote to the USDA for information regarding research on cooling plants in California. The USDA's experiments with precooling soft fruits that summer had proved so successful that it agreed to lend the Great Northern three men to help disseminate information during the 1913 season. The USDA also planned to send officials to the Wenatchee Valley to instruct growers on optimum methods for harvesting apples for shipment.[10]

This use of a federal agency, and deference to outside knowledge and expertise, extended beyond issues of fruit. While visiting Washington, D.C., in 1912, Chamberlain met with Secretary of Agriculture James "Tama Jim" Wilson, who promised the assistance of a department representative for two months to travel through irrigation districts "trying to prevail on them [the farmers] to use less water and follow better systems of tillage." Corporate stress on mainstream expertise was evident even when discussing railroad personnel. In 1913 Carl Gray boasted that the Great Northern employed "agricultural professors of national reputation." The acceptance of Progressive definitions of expertise had become all-prevailing.[11]

Having focused the company's research energies on increasing haulage, Great Northern personnel resorted to publicity campaigns to improve agricultural practices. In some ways, these attempts to reach farmers and settlers directly represented a return, on a corporate level, to a method James Hill had tried and abandoned in the 1880s. The railway's involvement in the "barberry eradication campaign" to stop wheat rust, from World War I into the 1950s, exemplified this revived strategy. However, while agents posted information on how to eradicate the rust, and the railroad lobbied for federal and state funding and research into the problem, corporate experimental work was notably absent.[12]

The company channeled other grassroots publicity efforts through extant educational and farmer organizations. At the instigation of General Manager Kenney and Fred S. Cooley, superintendent of the Montana Farmers' Institute, the railroad joined with the Montana Agricultural College in 1914 to coordinate a "Better Farming" train. The plans for the train demonstrated not only a change in the educational perspective of the corporation but also the growing influence of middle management, who formulated and implemented this part of railroad policy. Louis Hill and Carl Gray showed little interest in the train beyond costs. Similarly, when Kenney approached Louis Hill to discuss an agreement with a number of railroads to discontinue agricultural trains, Louis replied, "You may do as your judgment seems best in this connection." The Great Northern leadership had thus moved a considerable distance from the desire to improve farming that had been so central for James Hill.[13]

Through Cooley, the Great Northern also utilized their old antagonist, the Grange, to disseminate agricultural information. As the Grange had moved away from the political activism it had embraced in the 1870s, it returned to its earliest goals of education and entertainment, becoming an ideal vehicle for reaching farmers. In January 1914 the railroad offered reduced rates to farmers visiting the state Grange meeting in Bozeman, Montana. Later that year, Cooley recruited Thomas Shaw to be a keynote speaker at the Grange's 1915 state meeting. As with the agricultural trains, however, most speakers except Shaw were academics, not railroad employees.[14]

Part of Chamberlain's work also involved publicity, which often mirrored the agricultural and social engineering efforts of his predecessor and coworker, Thomas Shaw, and of James Hill himself. Chamberlain not only advised growers on methods but encouraged certain ethnic groups to migrate to specific areas, such as "Danes and Hollanders into the Kootenai and Spokane valleys." In addition, he also followed the circuit of county fairs and farmers' meetings, giving speeches and judging livestock throughout the railroad's territory.[15]

Chamberlain continued to represent the Great Northern at local fairs throughout the northern tier of states. However, this represented the extent of company involvement, as in 1915 Louis Hill discontinued financial support for fairs, asserting that the results no longer justified the expense. The same year, the Great Northern, in collaboration with the Northern Pacific, ended their support of the National Apple Show at Spokane. The event had "outlived its usefulness as a national event," and the railroads doubted "whether [they] ... receive very much benefit from it." This financial retreat diminished the line's ability to shape agricultural ideology. This was, perhaps, inevitable. Without the leadership of James J. Hill, the Great Northern moved away from a desire to make profit for the line in conjunction with promoting an agricultural ideology and toward a sole emphasis on economic pragmatism.[16]

Chamberlain broadened his publicity efforts and investment of time in ways that represented a sharp break from the past. In his first year he divided his efforts between the Pacific Northwest and attending land shows in the East. The land shows were a new, efficient means of luring settlers and investors to western lands. Unlike regional events with the semi-altruistic function of promoting scientific agriculture, eastern land shows were blatantly corporate phenomena, advertising western lands to the largest possible audience. For the first time in the history of the Great Northern, its main agricultural endeavors had shifted geographically away from the northern tier.[17]

Another, more problematic component of the corporation's agricultural publicity was Thomas Shaw. Through James Hill's influence he continued to be employed by the company and remained popular among Plains farmers. He was in great demand as a speaker among farming groups and other railroads, and he continued to write articles on the agricultural potential of the region, which he distributed to newspapers throughout the nation. As with his mentor, though, Shaw's influence as an expert was waning. Louis Hill and others in the railroad hierarchy worried about the information Shaw disseminated in speeches and in print. Shaw's word was no longer consid-

ered definitive, either inside or outside the corporation. In 1912, for example, Shaw sent an article to the Philadelphia *Saturday Evening Post* to correct some negative reports of dry farming, which the magazine had published
a few weeks earlier. Although Shaw accompanied his corrections with a letter from Louis, the paper refused to print his piece, temporizing in a letter
to the Great Northern management, "We recognize Professor Shaw as an
authority, but . . . we believe that a great deal of dissapointment [*sic*] and
injury has resulted from over enthusiastic representations." By March 1913
Louis had placed a careful watch on all of Shaw's reports, censoring those
that were "of such a nature that they would do us more harm than good if
published." Shaw's reports consistently painted glowing agricultural pictures
that stemmed from the antiquated agricultural ideology he shared with James
Hill. Indeed, Shaw himself recognized his archaic position. When the University of Minnesota's Agricultural Experiment Station approached the railroad to request help in hauling several demonstration cars, Shaw anticipated
that the only problem would be "that some of the people [professors] will
not be quite in accordance with Mr. Hill's views on cattle." As a friend of
James Hill, Shaw continued on the Great Northern's lecture circuit in 1915
and 1916, but almost immediately after James Hill's death, Louis Hill forced
the professor to retire.[18]

Therefore, during the years after James Hill's retirement as chairman in
1912, the Great Northern shifted its approach to agricultural development.
Instead of trying to persuade farmers to try new ways to develop the environment, the agricultural department devised ways to increase profits from
extant agriculture. This change in tactics aligned the railroad's agricultural
policy with prevailing attitudes toward professionalism. The department
abandoned most of its experimental work and hired university professors
to disseminate academic wisdom. The changes also marked the abandonment of James Hill's grand social vision. No longer would the Great Northern try to create an Eden filled with small-scale farms run by Jeffersonian
yeomen. Instead it focused on the narrow goal of corporate profit.

That the Hills never fully concurred with the Great Northern's adoption
of Progressive professionalism became evident in their relationships with
federal institutions, notably, the Reclamation Service. Continuing their battle with this organization, they viewed themselves as altruistic defenders of
western interests. Although ostensibly a proponent of Progressive efficiency,
objectivity, and corporate streamlining, Louis Hill's (and his father's) antagonism toward individuals within the Reclamation Service degenerated into

a vindictive personal diatribe, which the management of the Great Northern tried desperately to curtail.

Having failed to effect changes in federal policy and personnel, both Hills resorted in frustration to lambasting the Reclamation Service. Admitting that "I am one of the strong critizers [*sic*] of that service," Louis detailed, in a public speech in Oregon, the whole case against Frederick Haynes Newell, from the black tent shows, through the article promoting Canadian irrigation, to the failure by the service to follow through on irrigation works in Montana. Louis also spelled out actions taken by himself to correct the problems and to obtain Newell's dismissal. He framed the personal and corporate struggle as a battle against tyranny: "That man Newell is like a Russian politician; if things dont [*sic*] go his way he fires somebody. He ties the can to anybody who opposes his theory and to be perfectly frank and to use good English, when you corner him he lies out of it."[19]

The Hills continued to base their attacks on the Reclamation Service's incompetence and its failure to understand western needs. Having failed to initiate any action by badgering the Department of the Interior, by 1912 Louis Hill turned his attention to President William Taft's secretary, Charles Hilles. Concerned that the government had withdrawn twenty sections in northeastern Montana for irrigation purposes, and that homesteaders were being prevented from using the land even for grazing, Louis argued that it was "little things of this kind that antagonize the West against the Departments in Washington. The Reclamation Department are [*sic*] not only proving themselves of little practical benefit to our portion of the west, but they seem to take every means of antagonizing the settlers."[20]

The main grounds for attack, however, remained the article purportedly written by Frederick Newell, head of the Reclamation Service, promoting irrigation works in Canada. Louis Hill sent a copy to Hilles and claimed that "people of the west feel that Mr. Newell is not treating them right and they hold this against President Taft." When Hilles took the matter up with the Secretary of the Interior, Newell again denied authorship. Louis again tried to show him as a liar, assigning railroad personnel to track down the publication in Canadian Pacific literature. Despite considerable effort, Louis failed to prove Newell's authorship. Rather than give up, though, he next tried to portray Newell as unpatriotic, implying that he was to blame for overspending in the Reclamation Service and for its failure to complete projects. Louis sent information on the Reclamation Service's shortcomings to the editor of the *Great Falls Daily Tribune*, one William Bole. Bole tactfully demurred, pointing out that the material would "tend to scare away intended settlers on government irrigation projects, and that would not serve your purpose or mine."[21]

Through their continued personal antagonism toward Newell and the Reclamation Service, the Hills moved away from the increasingly professionalized approach of the Great Northern. This divergence appeared clearly in James Hill's actions and speeches. More interested in agricultural development than his son, Hill railed publicly at government failure. For example, in 1913 he attacked the Reclamation Service during a congressional hearing, contending that private irrigation projects in Canada had proved cheaper and more effective than those launched by the federal government. Hill focused on government inefficiency, saying, "I know that when private enterprises in Canada can sell the land and water for $30 an acre and the water on reclamation projects in the United States cost $45 an acre that there is some difference in the cost." Ironically, Frederick Newell, whom Louis Hill had been attacking for years for promoting Canadian irrigation, defended American irrigation. Newell asserted that Canadian projects were generally smaller and less well constructed than American projects, and so were cheaper, but not necessarily better. Secretary Franklin K. Lane finally judged that "the charges against the Reclamation Service have not been sustained."[22]

The position James Hill adopted in this case directly countered the interests of the Great Northern. Attacking the expense of irrigation on the northern Great Plains and comparing it unfavorably to Canadian projects was not calculated to increase settlement along the railroad. In retirement, Hill had allowed his concerns for the future of American agriculture to eclipse his love of the Great Northern, while Louis Hill's hatred of Newell colored his actions.

By 1913 the Hills' position with regards to the federal agency had diverged so far from Great Northern policies as to be an embarrassment. Great Northern middle management, such as L. C. Gilman, Gray's assistant, had worked closely with Newell, engineers, and settlers to complete various irrigation projects in Montana and establish necessary railroad easements across projects. Gilman did this by lobbying and building constituencies, as had been the railroad's practice for years, and although he did not personally like Newell or approve of his neglect of the northern Great Plains, he did recognize the importance of staying on good terms with the man. Thus, the

Hills' virulent attacks against Newell and the Reclamation Service struck Gilman as shortsighted. He warned Gray that "harm rather than good is done by constant criticism of the Reclamation Service. While personally I am of the opinion that its personnel might be very materially improved, I think there is little likelihood that it will be, and if we wish to accomplish anything it will be necessary to work with the tools we have." Others concurred. William Bole, the editor of the *Great Falls Daily Tribune*, wired Gray that President Taft had received a copy of a "very caustic interview on stupidity of reclamation service by J. J. Hill. Such stuff is used by our enemies and does harm it should stop."[23]

Despite the attempts of corporate professional management to circumvent such criticisms, James and Louis Hill continued to exacerbate the situation and to threaten the completion of irrigation projects in Montana. H. N. Savage, engineer with the Reclamation Service in charge of the Sun and Milk Rivers projects, wrote confidentially to Gilman that "The situation . . . is very precarious. The chronic adverse criticisms of Messrs. James J. and L. W. Hill which has extended over a period of years has become a very serious obstacle and may be the determining factor" in the projects' completion. Gilman and Gray managed to overcome the Hills' ill effects and persuaded Secretary Lane to invest more reclamation time and money in the projects in northern Montana.[24]

To be sure, James and Louis Hill were not the only voices complaining about Frederick Newell. Many western politicians, settlers, and newspapers attacked Newell for wasting money and for resisting attempts to ease the repayment burden on settlers. In 1914 these complaints finally culminated in Newell's firing. Although this must have provided immense satisfaction to the Hills, they remained silent and never claimed responsibility for the dismissal. Regardless of this long-demanded personnel change, the railroad men had little control over the Reclamation Service, its direction, or its employees.[25]

In all their attacks on the Reclamation Service and Newell, the Hills did adopt some constructive strategies. Although just threatening to take over irrigation works in Montana, in Washington they embarked again on railroad-financed irrigation. In the Okanogan Valley, north of Wenatchee, an area considered for irrigation since 1905, work finally started in 1916. As in Wenatchee and Adrian, the project was financed by a bond issue, with James Hill purchasing $490,000 of the bonds, his son-in-law Charles

Ffolliott purchasing $100,000, and the Great Northern Railway purchasing $10,000. As with earlier efforts to irrigate privately, the project showed some success, but at high and continuing cost.[26]

Having fought with farmers, the federal government, state universities, and booster groups, James Hill found at the end of his life that even his own railroad had abandoned his vision of American agriculture. Shunned by others, Hill retreated to his original position of trying to influence agricultural change through his own reputation.

Resuming action independent of the railroad, in 1913 Hill became chairman of the advisory committee of the National Soil Fertility League. Started in 1911, the league promoted agricultural education and was heavily funded by railroads. The advisory committee included William Taft, William Jennings Bryan, Charles Van Hise, W. D. Hoard, John H. Worst, and Henry C. Wallace. The principal aim of the organization was the enactment of the Lever bill or, as it became known, the Smith-Lever Act. This legislation proposed to give federal support and structure to agricultural extension programs that had been inaugurated by various institutions at the turn of the century.[27]

Hill's attraction to the concept of extension stemmed from his longstanding distrust of, and marginalization by, academics. He and many others felt that universities had neglected actual farming needs, postulated impractical systems, and patronized farmers. In 1908 Hill had lent his support to the Dolliver-Davis bill, which proposed a system of federally funded agricultural high schools. Hill hoped the measure would offer more practical agricultural education, but Congress did not pass it.[28]

Changing his focus to extension, Hill championed the same cause of grassroots education. In 1911 he financially supported the Better Farming Association in North Dakota, which instituted an extension program in that state. Hill also hoped that through the Lever bill, new scientific methods of farming could be disseminated effectively on a national level, using the extension model. He wanted extension programs to address practical farming issues, being "impressed with the possibility of work done by the farmer on his own land with his own hands under the direction of some one who knows of his own practice and not of what he has been told or what he has read out of books or newspapers." In 1914 the Smith-Lever Act passed, unifying and funding the county agent system and making it the responsibility of the land-grant colleges.[29]

This vision of a national extension system allied closely with Hill's ongoing belief in the efficacy of demonstration farms. Hill was disgusted with official agricultural education, but paradoxically believed that the federal government should remain responsible for this education. Such dichotomies had permeated his entire life. A believer in scientific and technological progress and expertise, Hill nevertheless saw agricultural knowledge as being gained through experience rather than formal teaching. By advocating a national extension service, Hill sought a middle ground where professionals could merely guide the experiential knowledge of farmers.

Hill's support of federal extension revisited his earlier contention that university professors were not fulfilling their professional mandate. Like many other "non-academics," he thought that productive farming could be guaranteed by individualized fertilizer prescriptions and good seed. Hill charged that university personnel should have provided this soil analysis and seed breeding, but that instead they had complained that these mundane demands of farmers for routine analyses cut into their research time. The Smith-Lever Act thus succeeded in straddling both camps. For those with Hill's perspective, the act provided a type of agricultural education and support that universities were reluctant to supply. For university personnel and their colleagues in the Office of Experiment Stations, the act freed them for research, passing educational responsibilities to the extension service. Hence, the act was well supported throughout the agricultural world, and Hill's backing was less than crucial.[30]

While gaining a victory of sorts through independent action with the Smith-Lever Act, James Hill also spent an increasing amount of time on his own farms in these last years. Returning to earlier ideas, he sought to educate local farmers through example and by providing them with high quality stock. Although his broad concerns of diversification through dual-purpose cattle and soil conservation had not changed, his methods did reveal the infiltration of some new ideas.

In addition to wheat farming in the Red River Valley, Hill returned to using his personal farms to promote his agrarian vision. Having profited considerably from the bonanza farming boom in the 1880s, Hill, in his seventies, decided to alter the purpose of his properties in the Red River Valley. Since the purchase of Humboldt, he had been selling the land off in small acreages, often equipped with new buildings, to foster his vision of Jeffersonian yeomen, but now he decided to use the farm to promote dual-purpose and blooded stock. In September 1910 Hill separated three thousand acres of the Humboldt farm, known as the Northcote division, and placed it under the management of his youngest son. Walter Hill was a twenty-five-year-old reputed alcoholic who was having trouble establishing himself. Walter told his father that he would like to try farming, so James Hill gave him the project of turning Northcote into a huge cattle station.[31]

James Hill's plans for Northcote involved local demonstrations and dissemination of knowledge. Walter Hill would experiment with different kinds of cattle feeds and then inform farmers of profitable combinations. James Hill also intended Northcote to function as a stock farm for breeding quality cattle. Both activities would help promote diversification through improvement and sale of available breeding stock. Thus, Hill once again tried to effect change through example. Under his son, however, the project consistently lost money, undermining the impact of the demonstration farm.[32]

It is unlikely that James Hill expected to make a profit in these endeavors, so the substantial losses should not automatically be blamed on Walter Hill's bad management. Stockbreeding was expensive because of the high cost of establishing a herd. In 1914, for example, the main expense for the farm was livestock purchases totaling more than $73,000. Separate from these costs was the building program Hill launched in 1912, intending to equip the new farm with the necessary buildings to make it a modern feed experiment station. By August 1914 Hill had constructed a cattle barn, silos, a root cellar, boarding house, power plant, dam, water system, a hog house, and twelve cottages, costing over $200,000.[33]

Hill's personal interest in livestock had regained momentum through association with Thomas Shaw in the years before Louis Hill fired him from railroad employment. In addition to working for the railway and for the Northern Pacific, Shaw had helped Hill with his personal agricultural endeavors. Like Hill, Shaw was convinced of the efficacy of dual-purpose cattle and, under his tutelage, Hill resumed his development of an effective breed. Shaw also helped reverse some of Hill's earlier ideas. Instead of starting with basic beef cattle, such as Shorthorns, and then breeding them for increased milk quality and yield, Shaw suggested working with dairy cattle to develop "good beef points."[34]

To build such a herd, Hill sent A. W. Shaw (apparently no relation to Thomas Shaw) to England in 1913 to buy cattle and horses. The stock arrived in Quebec, where problems arose with quarantine and tuberculin certification. A. W. Shaw eventually had to go to Washington, D.C., to sort out the problem. The stock remained in Quebec for a month while bureaucratic knots loosened. A. W. Shaw did not accompany the cattle to North Oaks, having accepted an assistant professorship at the University of Saskatchewan. The next year Thomas Shaw himself went to England to buy cattle and to hire cowhands. He purchased fifty Shorthorn bulls costing $17,345. Only five of these stayed at North Oaks; most were distributed along the lines of the Great Northern and Northern Pacific, with much more success than Hill's earlier distribution attempts.[35]

At the same time that Hill revived his interest in breeding cattle, he also resumed breeding other farm animals at North Oaks. Livestock registers detailed the purchase, breeding record, and death or sale for various breeds of pigs, sheep, and horses. By the time of Hill's death, North Oaks was once more a thriving stock farm, breeding high quality stock made available to the average farmer both through Hill's distribution scheme and through stud service.[36]

Hill also renewed agricultural experimentation. Despite his rejection of modern strictures on agricultural expertise, he had always supported the notion of scientific agriculture, and his internalization of changing scientific practices became apparent in the work at North Oaks. Unlike the experiments conducted in the 1880s, those started in 1914 were more systematic. The dairy kept weekly records of: pounds of milk received; average test of milk; pounds of cream received; average test of cream; pounds of butterfat from cream; and pounds of butter made. Two months later similar records were started for grade as well as thoroughbred cows. The farm experimented with different types of feed, and the superintendent proposed feeding milkers a mixture of oats, barley, and cowpeas after the grass died in the summer. Hill utilized F. R. Crane of the Great Northern agricultural extension department at North Oaks. Crane's studies for the railroad involved fertilizer work, and he frequently used North Oaks for testing.[37]

In these later years, Hill's Minnesota properties regained importance as part of his larger agricultural vision. When the railroad abandoned its idiosyncratic farming development policies, adopting a more mainstream Progressive approach, Hill returned to his position as a gentleman farmer utilizing North Oaks and Northcote for experimentation and demonstration. These educational endeavors met with no more success than Hill's earlier attempts. Hill never saw his plans for Northcote's development as a stock farm reach fruition. Although the farm did keep Walter Hill occupied, it failed to persuade area farmers of the importance of stock raising. In the 1880s farmers had passively refuted Hill's claims to agricultural expertise.

Some thirty years later, their opinion had not changed. In fact, Progressive definitions of expertise had given them considerable new ground to reject Hill's teachings, stemming as they did from experience rather than formal education.[38]

While his farms gained no effectiveness as teaching tools, their operations did demonstrate Hill's growing political impotence. In two cases involving Canadian employees on the Red River Valley estates, Hill tried and failed to leverage support from Minnesota's former governor, Senator Knute Nelson. The first problem began in 1913 when Walter Hill, at his father's insistence, hired a Canadian veterinarian recommended by Thomas Shaw and ran into problems with the Immigration Bureau. In March 1914 James Hill wrote to Nelson, asking him to intervene, but with no success. A similar conflict arose in 1915 on Hill's bonanza estate, Humboldt, which had remained primarily a productive wheat farm, raising extensive crops under hired management. In 1915 problems emerged with the farm's traditional Canadian labor force when the sheriff arrived in the middle of harvest and "took away four . . . shockers." They were charged as illegal aliens, but Hill's manager asserted that the men had been working on the farm without trouble for fifteen years. Hill again turned to Senator Nelson for help, but despite his protestations, the men were deported back to Canada. Hill did not let the matter rest. He asserted that immigration officials aimed to "make fees" by bothering "a number of poor men who . . . are trying to earn a living." The acting secretary of labor, J. B. Densmore, corrected Hill, pointing out that the agents did not profit from arrests; he then closed the case and refused to make further inquiries. Thus, by 1915 Hill's political influence had virtually vanished. Without the muscle of the railroad and with few federal connections, Hill found himself in the uncomfortable role of a private citizen, albeit a very rich one.[39]

James Hill's retirement from the board of the Great Northern Railway in 1912 marked the culmination of his "great adventure" and heralded his return to an earlier agricultural policy. With his retirement, the railroad gradually altered its development programs. Moving away from the social vision of Hill to a narrower economic focus, the Great Northern paid less attention to changing agricultural trends and more to maximizing profits from existing practices. The railroad's industrial department also increasingly mirrored university agricultural departments. As James Hill receded from everyday corporate affairs, the company began to accept Progressive notions of expertise and to focus attention on academic and federal professionals rather than the self-taught experts of Hill's day.

Diverging from the railroad policy for the first time, Hill returned to his position as a gentleman farmer. Once again he used his farms for experimentation and development. A crusty old man who had largely lost his political influence, Hill continued to berate agricultural practices and agencies with which he disagreed. Popular as a speaker, he maintained a forum for his ideas, which became an increasing liability for the Great Northern.

The failure of the elderly Hill to assume the position of a wise philanthropist among the farmers of his territory was compounded by his loss of political influence. By World War I, the "Empire Builder" had lost control of his empire, as international politics and immigration regulations superseded his authority.

Hill moved no closer to realizing his agrarian ideal. His vision of the Great Plains populated by Jeffersonian yeomen practicing scientific agriculture, taught to them by fellow farmers who were employed by sympathetic universities and federal bureaus, remained unattainable. A legend in his own lifetime, James Hill was valued as a character, a pioneer figure, and an empire builder, and his interest in farming was well known and appreciated. In terms of validity, however, he had become an anachronism. When he died, the new professionalized management of his railroad disassociated the corporation from Hill's attempts to effect agricultural change. His son, Louis Hill, abandoned even a pretense of interest in farming, and invested his energies instead in the development of tourism at Glacier National Park.[40]

8 / "The Voice of the Northwest"

One night in the late 1890s, Frederick Weyerhaeuser walked the short way up Summit Avenue in St. Paul to have dinner with his friend and neighbor, James Hill. After a lengthy meal in the sumptuous dining room, Hill ushered his guest into his cozy, book-lined den and plied him with whiskey. At this point, Hill began his pitch. Weyerhaeuser, he said, should invest in the Pacific Northwest. Lumbering had nearly exhausted the stands of timber in Minnesota, he argued, Michigan and Wisconsin forests had been extensively cut, and the future lay in the West. Weyerhaeuser hedged as his host poured them both another glass of his notoriously bad whiskey. He would need to think about it; he was not sure that his company had the capital to invest in expansion; he did not want to move to the coast. Hill persisted, arguing his case again and again. His guest was overwhelmed by exhaustion. Trying to escape, Weyerhaeuser pleaded the late hour and offered to resume the conversation another day. Hill remained firm, set on the task at hand, until finally Weyerhaeuser agreed to expand his company into the West, just to get away from his host and get to bed.

This partly apocryphal story, an urban legend from the powerhouse of Summit Avenue, illustrates the broad sweep of Hill's interests when it came to developing the West, at least that part of the West touched by his railroads. Weyerhaeuser followed through on his promise in early 1900 when his company bought 900,000 acres of the Northern Pacific's land grant, forested with prime timber, for $6 million. This sale proved pivotal to the development of the Pacific Northwest, helping the region overtake the Great Lakes area in lumber production by the early twentieth century. The lumber industry transformed the region, sparking a huge population influx and stimulating town growth, especially in Everett, Washington. It also provided substantial profits to both the Great Northern and the Northern Pacific railroads as they hauled lumber to eastern markets and workers and materials to the western forests. Thus, in the case of lumbering, Hill's push to develop the West and to alter its environment to generate more profit for his railroad, was an unquestionable success.[1]

Hill had a similar western development victory in his alliance with mining. In the mid-1880s Marcus Daly's Anaconda mine in Butte, Montana, had only two transportation options: the Northern Pacific and the Union Pacific. These railroads together agreed to set mutually beneficial, high freight rates. Daly turned to Hill for help, and Hill backed the construction of the Montana Central, which linked Butte to the Great Northern by 1888. This new line undercut the transportation rates offered by the Northern Pacific and the Union Pacific, and thus gained an effective monopoly of ore traffic from the mines. Hill also had close connections with other mining companies in Montana, such as the Boston and Montana Consolidated Copper and Silver Mining Company. He offered this firm the most competitive rates too, bringing considerable haulage to his line. Hill also benefited from the mining company's decision to site their new smelting and refining factories in Great Falls, as he held considerable real estate in the town.[2]

Therefore, in many other industries along the Great Northern, Hill was successful in promoting western development. From the Red River Valley fur trade of the 1880s to townsite planning to power companies, he frequently managed to stimulate the local economy along his line in ways that provided profit to him and growth to the region.

This generally successful track record, combined with his overall business acumen, has led many historians to misread his agricultural endeavors. Whether viewing his influence as positive or negative, most have agreed that Hill had considerable impact on farming practices in the territory of the Great Northern Railway. Joseph Gilpin Pyle, Hill's official biographer, claims that "The agricultural interest of the United States owes a lasting debt to the enthusiasm and the life-long labours of James J. Hill." Hill's later biographer, business historian Albro Martin, largely ignores his agricultural ventures but never contests Hill's authority or the inherent validity of his agricultural vision. Martin largely left Hill's farming interests to his graduate student, Howard Leigh Dickman, who, in 1977, finished his doctoral dissertation. Although acknowledging the failure of Hill's agricultural vision in the long term, Dickman never questions his influence on the major farming movements of his time: irrigation, conservation, and dryland farming.

Dickman's view is upheld by Roy V. Scott, who states that "Hill's reputation as a developer of [agriculture in] the Northwest was well deserved" and who holds Hill largely responsible for the flood of dryland farmers to Montana in the 1910s. In Michael P. Malone's recent and readable biography of the railroad magnate, Malone portrays Hill as an influential "advocate of model demonstration farms" and as leaving an "enduring legac[y]" from his "imperial promotion of modern agriculture across the breadth of his domain."[3]

Historians and others who are critical of Hill's agricultural involvement also give credence to his influence. Montana historian Joseph Kinsey Howard blames Hill for the influx of settlers into Montana who intended to practice dryland farming. He argues that Hill was thus responsible for the subsequent disaster, when a period of low rainfall from 1917 to 1922 burst the dryland farming boom and bankrupted thousands of homesteaders. Jonathan Raban popularized this interpretation of Hill's culpability in the dryland farming tragedy of the Plains in his 1996 novel, *Bad Land: An American Romance.*[4]

But on close examination, Hill's attempts to alter the agricultural development of the northern tier of states were not successful. His agrarian vision did not become a reality, and the ability of his railroad corporation and himself to change farming practices along the line proved decidedly limited. His failure to manipulate the development of agriculture contrasted distinctly with his successful development in other industries.

Part of the reason for Hill's failure to develop the West agriculturally lay in the idealized nature of his goal. Unlike his approach to other industries, Hill saw optimum farming as essential to social salvation as well as to economic success. He believed it necessary to populate the northern plains with small-scale yeomen farmers. He envisioned that these farmers, whether on reclaimed land or dryland, would practice diversified, efficient, commercial agriculture. Their work would be governed by basic, accessible principles, understandable to all. The agricultural experiment stations would aid these farmers by analyzing their soil and continuing to experiment with methods of maximizing production.

Hill had a variety of intertwined reasons for promoting the establishment of this dense rural settlement. Like others during the Progressive era, he saw one of the solutions to urban decay and political corruption in migration to the farm. Independent farm life provided the most natural human setting and, as such, the best training for active democratic participation.

According to Hill, an increased farm population would also meet the growing food needs of the country as well as solve the nation's urban and political problems. Calculating American population growth on the basis of the incredibly high immigration figures at the turn of the century, Hill worried about the decline in productivity of America's soils and predicted a time when the food supply would prove insufficient. The steady migration of rural people to the cities during this time period only heightened his concern. Hill thought that only by settling more people on the land to practice intensive, diversified agriculture would the United States avoid future dependency on other nations for food.

Hill articulated his concerns and solutions in many speeches. In 1913 he succinctly summarized his agrarian philosophy: "The change to a more intensive system, smaller farms, less ground planted to wheat, more to coarse grains and to forage plants, the keeping of cattle, the higher cultivation of the grain-producing area by soil study, fertilization, better tillage and all the methods included in modern scientific agriculture, will create a revolution in farm industry and at least double present yields and profits."[5]

Economic and technological factors ultimately thwarted Hill and other reformers. Mechanization, hybridization, fertilizers, and pesticides increased the transition to agrarian economies of scale. Monocropping remained feasible and popular, and rural labor needs diminished. Instead of regaining a place in the national economy, small-scale family farms found it hard to survive. Labor released from these farms by technological replacement continued to flow to the cities. And with the transition of America to an urban nation, as indicated by the census of 1920, those struggling with large-scale social reform focused their attention on the problems of the cities rather than the countryside.

Hill's neo-Malthusian vision of a nation unable to feed itself has proved no less false than his desire for a densely populated countryside. America's food production continued to grow, helped by science and technology. At the same time, the immigration rate, on which Hill had grounded his pessimism, declined sharply with legal restrictions and the advent of World War I. The Great Northern, Hill's fundamental concern, continued to make considerable profit from agricultural haulage, which remained one-third of its business until after World War II.[6]

In fact, the problem which confronted American food production in the twentieth century reversed Hill's predictions. From the rural depression of the 1920s on, the nation suffered from chronic overproduction. Farmers compensated for low prices by increasing productivity, which, in turn, further depressed prices. The federal government made various attempts to cure this problem, from Henry A. Wallace's orders to plow under crops and slaughter hogs to price supports and the purchase of farm surplus. Even with the development of a global economy, the problem remains.

Hill's vision of a densely settled rural America did not become reality. Although his idealism had always been combined with the fundamental pragmatism of a successful businessman, he failed to adapt his ideals to meet economic realities. Hill recognized early on that much of the territory of his railroad was most suited to agricultural production, and therefore he wanted it as populated as possible to maximize haulage both ways along his lines. As this dense settlement proved increasingly impossible to realize, Hill refused to compromise his principles by adopting an alternate developmental vision of western agriculture. One of the factors stymieing Hill in his desire to advance the farming industry along his line was the muddying of economic pragmatism with Jeffersonian idealism.

Another problem he faced lay in the nature of the farm audience. When promoting mining, lumbering, or the other industries in the northern tier, Hill negotiated with his peers. The deals and contracts of western industrial development in the late nineteenth and early twentieth centuries were forged among an elite group of businessmen. To promote agricultural change, however, Hill had to reach a large and varied group of farmers, all of whom had their own agendas. Evidence suggests that Hill had some influence on farmers. He was in great demand as a speaker, and local officials remarked on his expertise in their introductions of him. Private letters testified to the effectiveness of Hill's images. In 1902 a certain Edward Tuck told him, "it looks as though you know more about the farmers' business than the farmer does himself."[7]

Other evidence points to considerably less success. Hill and his railroad did not escape attack from various farmers' movements, such as the Grange, that swept the nation in the late nineteenth century. From 1882 to the end of the decade, Hill stayed in St. Paul when the legislature was in session to oppose passage of granger laws. Near the end of his life, the Great Northern faced opposition from the Nonpartisan League in North Dakota. In both cases, the farmers rebelled against railroad dominance in their state's economy. All of Hill's rhetoric about being one of the farmers did not prevent their attacks on the Great Northern.[8]

Another way of assessing Hill's influence is to examine the extent to which farmers adopted the systems he promoted. Dryland farming was probably the most popular idea he advocated. Favored by all railroads on the Great Plains, it also received approval from the experiment stations of the Great Plain states and the USDA. This general endorsement of the principles of dryland farming make it impossible to quantify Hill's particular influence, but also make it certain that it was far from unilateral.[9]

The other technique proposed by Hill that gained popularity among some farmers was irrigation. As with dryland farming, however, farmers' adoption of irrigation and their push for federal intervention hinged on factors other than Hill's advocacy. Consistent failure of private and state irrigation schemes made federal involvement necessary. Certainly, the National Irrigation Association, which included Hill, launched a useful lobbying campaign, but the impetus toward governmental involvement was already extant. The limits on the association's influence became apparent with its subsequent failure to modify the homesteading laws.

Hill's disillusionment with the Reclamation Service and his attempts to alter its irrigation priorities and its personnel met with continual failure. Without strong public opinion and a structured lobbying mechanism, his institutional influence was completely dissipated. Similarly, despite his optimism after being invited to the Governors' Conference on the Conservation of Natural Resources at the White House, Hill soon realized that he would have no success in changing the direction and aims of the national conservation movement.

Even philanthropy on a grand scale failed to alter farming practices as Hill wished. Believing that livestock would supplement farm income and provide valuable manure, Hill advocated the breeding of good quality animals to provide substantial quantities of milk as well as high quality meat. To this end, he gave purebred imported bulls to farmers along his line in the 1880s.[10] Hill's efforts failed as farmers throughout the Great Northern's territory refused to diversify. Reluctant to invest the time necessary to maintain quality stock, they usually slaughtered or sold the livestock Hill donated. Although some farmers continued to keep scrub cattle for home consumption, a concerted interest in mixed farming never materialized.[11]

Hill understood that his influence over farmers was less effective than he wished. Although his speeches celebrated farmers as the salt of the earth, he privately expressed exasperation, complaining about their resistance to scientific agriculture and stating that "Minnesota farmers have never shown a disposition as a whole to help themselves." Hill himself implicitly recognized his failure to influence agricultural change and continually altered his approach, adopting new strategies to try to reach farmers as the old ones failed.[12]

Hill's inability to influence farmer decisions was tied inextricably to his ineffectiveness to establish himself as an agricultural expert. He never encountered this problem when promoting other industrial development because his business credentials were impeccable. To gain the necessary agricultural reputation, he initially addressed the farming population directly, working from the position of a gentleman farmer. Finding this ineffective and costly, he shifted to creating alliances with other institutions, hoping to thus gain the authority and influence necessary to effect change. This proved effective for a brief period leading up to the Newlands Reclamation Act of 1902. The early twentieth century saw this policy break down. The agencies and organizations Hill had utilized to gain influence started to move in directions antagonistic to Hill's beliefs and goals, and he found that he lacked any control. As earlier partnerships disintegrated, Hill established his own agricultural institution within the corporation of the Great Northern to give his ideas credence. Yet farmers clearly perceived the vested interest of the railroad's development department and refused to make their farming decisions solely on the basis of information it provided. Finally, as management personnel of the Great Northern began to alienate themselves from Hill's ideas and mission, the old man resorted back to his role of gentleman farmer.

Hill's quest for agricultural authority proved elusive not only because of his own inadequacies but also because of the changing nature of expertise during his lifetime. Involved in a national struggle for the right to dictate the future of American agriculture, Hill ended up on the losing side. The laurels went to the academics and bureaucrats of the federal government.

Hill supported the idea of expertise in agriculture, but he opposed the narrowing of the term "expert." While never denying the importance of agricultural scientists and their institutions, he believed that farming expertise could also come through experience, thus qualifying himself and other farmers as experts. The science necessary for good farming was, Hill thought, easily within the reach of farmers. "It is true that the best methods of soil treatment and crop growing are scientific; but they require only that form of popular science which is within the comprehension and use of the uneducated man." He thought that most of the principles necessary to improve agricultural production in the United States were self-evident and could be learned by any observant, hardworking farmer.[13]

In addition, he agreed with farmer criticism that accused universities of indulging in theoretical and impractical work. While never dismissing them altogether, he certainly pointed out the limits of their help in practical agricultural development, especially when thwarted by universities or their personnel in implementing his vision. In 1911, for example, when financing the Better Farming Association's aims to provide a system of extension agents in North Dakota, Hill offered this patronizing view of university education. "Now, I do not want to take a shingle off the roof of an agricultural college in the world. I feel kindly toward them. I do wish that in place of putting on their spectacles and looking wise and talking in scientific terms and giving you the botanical names of plants and telling you they originated in some distant island of the sea, that they would get down and tell you what you can do on your own farm where you live."[14]

His actions and speeches reflected this dichotomy. While praising the work of agricultural scientists, he consistently attacked agricultural educators for their failure to convey simple improvements to the farming population and for their resistance to expertise gained through farming. By the time of his death in 1916, Hill was isolated as an agriculturist. This marginalization demonstrated both the triumph of a narrow definition of "expertise" and the alienation of farmers from primacy within their own profession.

By 1916 it was clear that the academicians and their political cohorts in the federal bureaucracy had seized control of the development of American agriculture. In capitulation, Hill's successors in the Great Northern corporation established a railroad agricultural department modeled after the university system, staffed it with academics, and fired the remnants of Hill's praetorian guard.

It would be wrong to assert that Hill had no influence over agricultural change. He was an intelligent and rich man whose railroad was significant enough to guarantee him at least an audience for his opinions. Hill's influence, however, proved minimal. Changes in the conceptualization of agricultural authority during the Progressive era left Hill chasing an illusive expertise.

Hill's inability to promote the agricultural development of the West can be tied to his idealism, his audience, and his lack of expertise, but it was also closely linked with the environment of the railroad. When sponsoring the lumber industry or the mining industry, Hill promoted the exploitation of natural resources that characterized western development. Nature had provided the essentials: the forests, the ores, the coal, the furs. All Hill added was capital and transportation. The farming industry envisioned by Hill proved very different. Capital was still problematic, but more so was the lack of water, the climate, and the poor soil. Like many of his contemporaries, Hill dismissed these problems, maintaining great faith in the triumph of humans over nature. And, like his contemporaries, his faith ultimately proved misplaced.

NOTES

1 / INTRODUCTION

1. "Métis," from the French word for half, were Canadians of mixed ancestry, either French-Indian or Scots-Indian. Riel's European background was French. Joseph Gilpin Pyle, *The Life of James J. Hill*, vol. 1 (Garden City, N.Y.: Doubleday, Page, & Co., 1917), 115–30; Michael P. Malone, *James J. Hill: Empire Builder of the Northwest* (Norman: University of Oklahoma Press, 1996), 24–26; Albro Martin, *James J. Hill and the Opening of the Northwest* (1976; reprint, St. Paul: Minnesota Historical Society Press, 1991), 72–76.

2. Pyle, *The Life of James J. Hill*, vol. 1, 115–30; Malone, *James J. Hill*, 24–26; Martin, *James J. Hill*, 72–76.

3. Ibid.

4. Pyle, *The Life of James J. Hill*, vol. 1, 115–30.

5. Robert G. Athearn, *The Mythic West in Twentieth-Century America* (Lawrence: University Press of Kansas, 1986), 10–23.

6. See, for example, Athearn, *The Mythic West*; Patricia Nelson Limerick, *The Legacy of Conquest: The Unbroken Past of the American West* (New York: W. W. Norton & Co., 1987); Gerald D. Nash, *The American West in the Twentieth Century: A Short History of an Urban Oasis* (Englewood Cliffs, N.J.: Prentice-Hall, Inc., 1973; reprint, Albuquerque: University of New Mexico Press, 1984); Richard White, *"It's Your Misfortune and None of My Own": A New History of the American West* (Norman: University of Oklahoma Press, 1991).

7. Walter Prescott Webb, *The Great Plains* (1931; reprint, Lincoln: University of Nebraska Press, 1959), 197, 273–80.

8. Ibid., 197; Lloyd J. Mercer, *Railroads and Land Grant Policy: A Study in Government Intervention* (New York: Academic Press, 1982), 4.

9. Benjamin Horace Hibbard, *A History of the Public Land Policies* (Madison: University of Wisconsin Press, 1965), 244; John Stover, *American Railroads* (1961; reprint, Chicago: University of Chicago Press, 1997), 81–83; White, *"It's Your Misfortune,"* 247; Mercer, *Railroads and Land Grant Policy*, 3.

10. White, *"It's Your Misfortune,"* 145–47.

11. Malcolm Rohrbough, *The Land Office Business: The Settlement and Administration of American Public Lands, 1789–1837* (New York: Oxford University Press, 1968), 1–25.

12. Ibid.; Hibbard, *A History of Public Land Policies*, 249–52; White, *"It's Your Misfortune,"* 248–49.

13. Julius Grodinsky, *Transcontinental Railway Strategy, 1869–1893: A Study of Businessmen* (Philadelphia: University of Pennsylvania Press, 1962).

14. White, *"It's Your Misfortune,"* 246–57.

15. For general information on the life of James J. Hill and his railroads, see Malone, *James J. Hill*; Martin, *James J. Hill*.

16. Malone, *James J. Hill*, 127–29, 149–50; White, *"It's Your Misfortune,"* 256.

17. White, *"It's Your Misfortune,"* 256.

18. Martin, *James J. Hill*, 301.

19. Alan Trachtenberg, *The Incorporation of America: Culture and Society in the Gilded Age* (New York: Hill and Wang, 1982), 7; David Noble, *The Progressive Mind, 1890–1917* (Chicago: Rand McNally & Co., 1970), 3–4; Robert C. McMath Jr., *American Populism: A Social History, 1877–1898* (New York: Hill and Wang, 1993), 3–7.

20. McMath, *American Populism*, 167–70; Lawrence Goodwyn, *The Populist Moment: A Short History of Agrarian Revolt in America* (New York: Oxford University Press, 1978), 90–93; David B. Danbom, *The Resisted Revolution: Urban America and the Industrialization of Agriculture, 1900–1930* (Ames: Iowa State University Press, 1979), 61–65; Stanford J. Layton, *To No Privileged Class: The Rationalization of Homesteading and Rural Life in the Early Twentieth-Century American West* (Salt Lake City: Charles Redd Center for Western Studies, Brigham Young University, 1988), 5–20.

21. William Cronon, *Nature's Metropolis: Chicago and the Great West* (New York: W. W. Norton & Co., 1991), 357–64; Danbom, *The Resisted Revolution*.

22. James J. Hill, *Highways of Progress* (Garden City, N.Y.: Doubleday, Page & Company, 1910), 40; Alan I Marcus, "The Wisdom of the Body Politic: The Changing Nature of Publicly Sponsored American Agricultural Research Since the 1830s," *Agricultural History* 62 (spring 1988): 7–9; Danbom, *The Resisted Revolution*; Alan I Marcus, *Agricultural Science and the Quest for Legitimacy: Farmers, Agricultural*

Colleges, and Experiment Stations, 1870–1890 (Ames: Iowa State University Press, 1985); Alan I Marcus, "The Ivory Silo: Farmer-Agricultural College Tensions in the 1870s and 1880s," *Agricultural History* 60 (spring 1986): 22–36; Jean-Noel Kapferer, *Strategic Brand Management: New Approaches to Creating and Evaluating Brand Equity* (New York: Free Press, 1992); Stanley M. Ulanoff, *Advertising in America: An Introduction to Persuasive Communication* (New York: Hastings House, 1977), 21; T. Dillon in *Advertising, Management, and Society: A Business Point of View,* ed. Francesco M. Nicosia (New York: McGraw-Hill, 1974), 55–60; Malone, *James J. Hill,* 12, 195–98; John C. Hudson, "North Dakota's Railway War of 1905," *North Dakota History* 48 (winter 1981): 7; Roy V. Scott, *Railroad Development Programs in the Twentieth Century* (Ames: Iowa State University Press, 1985), 7–8, 35, 38, 46.

2 / TRIAL AND ERROR, 1878–1893

1. The land grant of the St. Paul & Pacific had been originally given to the Minnesota & Pacific Railroad in 1857. This grant had been made by the territorial legislature using land it had received from the federal government for the specific purpose of constructing railroads. Ralph W. Hidy et al., *The Great Northern Railway: A History* (Boston: Harvard Business School Press, 1988), 2, 30; Albro Martin, *James J. Hill and the Opening of the Northwest* (1976; reprint, St. Paul: Minnesota Historical Society Press, 1991), 158.

2. Hidy et al., *The Great Northern Railway,* 305; Stanley Norman Murray, *The Valley Comes of Age: A History of Agriculture in the Valley of the Red River of the North, 1812–1920* (Fargo: North Dakota Institute for Regional Studies, 1967), 4–11.

3. Rhoda R. Gilman, Carolyn Gilman, and Deborah M. Stulz, *The Red River Trails: Oxcart Routes Between St. Paul and the Selkirk Settlement, 1820–1870* (St. Paul: Minnesota Historical Society Press, 1979), 2–8; Hiram M. Drache, *The Day of the Bonanza: A History of Bonanza Farming in the Red River Valley of the North* (Fargo: North Dakota Institute for Regional Studies, 1964), 19–20; Murray, *The Valley Comes of Age,* 59; Rhoda Gilman, "The Fur Trade in the Red River Valley" (paper presented at Teacher Conference at the Minnesota Historical Society, St. Paul, July 1993).

4. Drache, *The Day of the Bonanza,* 38–39, 43; Murray, *The Valley Comes of Age,* 104–6; Stanley N. Murray, "Railroads and the Agricultural Development of the Red River Valley of the North, 1870–1890," *Agricultural History* 31 (October 1957): 60.

5. Drache, *The Day of the Bonanza,* 71, 111, 119, 210; Murray, *The Valley Comes of Age,* 106.

6. Drache, *Day of the Bonanza,* 5, 8, 27.

7. Ibid., 4, 6; Martin, *James J. Hill,* 270.

8. Michael P. Malone, *James J. Hill: Empire Builder of the Northwest* (Norman: University of Oklahoma Press, 1996), 57–58, 89; Murray, "Railroads and the Agricultural Development of the Red River Valley," 63.

9. Murray, *The Valley Comes of Age*, 124–25; Russell S. Kirby, "Nineteenth-Century Patterns of Railroad Development on the Great Plains," *Great Plains Quarterly* 3 (summer 1983): 159.

10. James J. Hill to Henry C. E. Stewart, Credit Lyonnais, 16 April 1889, Letterpress Books, James J. Hill Papers, James J. Hill Library, St. Paul, Minn. (hereafter JJHP); John Luecke, "Minnesota Railroads" (paper presented at Teacher Conference at the Minnesota Historical Society, St. Paul, July 1993); Murray, "Railroads and the Agricultural Development of the Red River Valley," 58.

11. Hidy et al., *The Great Northern Railway*, 72–73; Martin, *James J. Hill*, 394.

12. Walter Prescott Webb, *The Great Plains* (1931; reprint, Lincoln: University of Nebraska Press, 1959), 273–74.

13. Robert F. Zeidel, "Peopling the Empire: The Great Northern Railroad and the Recruitment of Immigrant Settlers to North Dakota," *North Dakota History* 60 (spring 1993): 15–16.

14. Ibid., 15–16, 19; *Globe Gazette* (Wahpeton, N.D.), 30 September 1909; *23rd Annual Report of the Great Northern Railway Company*, 24, JJHP.

15. *St. Paul Pioneer Press*, 10 September 1910. The total cost for stock purchase and its transportation in 1886–87 was $15,667.80. In comparison, during the same two-year period, Hill spent in excess of $96,000 acquiring paintings for his art collection. North Oaks Receipts, 1886–1887, North Oaks Papers, JJHP; Sheila Ffolliott, "James J. Hill as Art Collector: A Documentary View," in Jane Hancock, Sheila Ffolliott, and Thomas O'Sullivan, *Homecoming: The Art Collection of James J. Hill* (St. Paul: Minnesota Historical Society Press, 1991), 25.

16. Marvin McInnis, "The Changing Structure of Canadian Agriculture, 1867–1897," *Journal of Economic History* 42 (March 1982): 194.

17. Eric Kerridge, *The Farmers of Old England* (Totowa, N.J.: Rowman and Littlefield, 1973), 64–65, 101–2, 132–33.

18. Henry F. May, *The Enlightenment in America* (New York: Oxford University Press, 1976), xiv; Ernest Cassara, *The Enlightenment in America* (Boston: Twayne Publishers, 1975), 49–67; August C. Miller Jr., "Jefferson as an Agriculturist," *Agricultural History* 16 (April 1942): 65–78; Avery O. Craven, *Edmund Ruffin, Southerner: A Study in Secession* (Baton Rouge: Louisiana State University, 1966), 49–72; Alan I Marcus, "The Wisdom of the Body Politic: The Changing Nature of Publicly Sponsored American Agricultural Research Since the 1830s," *Agricultural History* 62 (spring 1988): 4–26.

19. Tom Nesmith, "The Philosophy of Agriculture: The Promise of Intellect in Ontario Farming, 1835–1914" (Ph.D. diss., Carleton University, Ontario, 1988), 85–92; Thomas W. Irwin, "Government Funding of Agricultural Associations in Late Nineteenth-Century Ontario" (Ph.D. diss., University of Western Ontario, 1998), 58.

20. Clara Lindley, unpublished reminiscences, James J. Hill House, St. Paul, Minn., 124; Howard Leigh Dickman, "James Jerome Hill and the Agricultural Development of the Northwest" (Ph.D. diss., University of Michigan, 1977), 71–77, 310–13.

21. Dickman, "James Jerome Hill," 312; Journal 1881–1887, Humboldt Farm Papers, JJHP; Drache, *Day of the Bonanza,* 54–56, 71–75.

22. Hill to Richard Fitzgerald, railroad agent, 9 November 1882; to P. H. Tompkins, 19 December 1882, Letterpress Books, JJHP; Dickman, "James Jerome Hill," 77.

23. Hill to C. H. Burwell of Minnetonka, 2 May 1883; to Eugene Mehl, 27 July 1883; to W. T. McCollum of Howard Lake, 10 September 1883, Letterpress Books, JJHP; John Dalquest to Hill, 22 January 1903, General Correspondence, JJHP; Miscellaneous Bills of Purchase, North Oaks Papers, JJHP; Joan Brainard, "Bold Ventures Mark Local History," *North Oaks (Minn.) News,* February 1989, 2.

24. Hill to John Kennedy, 23 April 1883; to Van Fleet, 27 January 1885, Letterpress Books, JJHP; Order for quail, 23 February 1888, North Oaks Papers, JJHP; Mary Hill diaries, 1885, JJHP.

25. Chas. Maitland to Hill, 10 February 1887, General Correspondence, JJHP; Quarantine for stock—Port of Quebec form, 17 February 1887, North Oaks Papers, JJHP.

26. Hill to editor of *Farmers Advocate and Northwestern Stockman* (St. Paul), 17 May 1886, Letterpress Books, JJHP; Extracts from the *National Livestock Journal* (Chicago) sent to Hill by editor, 10 September 1888, North Oaks Papers, JJHP.

27. Hill to A. M. Sherman, 7 May 1886; to editor of *Farmers Advocate and Northwestern Stockman,* 17 May 1886, Letterpress Books, JJHP; "Crop and Live Stock in Ontario," Ontario Bureau of Industries, *Bulletin 56* (November 1895): 9–10; *Fifth Biennial Report of the Commissioner of Agriculture and Labor to the Governor of North Dakota for the Two Years Ending June 30, 1898* (Bismarck: Tribune, State Printers and Binders, 1898).

28. John Snell to John Gibson, superintendent at North Oaks, 7 December 1887; Memo regarding purchase of poultry 1888, North Oaks Receipts, 1887–1888, North Oaks Papers, JJHP; Ffolliott, "James J. Hill as Art Collector: A Documentary View," 25.

29. Hill to J. F. Harkness, 26 March 1884, Letterpress Books, JJHP; David B. Danbom, *The Resisted Revolution: Urban America and the Industrialization of Agriculture, 1900–1930* (Ames: Iowa State University Press, 1979), 88; John R. Stilgoe, "Plugging Past Reform: Small-Scale Farming Innovation and Big-Scale Farming Research," in *Scientific Authority and Twentieth-Century America,* ed. Ronald G. Walters (Baltimore: Johns Hopkins University Press, 1997), 121–22.

30. Dickman, "James Jerome Hill," 76; C. R. Gray to W. P. Kenney, 18 December 1913, Great Northern Railway Papers, Minnesota Historical Society, St. Paul, Minn. (hereafter GNRP); Robert Ankli, "Ontario's Dairy Industry, 1880–1920," *Canadian Papers in Rural History* 8 (1992): 261–76.

31. William Tomhave, "Pioneer in Animal Husbandry," in *Andrew Boss: Agricultural Pioneer and Builder, 1867–1947,* ed. Oscar B. Jesness (St. Paul: Itasca Press, 1950), 48.

32. Carl W. Thompson and G. P. Warber, *Social and Economic Survey of a Rural Township in Southern Minnesota* (Minneapolis: University of Minnesota, 1913), 34–35; C. W. Crickman, George A. Sallee, and W. H. Peters, "Beef Cattle Production in Minnesota," Agricultural Experiment Station, University of Minnesota, *Bulletin 301* (February 1934): 24–26.

33. Hill to Andrew Nelson, Litchfield, Minn., 4 January 1884, North Oaks Papers, JJHP.

34. Charles Rosenberg, *No Other Gods: On Science and American Social Thought* (Baltimore: Johns Hopkins University Press, 1961), 12–18, 143–84; Alan I Marcus and Howard P. Segal, *Technology in American Life: A Brief History* (Fort Worth: Harcourt Brace Jovanovich, 1989), 165–77.

35. Hill to Samuel Thorne, 19 January 1883; to Col. C. A. DeGraff, spring 1883; to N. J. Stubbs, 16 October 1884; to W. G. Trotman, 27 January 1886; to Robert Auketell, 28 May 1886; to H. W. Donaldson, 8 April 1889; to N. J. Stubbs, 13 April 1889, Letterpress Books, JJHP; miscellaneous bills with notes in Hill's hand, North Oaks Papers, JJHP.

36. Catalog mailing list, 1887, North Oaks Papers, JJHP; Hill to Robert Campbell, 31 December 1885, Letterpress Books, JJHP; Charles Mills to Hill, 21 November 1887; North Oaks Receipts, 1889, North Oaks Papers, JJHP.

37. Darwin S. Hall and R. I. Holcombe, *History of the Minnesota State Agricultural Society from Its Organization in 1854 to the Annual Meeting of 1910* (St. Paul: McGill-Warner Company, 1910), 200, 273; "An Hour At North Oaks," *Breeder's Gazette* (Chicago), 30 September 1886.

38. Theophilus Haecker to James J. Hill, 24 November 1893, General Correspondence, JJHP; letter, 15 October 1887, North Oaks Papers, JJHP; Philip Armour

to James J. Hill, 1 December 1885, General Correspondence, JJHP; Hall and Holcombe, *History of the Minnesota State Agricultural Society*, 186, 298.

39. *Anaconda (Mont.) Standard*, 27 October 1909; Hill to R. S. Bull, 18 June 1886, Letterpress Books, JJHP; *Globe-Gazette* (Wahpeton, N.D.), 30 September 1909; *Minot (N.D.) Daily Optic*, 28 September 1909; *St. Paul Dispatch*, 19 November 1912 and 14 January 1914; *Seattle Post-Intelligencer*, 1 November 1907 and 6 September 1910; *Omaha Daily News*, 9 December 1909; *St. Paul Pioneer Press*, 6 September 1910.

40. *Record* (Fargo, N.D.), September 1897; *St. Paul Dispatch*, 19 November 1912; *Post and Record* (Rochester, Minn.), 1 October 1909; *Butte (Mont.) Evening News*, 6 October 1909; *Anaconda (Mont.) Standard*, 27 October 1909; *The Dakota Farmer* (Aberdeen, S.D.), 1 June 1909.

41. Hill to Robert Auketell, 28 May 1886, Letterpress Books, JJHP; *Ariel* (Minneapolis) 14, no. 6 (1890–91): 89; Hill to anon., 21 December 1885; to R. S. Bull, 18 June 1886; to C. C. Andrews, 22 May 1884, Letterpress Books, JJHP; C. C. Andrews to Hill, 5 March 1883 and 19 April 1884, General Correspondence, JJHP.

42. Danbom, *The Resisted Revolution*, 92; Stilgoe, "Plugging Past Reform," 119.

43. Hill to Andrew Nelson, Litchfield, Minn., 1 April 1884, North Oaks Papers, JJHP.

44. Hill to P. S. Lay, 28 November 1885, Letterpress Books, JJHP; "Contracts" in the North Oaks Papers, JJHP.

45. Hill's official biographer, Joseph Gilpin Pyle, claims that Hill distributed nine hundred bulls between 1885 and 1886 at a cost of $150,000. Hill himself claimed in later life that the distributions for these two years approximated eight hundred bulls donated. These figures seem unreasonably high, given all the information contemporary to the distributions, and I have relied on the latter figures. Joseph Gilpin Pyle, *The Life of James J. Hill*, vol. 1 (Garden City: Doubleday, Page & Company, 1917), 367; *Orange Judd Farmer* (Chicago), 6 September 1890; Hill to Onsted [*sic*], 8 May 1885; to Gilbert Pierce, 17 October 1885; to C. D. Baker, 4 August 1886; to Knute Nelson, 30 March 1914, Letterpress Books, JJHP; "Contracts" in the North Oaks Papers, JJHP.

46. David B. Danbom, "The North Dakota Agricultural Experiment Station and the Struggle to Create a Dairy State," *Agricultural History* 63 (spring 1989): 178, 180–82; Thompson and Warber, *Social and Economic Survey of a Rural Township in Southern Minnesota*, caption on photograph between pages 20 and 21.

47. John J. Toomey, 16 February 1899, General Correspondence, JJHP; Toomey to James McClure, 24 January 1900, North Oaks Papers, JJHP.

48. James J. Hill, speech in Williston, N.D., 27 November 1911, Louis W. Hill Papers, James J. Hill Library, St. Paul, Minn.; Danbom, "The North Dakota Agricultural Experiment Station," 176–78.

49. John J. Toomey, 16 February 1899, General Correspondence, JJHP; Toomey to James McClure, 24 January 1900; "Contracts," North Oaks Papers, JJHP.

50. In contrast, the *Michigan Farmer* (Detroit) had a circulation of 12,000 in 1857, the *Southern Cultivator* (Atlanta) had 10,000 in 1852, and the *American Agriculturist* (Ithaca, N.Y.) had 45,125 in 1859. Later, under the direction of Herbert Myrick, the *Farmer* (St. Paul and Chicago) reached a subscription figure of 90,000. Albert Lowther Demaree, *The American Agricultural Press, 1819–1860* (New York: Columbia University Press, 1941), 351, 375, 385; Herbert Myrick to Hill, 5 December 1905, GNRP; George W. Hill to Hill, 11 April 1887 and 5 May 1887, General Correspondence, JJHP.

51. George W. Hill to Hill, 5 May 1887, General Correspondence, JJHP.

52. Ibid.; *Farmer* (St. Paul and Chicago), 6 January 1887, 13 January 1887, 27 January 1887, 3 February 1887, 10 February 1887, 16 March 1887, 14 April 1887, 28 April 1887, 2 June 1887, 9 June 1887.

53. *Farmer* (St. Paul and Chicago), 6 January 1887, 10 February 1887; Thompson and Warber, *Social and Economic Survey of a Rural Township in Southern Minnesota,* 46–47.

54. Orange Judd to Hill, 8 September 1888 and 23 April 1889, General Correspondence, JJHP; William Edward Ogilvie, *Pioneer Agricultural Journalists: Brief Biographical Sketches of Some of the Early Editors in the Field of Agricultural Journalism* (Chicago: Arthur G. Leonard, 1927), 33–37.

55. Judd to Hill, 23 April 1889 and 30 January 1891; to W. A. Stephens, 27 February 1891 and undated, General Correspondence, JJHP; Ogilvie, *Pioneer Agricultural Journalists,* 37.

56. Ben Palmer, "Swamp Land Drainage with Special Reference to Minnesota," University of Minnesota, Studies in the Social Sciences, *Bulletin 5* (March 1915): 64; Ann Vileisis, *Discovering the Unknown Landscape: A History of America's Wetlands* (Washington, D.C.: Island Press, 1997), 122–27.

57. Palmer, "Swamp Land Drainage," 64; Dickman, "James Jerome Hill," 22; Hill to Christopher Stevenson, 17 March 1886; Letterpress Books, JJHP.

58. Palmer, "Swamp Land Drainage," 64; Vileisis, *Discovering the Unknown Landscape,* 122–27; Hill to Christopher Stevenson, 17 March 1886; to John M. Martin, 26 November 1886; to H. W. Donaldson, 19 June 1893, Letterpress Books, JJHP.

59. Hill to Donaldson, 19 June 1893, Letterpress Books, JJHP; Palmer, "Swamp Land Drainage," 65–66; Dickman, "James Jerome Hill," 23.

60. Palmer, "Swamp Land Drainage," 66–69; *General Laws of Minnesota for 1893,* Chapter 221, "An Act to Appropriate Moneys for the Purpose of Opening of Closed Watercourses," 371–72.

61. Hill to Donaldson, 19 June 1893, Letterpress Books, JJHP; Knute Nelson to

Hill, 15 July 1893, General Correspondence, JJHP; Malone, *James J. Hill*, 128–29; Lloyd J. Mercer, *Railroads and Land Grant Policy: A Study in Government Intervention* (New York: Academic Press, 1982), 58–59 (Mercer's book gives the year of incorporation of the Great Northern as 1885, all other references give 1889); Martin, *James J. Hill*, 376–78; Hidy et al., *The Great Northern Railway*, 72–73.

62. Hill to M. S. Merager, 21 May 1889, Letterpress Books, JJHP.

63. *Breeders' Gazette* (Chicago), 30 September 1886; *Third Annual Report of the Bureau of Animal Industry for the Year 1886,* Bureau of Animal Industry, USDA (Washington, D.C.: Government Printing Office, 1887), 11–12, 15; *Fourth and Fifth Annual Reports of the Bureau of Animal Industry for the Years 1887 and 1888,* Bureau of Animal Industry, USDA (Washington, D.C.: Government Printing Office, 1889), 9–12.

64. *Fourth and Fifth Annual Reports,* 10; *Tenth and Eleventh Annual Reports of the Bureau of Animal Industry for the Years 1893 and 1894,* Bureau of Animal Industry, USDA (Washington, D.C.: Government Printing Office, 1896), 8; Pearson, Murray, Atkinson, Lowe, Harbaugh, Law, Dickson, Mohler, Trumbower, Salmon, Smith, and Stiles, *Special Report on Diseases of Cattle,* Bureau of Animal Industry, USDA (Washington, D.C.: Government Printing Office, 1904), 364–67; *Farmer* (St. Paul and Chicago), 27 January 1887; *Congressional Record,* 49th Cong., 2nd sess., 1887, 18: 272, 1854, 2122–24, 2175, 2182–98, 2386, 2554; *Fourth and Fifth Annual Reports,* 10; *Congressional Record,* 50th Cong., 1st sess., 1888, 18: 88.

65. *Eighth and Ninth Annual Reports of the Bureau of Animal Industry for the Years 1891 and 1892,* Bureau of Animal Industry, USDA (Washington, D.C.: Government Printing Office, 1893), 74.

66. Tamara Plakins Thornton, *Cultivating Gentlemen: The Meaning of Country Life Among the Boston Elite, 1785–1860* (New Haven: Yale University Press, 1989), 201–12; George T. Clark, *Leland Stanford: War Governor of California, Railroad Builder, and Founder of Stanford University* (Stanford: Stanford University Press, 1931), 341–63; Jerry E. Patterson, *The Vanderbilts* (New York: Harry N. Abrams, Inc., 1989), 162–86; Stow Persons, *The Decline of American Gentility* (New York: Columbia University Press, 1973).

67. Hill to C. O. Gregg, 15 April 1887, Letterpress Books, JJHP.

3 / COOPERATION AND SUCCESS, 1893–1902

1. W. Thomas White, "A Gilded Age Businessman in Politics: James J. Hill, the Northwest, and the American Presidency, 1884–1912," *Pacific Historical Review* 57 (November 1988): 439–45; Albro Martin, *James J. Hill and the Opening of the*

Northwest (1976; reprint, St. Paul: Minnesota Historical Society Press, 1991), 415–16.

2. Agreement, 2 April 1896, Northern Pacific Reorganization Papers, James J. Hill Papers, James J. Hill Library, St. Paul, Minn. (hereafter JJHP); Senate, *Bills and Debates in Congress Relating to Trusts,* 57th Cong., 2nd sess. (Washington, D.C.: Government Printing Office, 1903), vol. I, 91, 94; Michael P. Malone, *James J. Hill: Empire Builder of the Northwest* (Norman: University of Oklahoma Press, 1996), 178–82; Gabriel Kolko, *The Triumph of Conservatism: A Reinterpretation of American History, 1900–1916* (New York: Free Press, 1963), 60–70.

3. Malone, *James J. Hill,* 178–82, 217–18; Martin, *James J. Hill,* 443–64.

4. *Anaconda (Mont.) Standard,* 27 October 1909.

5. Benjamin Horace Hibbard, *A History of Public Land Policies* (Madison: University of Wisconsin Press, 1965), 426–27.

6. William Liggett, board of managers of Minnesota State Agricultural Society, to F. I. Whitney, general passenger agent on Great Northern Railway, 15 August, 1896; J. C. Hanley to Hill, 8 February 1899; Liggett to Hill, 16 November 1899; Edward Tuck to Hill, 31 December 1902, General Correspondence, JJHP; *Record* (Fargo, N.D.), September 1897.

7. Mary T. Hill's diaries, 13 July 1885, 28 April, 3 May, 7 June, 4, 16 July, and 21 October 1899, JJHP; *St. Paul Pioneer Press,* 19 October 1896.

8. Howard Leigh Dickman, "James Jerome Hill and the Agricultural Development of the Northwest" (Ph.D. diss., University of Michigan, 1977), 24; Erza Valentine to Hill, 3 January 1902, General Correspondence, JJHP.

9. Anon., "The Northwestern Experiment Station," p. 37, undated mss., Institute of Agriculture Files, University of Minnesota Archives, Minneapolis, Minn.(hereafter UMA); Willet Hays, "Early History of the Northwest Agricultural School and Experiment Station," p. 7, 10–11, undated mss., Early Papers and Correspondence, Agricultural Experiment Station Papers, UMA.

10. Hays, "Early History of the Northwest Agricultural School and Experiment Station," p. 10–11, UMA; Anon.,"Northwest Experiment Station," p. 11, undated mss., History 1908–1938; Conrad Selvig, "The Northwest Experiment Station at Crookston," p. 3, undated mss.; Andrew Boss to Selvig, 2 July 1924, Early Papers and Correspondence, Agricultural Experiment Station Papers, UMA.

11. Hays, "Early History of the Northwest Agricultural School and Experiment Station," p. 10–11; "Northwest Experiment Station," p. 11; Selvig, "The Northwest Experiment Station at Crookston," p. 3; Boss to Selvig, 2 July 1924, UMA.

12. Letter from Hays, 1 October 1908, Institute of Agriculture Files, UMA.

13. John Luecke, "Minnesota Railroads," August 1993, Teacher Conference at the Minnesota Historical Society, St. Paul, Minn.; Martin, *James J. Hill*, 221.

14. Charles E. Rosenberg, *No Other Gods: On Science and American Social Thought* (Baltimore: Johns Hopkins University Press, 1961), 143–49.

15. James J. Hill, *Highways of Progress*, (Garden City, N.Y.: Doubleday, Page & Company, 1910), 59; James J. Hill, Speech to the Farmers' National Congress, Madison, Wisconsin, 24 September 1908, Louis W. Hill Papers, James J. Hill Library, St. Paul, Minn.

16. Boss to Selvig, 2 July 1924, UMA.

17. Selvig, "The Northwest Experiment Station at Crookston," p. 3, UMA; Norene Roberts and Claire Strom, "Statement of Content, National Register Nomination for University of Minnesota," p. 29, mss., State Historic Preservation Office, Minnesota Historical Society, St. Paul, Minn.

18. Conrad Selvig, "Early Days," undated mss., p. 1, Early Papers and Correspondence, Agricultural Experiment Station Papers, UMA.

19. Ibid.

20. William Tomhave, "Pioneer in Animal Husbandry," in *Andrew Boss: Agricultural Pioneer and Builder, 1867–1947,* ed. Oscar Jesness (St. Paul: Itasca Press, 1950), 48.

21. Charles E. Rosenberg, *No Other Gods: On Science and American Social Thought,* (Baltimore: Johns Hopkins University Press, 1961), 154–70; David B. Danbom, *"Our Purpose is to Serve": The First Century of the North Dakota Agricultural Experiment Station,* (Fargo: North Dakota Institute for Regional Studies, 1990), 16–19.

22. *The Beet Sugar Story* (Washington, D.C.: United States Beet Sugar Association, 1959), 48; R. A. McGinnis, ed. *Beet-Sugar Technology* (New York: Reinhold Publishing Corporation, 1951), 14, 134–36; John Worst to Hill, 20 May 1897; Hill to Worst, 24 May 1897, Great Northern Railway Papers, Minnesota Historical Society, St. Paul, Minn. (hereafter GNRP); Terry L. Shoptaugh, *Roots of Success: A History of the Red River Valley Sugarbeet Growers* (Fargo, N.D.: Institute for Regional Studies, 1997), 14–39. Sugar beet growing was successfully established in the Red River Valley in the fifteen years following World War I. However, the American sugar industry, as a whole, continued to suffer from European competition until World War II. The Spanish-American War and the consequent acquisition of the Philippines also jeopardized beet sugar production by reducing the tariff on sugar from this nation.

23. Robert F. Zeidel, "Peopling the Empire: The Great Northern Railroad and the Recruitment of Immigrant Settlers to North Dakota," *North Dakota History* 60

(spring 1993): 14; Karel Denis Bicha, "The American Farmer and the Canadian West, 1896–1914: A Revised View," *Agricultural History* 38 (January 1964): 43–46; Marvin McInnis, "The Changing Structure of Canadian Agriculture, 1867–1897," *Journal of Economic History* 42 (March 1982): 192; Thorstein Veblen, "The Food Supply and the Price of Wheat," *Journal of Political Economy* 1 (1892–93): 365–79; Mary Wilma M. Hargreaves, *Dry Farming in the Northern Great Plains, 1900–1925* (Cambridge: Harvard University Press, 1957), 17; John Fahey, *The Inland Empire: Unfolding Years, 1879–1929 (Seattle: University of Washington Press)*, 16–18.

24. The information on the geography and agricultural history of the Columbia Basin comes from Donald W. Meinig, *The Great Columbia Plain: A Historical Geography, 1805–1910* (Seattle: University of Washington Press, 1968).

25. Meinig, *The Great Columbia Plain*; William G. Robbins, *Landscapes of Promise: The Oregon Story, 1800–1940* (Seattle: University of Washington Press, 1997), 147; David Vaught, *Cultivating California: Growers, Specialty Crops, and Labor, 1875–1920* (Baltimore: Johns Hopkins University Press, 1999), 11–15; Steven Stoll, *The Fruits of Natural Advantage: Making the Industrial Countryside in California* (Berkeley: University of California Press, 1998), 30–31.

26. "Northern Pacific Early Development of the Yakima Valley"; "Yakima," Northern Pacific Papers, Minnesota Historical Society, St. Paul, Minn.; W. D. Lyman, *History of the Yakima Valley, Washington, Comprising Yakima, Kittitas and Benton Counties* (n.p.: S. J. Clarke Publishing, 1919), 355–69.

27. Keith A. Murray, "The Highline Canal: Irrigation Comes to Wenatchee," *Columbia* 9 (winter 1995/96): 20; Burke to Hill, 8 June 1891 and 5 May 1892, Thomas Burke Papers, University of Washington Archives, Seattle, Washington (hereafter UWA).

28. *Columbia River and its Tributaries, Northwestern United States*—Vol. III, 81st Cong., 2nd sess., 1950, H. Doc. 531, 970–78; Lieutenant Thomas W. Symons, *Report of An Examination of the Upper Columbia River and the Territory in its Vicinity in September and October, 1881, to Determine its Navigability and Adaptability to Steamboat Transportation. Made by Direction of the Commanding General of the Department of the Columbia*, 47th Cong., 1st sess., 1881, Ex. Doc. No. 186, 43; Murray, "The Highline Canal," 18–19.

29. Manuscript History of the Wenatchee Development Company, GNRP; Accounting Department of Great Northern to secretary of Wenatchee Development Company, 19 May 1892; Arthur Gunn to Burke, 4 October 1894, 11 May, 11, 15, 16, 26, 27 June, 2, 6, 16, 21 July, 16 and 21 November 1895; Memoranda, Papers of Wenatchee Development Company, 1896, Thomas Burke Papers, UWA.

30. Murray, "The Highline Canal," 21; Lindley M. Hull, ed., *A History of Central*

Washington Including the Famous Wenatchee, Entiat, Chelan and the Columbia Valleys with an Index and Eighty Scenic Historical Illustrations (Spokane, Wash.: Shaw and Borden Co., 1929), 540–41, 557; Burke to Hill, 8 October 1894; Manuscript History of the Wenatchee Waterpower Company, GNRP.

31. William Samuel Bryans, "A History of Transcontinental Railroads and Coal Mining on the Northern Great Plains to 1920" (Ph.D. diss., University of Wyoming, 1987), 64–221; Gunn to R. I. Farrington, 30 January 1900; Manuscript History of the Wenatchee Waterpower Company, GNRP; Farrington to Burke, 23 June 1890; Gunn to Hill, 7 June 1898, Thomas Burke Papers, UWA.

32. Murray, "The Highline Canal," 22; Hull, *A History of Central Washington,* 541, 567–69; Burke to W. T. Clark, 7, 12 April, 19 May 1902, Thomas Burke Papers, UWA.

33. Manuscript History of Wenatchee Waterpower Company, GNRP; Farrington to Burke, 11 March 1898, Thomas Burke Papers, UWA.

34. Murray, "The Highline Canal," 22; Burke to Hill, 6 June 1902, GNRP.

35. Agreement between Clark and the Wenatchee Development Company, 10 May 1902, GNRP.

36. Hull, *A History of Central Washington,* 556A, 560; Burke to Hill, 8 July 1902, GNRP. In 1904 the Great Northern shipped 1,663,944 lbs. of apples from the valley in the month of October, with a total freight charge of $9,125.66. Four years later, 13,757,855 lbs. were shipped at a cost of $107,641.39. "Apple Shipments from Wenatchee During the Month of October 1904, 1905, 1906, 1907, 1908," GNRP.

37. Symons, *Report of An Examination of the Upper Columbia River,* 971; Burke, Shepard & McGilvra to F. E. Ward, 16 December 1897; Hill to J. D. McIntyre, 6 March 1896; Great Northern to McIntyre, 11 August 1896, GNRP.

38. Nathan Butler to Hill, 11 June 1896; R. Harding to W. H. Newman, Second vice president, 9 January 1897; Jonathan Stevens to F. E. Ward, assistant to the president, 15 July 1897, GNRP.

39. Burke, Shepard & McGilvra to Ward, 16 December, 30 December 1897, 14 January 1898; Ward to Burke, Shepard & McGilvra, 25 January 1898, GNRP.

40. Gunn to Hill, 31 August 1898; Gunn to Farrington, 5 December 1899, GNRP.

41. Daniel E. Willard, *Montana: The Geological Story* (Lancaster, Penn.: Science Press, 1935), 27; Michael P. Malone and Richard B. Roeder, *Montana: A History of Two Centuries* (Seattle: University of Washington Press, 1976), 180.

42. Gladys R. Costello, "Irrigation History and Resettlement on the Milk River Project, Montana," *Reclamation Era* 40 (May 1940): 136–37; John Shurts, *Indian Reserved Water Rights: The Winters Doctrine in Its Social and Legal Context, 1880s-1930s* (Norman: University of Oklahoma Press, 2000), 29.

43. Shurts, *Indian Reserved Water Rights,* 29.

44. A. A. Den Otter, "Adapting the Environment: Ranching, Irrigation, and Dry Land Farming in Southern Alberta, 1880–1914," *Great Plains Quarterly* 6 (summer 1986): 179; Hill to W. M. Wooldridge, 19 August 1898 and 6 August 1899, GNRP.

45. R. F. Pettigrew to Hill, 4 December 1899; Hill to Pettigrew, 7 December 1899, GNRP.

46. For discussions of the move toward federal intervention, see Donald J. Pisani, *To Reclaim a Divided West: Water, Law, and Public Policy, 1848–1902* (Albuquerque: University of New Mexico Press, 1992); William D. Rowley, *Reclaiming the Arid West: The Career of Francis G. Newlands* (Bloomington: Indiana University Press, 1996); Donald Worster, *Rivers of Empire: Water, Aridity, and the Growth of the American West* (New York: Pantheon Books, 1985); Michael C. Robinson, *Water for the West: The Bureau of Reclamation, 1902–1977* (Chicago: Public Works Historical Society, 1979).

47. Louis N. Hafermehl, "To Make the Desert Bloom: The Politics and Promotion of Early Irrigation Schemes in North Dakota," *North Dakota History* 59 (summer 1992): 13–27; James J. Hill, *Highways of Progress,* 189–90.

48. J. Kruttschnitt, assistant to the president of the Southern Pacific Company, to Hill, 6 April 1903, GNRP.

49. Andrew Hudanick Jr., "George Hebard Maxwell: Reclamation's Militant Evangelist," *Journal of the West* 14 (July 1975): 108–21; Robinson, *Water for the West,* 9.

50. Pisani, *To Reclaim a Divided West,* 235, 308–9; Paris Gibson to Hill, 27 November 1901, GNRP.

51. William E. Doughterty to Hill, 22 April 1884; Hill to H. E. Fletcher, 26 May 1886, General Correspondence, JJHP; *Havre (Mont.) Plaindealer,* 20 February 1904.

52. *Havre (Mont.) Plaindealer,* 20 February 1904; Gibson to Hill, 20 August and 27 November 1901; Hill to St. Clair McKelway, 29 November 1901, GNRP; Bicha, "The American Farmer and the Canadian West," 43–46; Hill to George Maxwell, 16 April 1902, Letterpress Books, JJHP.

53. Hudanick, "George Hebard Maxwell," 116; Pisani, *To Reclaim a Divided West,* 303.

54. Martin, *James J. Hill,* 516; Henry Hansbrough to Hill, 3 December 1901; Gibson to Hill, 4 January 1902; Hansbrough to D. S. Lamont, 11 February 1902; Maxwell to Hill, 12 April 1902, GNRP.

55. Pisani, *To Reclaim a Divided West,* 315–19; Hill to Lamont, 13 February 1902; Gibson to Hill, 9 April 1902 and 3 May 1902; Maxwell to Hill, 12 April 1902, GNRP.

56. Maxwell to Hill, 28 June 1902; Darius Miller, vice president of the CB&Q, to Hill, 20 July 1902, GNRP.

4 / "THE NATION'S FUTURE," 1902–1907

The chapter title is from James J. Hill, *Highways of Progress* (Garden City, N.Y.: Doubleday, Page & Company, 1910), chapt. 1.

1. Ralph W. Hidy et al., *The Great Northern Railway: A History* (Cambridge: Harvard Business School Press, 1988), 117; Michael P. Malone, *James J. Hill: Empire Builder of the Northwest* (Norman: University of Oklahoma Press, 1996), 261.

2. W. Thomas White, "A Gilded Age Businessman in Politics: James J. Hill, the Northwest, and the American Presidency, 1884–1912," *Pacific Historical Review* 57 (November 1988): 444–47; Lewis L. Gould, *The Presidency of Theodore Roosevelt* (Lawrence: University Press of Kansas, 1991), 5–8; George E. Mowry, *The Era of Theodore Roosevelt, 1900–1912* (New York: Harper & Row, 1958), 107–8. Quotations attributed to Marcus Hanna, see Henry Pringle, *Theodore Roosevelt: A Biography* (New York: Harcourt, Brace and Company, 1931), 223, 239.

3. Samuel P. Hays, *The Response to Industrialism, 1885–1914* (Chicago: University of Chicago Press, 1957), 138–39; Gabriel Kolko, *The Triumph of Conservatism: A Reinterpretation of American History, 1900–1916* (New York: Free Press, 1963), 61–62; Albro Martin, *James J. Hill and the Opening of the Northwest* (1976; reprint, St. Paul: Minnesota Historical Society Press, 1991), 514; John E. Stover, *American Railroads* (1961; reprint, Chicago: University of Chicago Press, 1997), 128–29.

4. Howard Elliott to Hill, 5 November 1903, General Correspondence, James J. Hill Papers, James J. Hill Library, St. Paul, Minn. (hereafter JJHP); Malone, *James J. Hill*, 8, 222; Martin, *James J. Hill*, 514–17.

5. Hill to Mary Hill, 30 October 1901, privately owned, cited in Martin, *James J. Hill*, 517.

6. Charles R. Flint, James J. Hill, et al., *The Trust: Its Book* (New York: Doubleday, Page & Company, 1902); *St. Paul Globe*, 21, 22 October 1902.

7. K. Ross Toole, *Twentieth-Century Montana: A State of Extremes* (Norman: University of Oklahoma Press, 1972), 34.

8. James J. Hill, Speech at National Irrigation Congress in Portland, Oregon, 1905, Louis W. Hill Papers, James J. Hill Library, St. Paul, Minn. (hereafter LWHP); White, "A Gilded Age Businessman in Politics," 448–50; Hill, *Highways of Progress*, 79–80, 321.

9. In 1907 the Service became an independent agency and, in 1923, was renamed Bureau of Reclamation. Donald Worster, *Rivers of Empire: Water, Aridity, and the Growth of the American West* (New York: Pantheon Books, 1985), 155–70.

10. Louis N. Hafermehl, "To Make the Desert Bloom: The Politics and Promotion of Early Irrigation Schemes in North Dakota," *North Dakota History* 59 (summer

1992): 13–27. For rainfall in the late 1920s, see E. G. Schollander, "Williston Substation Report for April 1, 1927 to March 31, 1928," North Dakota Agricultural College, *Bulletin 219* (May 1928): 4.

11. Hafermehl, "To Make the Desert Bloom," 13–27; James J. Hill, Speech at National Irrigation Congress in Portland, Oregon, 1905, LWHP.

12. E. A. Williams to Louis Hill, 19 January 1905, Outgoing Correspondence, Erastus A. Williams Papers, Hafermehl, "To Make the Desert Bloom," 13–27; State Historical Society of North Dakota, Bismarck, N.D. (hereafter SHSND); *Fargo (N.D.) Forum and Daily Republican,* 21 and 22 October 1903; Elwyn B. Robinson, *History of North Dakota* (Lincoln: University of Nebraska Press, 1966), 219–20, 230, 241; James J. Hill, Speech at National Irrigation Congress in Portland, Oregon, 1905, LWHP.

13. Hafermehl, "To Make the Desert Bloom," 13–27; Donald J. Pisani, *To Reclaim a Divided West: Water, Law, and Public Policy, 1848–1902* (Albuquerque: University of New Mexico Press, 1992), 303.

14. William C. Hunter, *Beacon Across the Prairie: North Dakota's Land-Grant College* (Fargo: North Dakota Institute for Regional Studies, 1961), 52–55; David B. Danbom, *"Our Purpose is to Serve": The First Century of the North Dakota Agricultural Experiment Station* (Fargo: North Dakota Institute for Regional Studies, 1990), 20–22, 28, 32, 35, 40–41, 53–54.

Historians debate when the work of agricultural scientists became accepted by the majority of the rural population. David Danbom argues that farmers relinquished their independence only after the agricultural depression of the 1920s. At the other extreme, Alan Marcus and Howard Segal postulate farmer dependence on experts by the early twentieth century. Neither argument is persuasive. Farmer deference to agricultural scientists was a gradual and regional process. Many variables, including the personnel of specific agricultural colleges, the general state of the local farm economy, and the success of their methods in meeting farmer needs, affected the rate of grassroots acceptance of academic expertise. Certainly, by the early twentieth century, the Farmers' Institute movement had become well established, and farmer attendance at meetings grew.

In North Dakota, Farmers' Institutes started out as voluntary endeavors by the North Dakota Agricultural College's staff. Their popularity led to state funding and a growing trust between some farmers and educators such as Torger Hoverstad, who took over as superintendent of the institutes in 1907. The University of Minnesota had fired Hoverstad in 1906 for failure to drain the saturated lands at the Crookston Experiment Station. Hoverstad had a wealth of experience from farming in the Red River Valley, which North Dakota farmers recognized and appreciated when he crossed the River. David B. Danbom, *The Resisted Revolution: Urban America and the Industrialization of Agriculture, 1900–1930* (Ames: Iowa State University Press, 1979), 138–45; Alan I Marcus and Howard P. Segal, *Technology in American Life: A Brief History* (Fort Worth: Harcourt Brace Jovanovitch, 1989), 192–93; Roy V. Scott, *The Reluctant Farmer: The Rise of Agricultural Extension to 1914* (Urbana: University of Illinois Press, 1970), 106–7.

15. F. B. Linfield, "Agricultural Development in Montana," n.d., mss., Montana State University Archives, Bozeman, Mont. (hereafter MSU); W. M. Wooldridge to Williams, 16 September and 15 December 1904, E. A. Williams Papers, SHSND.

16. Anon., "The Williston and Buford-Trenton Irrigation Projects," *North Dakota Magazine* (Bismarck) 2 (August 1907): 1–8; William Samuel Bryans, "A History of Transcontinental Railroads and Coal Mining on the Northern Great Plains to 1920" (Ph.D. diss., University of Wyoming, 1987), 27–63.

17. Anon., "The Williston and Buford-Trenton Irrigation Projects," 1; "Missouri River Pumping Projects, North Dakota," n.d., mss., MSU.

18. Linfield, "Agricultural Development in Montana," MSU.

19. Worster, *Rivers of Empire*, 158, 182–83; Pisani, *To Reclaim a Divided West*, 60–64, 307–9.

20. Pisani, *To Reclaim a Divided West*, 307–9; Worster, *Rivers of Empire*, 173; Letter from Maxwell, 11 February 1903, Great Northern Railway Papers, Minnesota Historical Society, St. Paul, Minn. (hereafter GNRP).

21. Maxwell to J. H. Hannaford, to W. H. Phipps, to F. I. Whitney, to D. Miller, to Hill, 8 January 1903; to Hill, 14 February 1903; press release enclosed with Maxwell to Hill, 14 February 1903, GNRP; Hill to C. S. Mellen, 12 January 1903, Letterpress Books, JJHP; *House Journal of the Eighth Regular and Extraordinary Sessions of the Legislative Assembly of the State of Montana* (Helena: State Publishing Co., 1903).

22. Stanley W. Howard, *Green Fields of Montana: A Brief History of Irrigation* (Manhattan, Kans.: Sunflower Press, 1974), 31; *Hearings Before the Committee on Irrigation of Arid Lands of the House of Representatives Related to Projects for the Irrigation of Arid Lands Under the National Irrigation Act and the Work of the Division of Irrigation Investigations of the Agricultural Department in Connection with Irrigation of Arid Lands*, 58th Cong., 3rd sess., 1904, H. Doc. 381.

23. Howard, *Green Fields of Montana*, 31; *Hearings Before the Committee on Irrigation of Arid Lands*, 1904.

24. John Shurts, *Indian Reserved Water Rights: The Winters Doctrine in Its Social and Legal Context, 1880s-1930s* (Norman: University of Oklahoma Press, 2000), 3–4, 75–76.

25. Shurts, *Indian Reserved Water Rights*, 77–78; *Hearings Before the Committee on Irrigation of Arid Lands*, 1904; Howard, *Green Fields of Montana*, 31.

26. *Hearings Before the Committee on Irrigation of Arid Lands,* 1904.

27. James J. Hill, Speech at National Irrigation Congress in Portland, Oregon, 1905, LWHP; Pisani, *To Reclaim a Divided West,* 90, 165.

28. Ernest Staples Osgood, *The Day of the Cattleman* (1929; reprint, Chicago: University of Chicago Press, 1970), 197–211, 230; Edward Everett Dale, *The Range Cattle Industry: Ranching on the Great Plains from 1865–1925* (Norman: University of Oklahoma Press, 1960).

29. Benjamin Horace Hibbard, *A History of the Public Land Policies* (Madison: University of Wisconsin Press, 1965), 386–88, 426–29, 465–66; *Congressional Record,* 58th Cong., 1st sess., 1903, 37, pt. 1: 246.

30. Maxwell to Hill, 27 May 1903; Maxwell to L. W. Hill and to J. W. Cooper, 6 August 1903; Press Release, no date; Paris Gibson to Maxwell, 27 July 1903, GNRP; James J. Hill, Speech at National Irrigation Congress in Portland, Oregon, 1905, LWHP; Gifford Pinchot, W. A. Richards, and Frederick Haynes Newell, *The Second Partial Report of the Public Lands Commission, appointed October 22, 1903, to Report Upon the Condition, Operation, and Effect of the Present Land Laws,* 58th Cong., 3rd sess., 1905, S. doc. 154.

31. Robinson, *History of North Dakota,* 230; Maxwell to L. W. Hill, 6 August 1903, GNRP.

32. Maxwell to Cooper, 6 August 1903, GNRP; *Congressional Record,* 58th Cong., 1st sess., 1903, 37, pt. 1: 181; Hansbrough to Hill, 12 October 1903; Gibson to Hill, 21 24 October 1903, General Correspondence, JJHP; *Great Falls (Mont.) Daily Tribune,* 21 October 1903; *Fargo (N.D.) Forum and Daily Republican,* 20 October 1903; H. G. Hansbrough to Williams, 9 December 1903, E. A. Williams Papers, SHSND.

33. Gibson to Hill, 21 and 24 October 1903, General Correspondence, JJHP.

34. *St. Paul Globe,* 14 January 1904; *Daily Pioneer Press* (St. Paul), 14 January 1904; James J. Hill, Speech at National Irrigation Congress in Portland, Oregon, 1905, LWHP; *Congressional Record,* 58th Cong., 1st sess., 1903, 37, pt. 1: 478; *Congressional Record,* 58th Cong., 2nd sess., 1904, 38, pt. 4: 3376.

35. *Morning Oregonian* (Portland), 22, 23, and 24 August 1905.

36. Mary Wilma M. Hargreaves, *Dry Farming in the Northern Great Plains, 1900–1925* (Cambridge: Harvard University Press, 1957), 85–86.

37. F. B. Linfield and Alfred Atkinson, "Dry Farming in Montana," Montana Agricultural College Experiment Station, *Bulletin 63* (January 1907): 17–29.

38. Hargreaves, *Dry Farming,* 86–87, 90, 92–94.

39. Ibid; Hardy W. Campbell to Hill, 26 January 1895; J. W. Kendrick, general manager of Northern Pacific, to Hill, 25 March 1895, GNRP.

40. Contract signed by B. S. Rufsel, 15 February 1897, GNRP.

41. Howard Leigh Dickman, "James Jerome Hill and the Agricultural Development of the Northwest" (Ph.D. diss., University of Michigan, 1977), 35–40; *Havre (Mont.) Plaindealer,* 20 February 1904.

42. Thomas Cooper to president, State Agricultural College, 29 November 1904, MSU; Linfield and Atkinson, "Dry Farming in Montana," 13; anon. "Co-operative Work in Dry Farming in Montana," n.d., GNRP.

43. Karl Quisenberry, "The Dry Land Stations: Their Mission and Their Men," *Agricultural History* 51 (January 1977): 219; W. W. Laughlin to M. J. Costello, 21 October 1905; Linfield to Elwood Mead, 2 December 1905, MSU; Linfield and Atkinson, "Dry Farming in Montana."

44. Cooper to Linfield, 1 February 1906, MSU; Linfield and Atkinson, "Dry Farming in Montana," 13–14; B. Campbell, Fourth Vice President, to L. W. Hill, 10 March 1906; W. W. Broughton, General Traffic Manager, to L. W. Hill, 26 December 1907; anon., "Co-operative Work in Dry Farming in Montana," n.d., GNRP.

45. Linfield and Atkinson, "Dry Farming in Montana," 14; anon., "Co-operative Work in Dry Farming in Montana," n.d.; B. Campbell to L. W. Hill, 23 August 1906, GNRP.

46. E. C. Chilcott to C. W. Mott, 30 November 1906, MSU.

47. For example, Linfield and Atkinson, "Dry Farming in Montana."

48. Dickman, "James Jerome Hill," 35–40; *Havre (Mont.) Plaindealer,* 20 February 1904; James J. Hill, Speech at National Irrigation Congress in Portland, Oregon, 1905, LWHP.

49. C. H. Honey to Hill, 21 July 1902 and 23 July 1903; "Resolutions," n.d., GNRP; Hafermehl, "To Make the Desert Bloom," 27; Linfield to Cooper, 5 April 1909, MSU; *Seventeenth Annual Report of the North Dakota Agricultural Experiment Station, Agricultural College, North Dakota, to the Governor of North Dakota, 1907* (Fargo, N.D.: Walker Bros. & Hardy, 1907), 14, 66–89; Jeffrey B. Roet, "Agricultural Settlement on the Dry Farming Frontier, 1900–1920" (Ph.D. diss., Northwestern University, 1982), 246–49.

50. Alexander M. Ross, *The College on the Hill: A History of the Ontario Agricultural College, 1874–1974* (Vancouver: Copp Clark Publishing, 1974), 29–99; F. B. Linfield, "A Talk Prepared for the Quarter Century Club, But Not Given," undated mss., MSU; H. M. Creel to L. W. Hill, 6 February 1907, GNRP; Robert L. Morlan, *Political Prairie Fire: The Nonpartisan League, 1915–1922* (1955; reprint, St. Paul: Minnesota Historical Society Press, 1983), 3, 42, 250; Danbom, *"Our Purpose is to Serve",* 58–76.

51. *Seventeenth Annual Report of the North Dakota Agricultural Experiment Station,* 14, 66–89.

52. L. W. Hill to B. Campbell, 3 April 1905; Campbell to L. W. Hill, 14 April and 1 May 1905; L. W. Hill to B. Campbell, 17 April 1905, GNRP.

53. John Henry Worst to Hill, 9 June and 19 September 1902; Secretary to the president to Worst, 12 June 1902; Jonathan Stevens to L. W. Hill, 13 September 1902; L. W. Hill to Worst, 18 September 1902; Campbell to L. W. Hill, 1 May 1905; F. E. Ward to L. W. Hill, 16 May 1905; L. W. Hill to F. E. Ward, 18 May 1905, GNRP.

54. The Great Northern ran a Good Soil Special around this time. The use of informational trains probably started in 1891 when the Agricultural College at Guelph, Ontario, sent two lecturers out on a wagon. As Hill's friend Thomas Shaw came from that college, the launching of Great Northern trains reflected the influence of his Canadian network. Hill also could have been following the lead of the Burlington, which launched informational trains in four states in 1904. The presence of agricultural trains in North Dakota run by the competitive Soo line added incentive. Campbell to L. W. Hill, 29 March 1906, GNRP; *Iowa State Register* (Des Moines), 12 May 1905; Scott, *Railroad Development Programs*, 40.

55. Campbell to L. W. Hill, 29 March 1906; Herbert Myrick to Hill, 27 January 1906, GNRP; Hargreaves, *Dry Farming*, 180; Vermillion, South Dakota to Board of Regents, 1 December 1899, Thomas Shaw Biography file, Institute of Agriculture Files, University of Minnesota Archives, Minneapolis, Minn. (hereafter UMA).

56. R. S. Shaw, Thomas Shaw's son, to C. A. Franzman at the University of Minnesota, n.d., Thomas Shaw Biography file, Institute of Agriculture Files, UMA.

57. Despite the engineering of hardy hybrids, corn is still a difficult crop to grow in the upper tier. In Montana, for example, in 1995, only sixty thousand acres of corn were grown, all in the extreme south of the state. By comparison, farmers grew over five-and-a-half million acres of wheat. *Montana Agricultural Statistics Bulletin, 1995* (Helena: State Department of Agriculture, 1996).

58. Dickman, "James Jerome Hill," 90–91; North Oaks Experiment File, 13 and 18 April 1905, North Oaks Papers, JJHP.

59. Dickman, "James Jerome Hill," 91; Andrew Boss to Toomey, 26 February 1906, North Oaks Experiment File, North Oaks Papers, JJHP.

60. Corn Experiments file, 1905; J. H. Shepperd of the North Dakota Agricultural College, to John J. Toomey, 13 November 1906, Corn Experiments file, North Oaks Papers, JJHP.

61. John R. Stilgoe, "Plugging Past Reform: Small-Scale Farming Innovation and Big-Scale Farming Research," in *Scientific Authority and Twentieth Century America*, ed. Ronald G. Walters (Baltimore: Johns Hopkins University Press, 1997), 119–47; Pete Daniels, *Breaking the Land: The Transformation of Cotton, Tobacco, and Rice Cultures Since 1880* (Urbana: University of Illinois Press, 1985), 3–22.

62. Thomas Shaw to Hill, 5 December 1905, GNRP.

63. James J. Hill, Address at dedication of Stephens Hall, Crookston, Minn., 17 September 1908, LWHP; Thomas Shaw, press release, n.d., "Prizes for Farms in Minnesota and the Dakotas"; Shaw to Hill, 22 January 1906; Clarence A. Shamel [*sic*] to L. W. Hill, 9 March 1906, GNRP; *Farmer* (St. Paul), 17 November 1906.

64. *Farmer* (St. Paul), 17 November 1906; D. K. Tallman to Hill, 5 December 1906, General Correspondence, JJHP; *St. Paul Dispatch*, 15 November 1906.

65. Hill, *Highways of Progress*, 5; Charles A. Dalich, "Dry Farming Promotion in Eastern Montana, 1907–1916" (M.A. thesis, University of Montana, 1968), 21–25.

66. This situation continued, with England buying an average of $23,353,000 of wheat from America in 1912 to 1914, as compared with $3,473,000 bought by France, and $5,762,000 of wheat purchased by Japan. *Trends in the Foreign Trade of the United States* (New York: National Industrial Conference Board, 1930), 29, 31, 116; Denis Judd, *Radical Joe: A Life of Joseph Chamberlain* (London: Hamish Hamilton, 1977), 237, 263–64, 244–72.

67. *Havre (Mont.) Plaindealer*, 20 February 1904.

68. John Fahey, *The Inland Empire: Unfolding Years, 1879–1929* (Seattle: University of Washington Press, 1986), 16–18; Howard Schonberger, "James J. Hill and the Trade with the Orient," *Minnesota History* 41 (winter 1968): 178–90; Thomas Burke to Hill, 4 July 1893; Hill to Burke, 10 August 1894, Thomas Burke Papers, University of Washington Archives, Seattle, Washington.

69. Quoted in Malone, *James J. Hill*, 153; "Speech of the Honorable Thomas Burke, of Seattle, Washington, at the Launching of the S. S. Minnesota, at Groton, Conn., Thursday April 16th, 1903," General Correspondence, JJHP.

70. Barbara L. Bender, "Historic 'Sisters' on Puget Sound," *Portage* 8 (fall 1986): 14–17; Malone, *James J. Hill*, 96.

71. J. H. Isherwood, "Great Northern Liner: 'Minnesota of 1904,'" *Sea Breezes* (November 1970): 670–75; "Speech of the Honorable Thomas Burke, of Seattle, Washington, at the Launching of the S. S. 'Minnesota,' at Groton, Conn., Thursday April 16th, 1903," General Correspondence, JJHP; Bender, "Historic "Sisters" on Puget Sound," 14–17.

72. James M. Morris, *Our Maritime Heritage: Maritime Developments and Their Impact on American Life* (Washington, D.C.: University Press of America, 1979), 189–206; *U.S. Shipping and Shipbuilding: Trends and Policy Choices* (Washington, D.C.: Government Printing Office, 1984), 8–10.

73. *Havre (Mont.) Plaindealer*, 20 February 1904; *Minot (N.D.) Daily Reporter*, 30 September 1909; *Philadelphia Press*, 19 September 1909; Hill, *Highways of Progress*, 38; *Sioux City (S.D.) Tribune*, 8 September 1906.

5 / CONFLICT AND DISILLUSION, 1907–1912

1. John Milton Cooper, Jr., *Pivotal Decades: The United States, 1900–1920* (New York: W. W Norton & Co., 1990), 113–14.

2. Michael P. Malone, *James J. Hill: Empire Builder of the Northwest* (Norman: University of Oklahoma Press, 1996), 228–42; Ralph W. Hidy et al., *The Great Northern Railway: A History* (Cambridge: Harvard Business School Press, 1988), 102; Howard Leigh Dickman, "James Jerome Hill and the Agricultural Development of the Northwest" (Ph.D. diss., University of Michigan, 1977), 359.

3. Albro Martin, *James J. Hill and the Opening of the Northwest* (1976; reprint, St. Paul: Minnesota Historical Society Press, 1991), 576.

4. Like his elder brother, James Norman, Louis had attended Exeter prep school in New England. Unlike his brother, he failed to obtain the necessary languages for admission to Yale and so attended Yale's Sheffield Scientific School. This provided many years more education than his father had ever received and exposure to the eastern elite at an impressionable age. Ibid., 352–54, 421–21; Malone, *James J. Hill,* 249–50, 265–66.

5. James J. Hill, *Highways of Progress,* (Garden City, N.Y.: Doubleday, Page, & Company, 1910), 40–41; *Chicago Daily Tribune,* 16 September 1909.

6. Samuel P. Hays, *Conservation and the Gospel of Efficiency: The Progressive Conservation Movement, 1890–1920* (Cambridge: Harvard University Press, 1959), 23–36, 72–89, 136.

7. Ibid., 148–52, 162–63; Harold K. Steen, *The U.S. Forest Service: A History* (Seattle: University of Washington Press, 1976), 81–84.

8. Hays, *Conservation and the Gospel of Efficiency,* 153–72; Steen, *The U.S. Forest Service,* 100–102.

9. L. W. Hill to Hill, 12 February 1908; to D. Miller, 17 September 1909, Great Northern Railway Papers, Minnesota Historical Society, St. Paul, Minn. (hereafter GNRP); *Investigation of the Department of the Interior and of the Bureau of Forestry,* 61st Cong., 3rd sess., 1911, S. doc. 719, p. 85.

10. Perkins to Ballinger, 1910, Richard Ballinger Papers, University of Washington Archives, Seattle, Washington (hereafter UWA); *Investigation of the Department of the Interior and of the Bureau of Forestry,* p. 85.

11. "Missouri River Pumping Projects, North Dakota," n.d., Montana State University Archives, Bozeman, Mont.; Report of meeting of the Williston Water Users' Association held on 7 January 1910, GNRP.

12. J. W. Jackson to Hill, 30 November 1910; L. W. Hill to Jackson, 8 December 1910; L. C. Gilman, assistant to the president of the Great Northern, to L. W. Hill,

8 December 1910; Gilman to W. E. Humphrey, 9 December 1910; Jackson to Gilman, 22 April 1911, GNRP; Paul Edward Kelly, "Under the Ditch: Irrigation and the Garrison Diversion Controversy" (M.A. thesis, North Dakota State University, 1989), 9–24; *U.S. Statutes at Large, Vol. 36, Part I* (Washington, D.C.: Government Printing Office, 1911), 902.

13. A. P. Davis, chief engineer of the Reclamation Service, to L. W. Hill, 2 March 1910; L. W. Hill to Davis, 14 March 1910; to Thomas Carter, 7 February 1910, GNRP; John Shurts, *Indian Reserved Water Rights: The Winters Doctrine in Its Social and Legal Context, 1880s–1930s* (Norman: University of Oklahoma Press, 2000), 77–78, 149; "Treaty between the United States and Great Britain Relating to the Boundary Waters between the United States and Canada," *The Statutes at Large of the United States of America, From March, 1909, to March, 1911, Concurrent Resolutions of the Two Houses of Congress, and Recent Treaties, Conventions, and Executive Proclamations* 36:2 (Washington, D.C.: Government Printing Office, 1911), 2448–55; Gladys R. Costello, "Irrigation History and Resettlement on the Milk River Project, Montana," *Reclamation Era* 40 (May 1940): 138.

14. Gilman to L. W. Hill, 7 October 1909; W. M. Wooldridge to L. W. Hill, 13 November 1909; L. W. Hill to W. W. Broughton (with enclosures), 21 October 1909; to Davis, 26 February 1910; to Darius Miller, CB&Q, 17 September 1909, GNRP.

15. L. W. Hill to Miller, 17 September 1909, GNRP.

16. Davis to L. W. Hill, 2 March 1910; L. W. Hill to Davis, 14 March 1910, Ballinger Papers, UWA.

17. Louis Hill to Thomas Carter, 16 September 1909, GNRP.

18. Edmund Taylor Perkins to E. L. Lomax, Union Pacific, 9 August 1909; to P. S. Eustis, CB&Q, 10 August 1909; to A. M. Cleland, Northern Pacific, 21 September 1909; Eustis to J. S. Woodworth, Northern Pacific, and Broughton, Great Northern, 12 August 1909; Broughton to Miller, 13 September 1909; Miller to Broughton, 15 September 1909, GNRP.

19. *Investigation of the Department of the Interior and of the Bureau of Forestry*, p. 1796–1800; L. W. Hill to Thomas Carter, 16 September 1909; to Miller, 17 September 1909; Circular issued by the St. Paul Jobbers and Manufacturers' Association, September 1909; C. L. Kluckhorn, president of the St. Paul Jobbers and Manufacturers' Association, to Perkins, 27 September 1909, GNRP.

20. L. W. Hill to Kluckhorn, 25 September 1909, GNRP.

21. Ibid.; F. H. Newell to Thomas Cooper, Great Northern, 28 September 1909; Perkins to Broughton, 4 October 1909; Eustis to Miller 5 October 1909, GNRP.

22. J. H. Beek, Minnesota State Fair Association, to Reclamation Service, n.d.; to Perkins, 27 September 1909, GNRP.

23. L. W. Hill to Miller, 28 September 1909, GNRP.

24. L. W. Hill to Miller, 5 April 1910; to D. M. Hoyt, E. H. Cooney, Governor Norris, *Helena Independent,* W. B. George, 5 April 1910, GNRP.

25. *Investigation of the Department of the Interior and of the Bureau of Forestry,* p. 84; Perkins to Ballinger, 1910, Ballinger Papers, UWA.

26. Pinchot to Taft, 4 November 1909; Article by Roy Crandall, sent to E. C. Brainerd, editor of the *Post-Intelligencer,* 14 August 1909, Ballinger Papers, UWA.

27. Senate, *Investigation of the Department of the Interior and of the Bureau of Forestry,* p. 1836–38.

28. Ibid., p. 1842–49.

29. L. W. Hill to Charles B. Nichols, *Leslie's Weekly,* 6 April 1910; to D. M. Hoyt, E. H. Cooney, Governor Norris, *Helena Independent,* W. B. George, 5 April 1910, GNRP.

30. L. W. Hill to Nichols, 6 April 1910; to M. J. Costello, 28 June 1910, GNRP.

31. McKinney, McKinney, Hobbs & Mass, to L. W. Hill, 6 and 18 June 1910; L. W. Hill to Nichols, 28 June 1910; Ballinger to L. W. Hill, 6 August 1910, GNRP.

32. Perkins to Ballinger, 9 June 1910; to Senator Weldon B. Heyburn of Idaho, 9 June 1910, Ballinger Papers, UWA; H. H. Parkhouse to L. W. Hill, n.d., GNRP.

33. Elmo R. Richardson, *The Politics of Conservation: Crusades and Controversies, 1897–1913* (Berkeley: University of California Press, 1962), 78–9, 113, 117, 123–29, 134–35.

34. Ibid., 15; *Proceedings of the First State Irrigation Congress Held at Bismarck, N.D., October 20th and 21st, 1903* (Bismarck: State Irrigation Congress, 1903), 21–22; Hill, *Highways of Progress,* 17–18; Theodore M. Porter, *Trust in Numbers: The Pursuit of Objectivity in Science and Public Life* (Princeton: Princeton University Press, 1995), 74; Christopher Lasch, *The True and Only Heaven: Progress and Its Critics* (New York: W. W. Norton & Co., 1991), 125.

35. Hill, *Highways of Progress,* 38, 50.

36. *St. Paul Pioneer Press,* 6 September 1910; *Omaha Daily News,* 9 December 1909; *Chicago Daily News,* 30 October 1909; *News-Messenger* (Marshall, Minn.), 8 October 1909; *Seattle Post-Intelligencer,* 6 September 1910.

37. Milton Whitney, "The Chemistry of the Soil as Related to Crop Production," Bureau of Soils, USDA, *Bulletin 22* (1903): 55–56, 64; Cyril Hopkins, "The Duty of Chemistry to Agriculture," University of Illinois Agricultural Experiment Station, *Circular 105* (November 1906): 4.

38. Cyril Hopkins, "Chemical Principles of Soil Fertility," University of Illinois Agricultural Experiment Station, *Circular 124* (November 1908): 2; Whitney, "The Chemistry of the Soil as Related to Crop Production"; Hopkins, "The Duty of Chemistry to Agriculture," 25–27.

39. Hopkins, "The Duty of Chemistry to Agriculture," 25–27; Eugene Davenport, University of Illinois Agricultural Experiment Station, *Circular 123* (1908).

40. Hopkins, "The Duty of Chemistry to Agriculture," 14; Davenport, *Circular 123*; Hopkins, "Chemical Principles of Soil Fertility," 1–4.

41. *Report of the National Conservation Commission with Accompanying Papers, February 1909,* 60th Cong., 2nd sess., 1909, S. doc. 676, 3: 108; Milton Whitney, "A Study of Crop Yields and Soil Composition in Relation to Soil Productivity," USDA, Bureau of Soils, *Bulletin 57* (October 1909).

42. Davenport, *Circular 123,* 5; Theodore Roosevelt to Hill, 4 March 1908, General Correspondence, James J. Hill Papers, James J. Hill Library, St. Paul, Minn. (hereafter JJHP); Hill to Roosevelt, 20 March 1908, Letterpress Books, JJHP.

43. *Baltimore American,* 14 May 1908; W. J. McGee, ed., *Proceedings of a Conference of Governors in the White House, Washington, D.C. May 13–15, 1908* (Washington, D.C.: Government Printing Office, 1909), vi, viii–ix, xix, xxv–xxxi, 37–39, 63–75; *Chicago Record-Herald,* 15 May 1908; *Augusta (Ga.) Chronicle,* 18 May 1908; *Sun* (New York), 15 May 1908.

44. McGee, *Proceedings of a Conference of Governors,* xxv, 96, 203, 432; Roosevelt to Hill, 8 June 1908, General Correspondence, JJHP.

45. *Minot (N. D.) Daily Optic,* 28 September 1909; *News-Messenger* (Marshall, Minn.), 8 October 1909; *Helena (Mont.) Independent,* 28 September 1909; *Post and Record* (Rochester, Minn.), 1 October 1909; Hill, *Highways of Progress.*

46. J. P. Morgan to Hill, 7 December 1909, Hopkins to Hill, 21 and 29 December 1909, General Correspondence, JJHP; Hill to Hopkins, 29 December 1909; Hopkins to Hill, 3 January 1910, GNRP; Charles R. Van Hise, "Conservation of Soils," in *Proceedings of a Conference of Governors,* 431–22.

47. Richardson, *Politics of Conservation,* 60–80; Lawrence Rakestraw, "The West, States' Rights, and Conservation: A Study of Six Public Land Conferences," *Pacific Northwest Quarterly* 48 (July 1957): 89–99.

48. L. W. Hill to C. G. Goodrich, E. Pennington, W. A. McGonagle, F. E. House, A. J. Earling, and Marvin Hughitt, 16 February 1910; to Costello, 28 June 1910; to Carter, 28 June 1910, GNRP.

49. B. N. Baker to Hill, 30 June 1910; L. W. Hill to Charles Norton, 13 July 1910; Knute Nelson to L. W. Hill, 19 July 1910; Nelson to L. W. Hill, 19 July 1910, GNRP.

50. H. J. Bergman, "The Reluctant Dissenter: Governor Hay of Washington and the Conservation Problem," *Pacific Northwest Quarterly* 62 (January 1971): 27–33.

51. L. W. Hill to Edwin Norris, governor of Montana, 12 August 1910, (two letters); to Charles Norton, 16 August 1910, GNRP.

52. Bergman, "The Reluctant Dissenter," 27–33; Hay to Dr. F. O. Hudnutt, 15 September 1910, Hay Papers, Washington State Archives, Olympia, Washington; Richardson, *Politics of Conservation,* 100–101.

53. *Seattle Post-Intelligencer,* 8 September 1910; *Saint Paul Pioneer Press,* 7 and 9 September 1910; *Minneapolis Morning Tribune,* 8 September 1910.

54. *Leslie's Weekly* (Chicago), 22 September 1910; *Saint Paul Pioneer Press,* 10 September 1910.

55. Bergman, "The Reluctant Dissenter," 30; Henry C. Wallace to Hill, 11 March 1911, 5 and 12 August 1911; Hill to Wallace, 16 March 1911, 7 and 28 August 1911; to Thomas Shipp, 30 September 1912, General Correspondence, JJHP.

56. James J. Hill, "Minnesota's Agriculture, Speech at the Second Minnesota Conservation and Agricultural Development Congress, Minneapolis, Minn., 19 November 1912," Louis W. Hill Papers, James J. Hill Library, St. Paul, Minn.

57. Gifford Pinchot, W. A. Richards, and Frederick Haynes Newell, *The Second Partial Report of the Public Lands Commission, appointed October 22, 1903, to Report Upon the Condition, Operation, and Effect of the Present Land Laws,* 58th Cong., 3rd sess., 1905, S. doc. 154.

6 / ISOLATION AND EXPERTISE, 1907–1912

1. Jeffrey B. Roet, "Agricultural Settlement on the Dry Farming Frontier 1900–1920" (Ph.D. diss., Northwestern University, 1982), 159–61.

2. F. B. Linfield, "Fourteenth Annual Report for the Fiscal Year ending June 30, 1907," Montana Agricultural College Experiment Station, February 1908, 164; W. W. Broughton to L. W. Hill, 26 December 1907, Great Northern Railway Papers, Minnesota Historical Society, St. Paul, Minn., (hereafter GNRP); "Co-operative Work in Dry Farming in Montana," anon., undated, GNRP. In 1907 the Northern Pacific contributed three thousand dollars to dryland farming experimentation, and the state of Montana gave two thousand dollars. The state also gave two thousand dollars to start a station in Fergus County, not far from Moccasin in the Judith Basin, on a branch line of the Great Northern. All parties found the work generally satisfactory despite some personnel problems at the Shelby station. In 1908 the Northern Pacific's contribution dropped back to $2,500, and the Shelby station along the Great Northern was discontinued. In 1909 the state increased its contribution to nine thousand dollars and the Northern Pacific to five thousand, with two more stations being established along its line. The Chicago, Milwaukee and St. Paul Railway also committed two thousand dollars per year for two stations on its road.

3. L. W. Hill to Broughton, 21 February 1910; Thomas Shaw to L. W. Hill, 1 October

1909, GNRP. In 1910 James J. Hill published his collection of speeches, *Highways of Progress* (Garden City, N.Y.: Doubleday, Page & Company, 1910). In it he demonstrated his concern with wheat yields, saying, "The average wheat yield per acre in the United States in 1907 was 14 bushels. The average for the last ten years is 13.88.... It is a disgraceful record" (p. 75).

4. Linfield to E. C. Leedy, 28 January 1910, Montana State University Archives, Bozeman, Mont.; Howard Leigh Dickman, "James Jerome Hill and the Agricultural Development of the Northwest" (Ph.D. diss., University of Michigan, 1977), 173–74; L. W. Hill to Edwin Norris, 8 February 1910, GNRP.

5. Thomas Cooper, land commissioner of Great Northern, to Howard Elliott, president of Northern Pacific, 15 December 1908, GNRP.

6. *Proceedings of the Trans-Missouri Dry Farming Congress. Held at Denver, Colorado, January 24, 25, 26, 1907* (Denver Chamber of Commerce, 1907), 3–4; Charles A. Dalich, "Dry Farming Promotion in Eastern Montana (1907–1916)" (M.A. thesis, University of Montana, 1968), 66.

7. Jardine was American secretary of agriculture from 1925–29; Roet, "Agricultural Settlement on the Dry Farming Frontier," 227; Gladys Baker et al. *A Century of Service: The First 100 Years of the United States Department of Agriculture* (Washington, D.C.: U. S. Department of Agriculture, 1963), 45; *Proceedings of the Trans-Missouri Dry Farming Congress, 1907*, 16–27, 32–35, 72–76, 126–29, 146–48.

8. *Fourth Dry Farming Congress Will Convene in Billings, Montana, U. S. A. October 26th, 27th and 28th, 1909,* (Helena: Montana Board of Control, 1909).

9. Charles E. Rosenberg, *No Other Gods: On Science and American Social Thought* (Baltimore: Johns Hopkins University Press, 1961), 12; Robert H. Wiebe, *The Search for Order, 1877–1920* (New York: Hill and Wang, 1967), 145–46; Margaret Rossiter, "The Organization of the Agricultural Sciences," in *The Organization of Knowledge in Modern America, 1860–1920,* ed. Alexandra Oleson and John Voss (Baltimore: Johns Hopkins University Press, 1979), 211–48.

10. Hill, *Highways of Progress,* 40, 62.

11. Mary Wilma M. Hargreaves, *Dry Farming in the Northern Great Plains, 1900–1925* (Cambridge: Harvard University Press, 1957), 101–4; Stanford J. Layton, *To No Privileged Class: The Rationalization of Homesteading and Rural Life in the Early Twentieth-Century American West* (Salt Lake City: Charles Redd Center for Western Studies, Brigham Young University, 1988), 25; Roet, "Agricultural Settlement on the Dry Farming Frontier," 228.

12. Hargreaves, *Dry Farming in the Northern Great Plains,* 63.

13. L. W. Hill to John T. Burns, Secretary-Treasurer, Fourth Dry Farming Congress in Billings, 4 May 1909; Broughton to L. W. Hill, 9 June 1909, GNRP.

14. Burns to Hill, 10 December 1909; L. W. Hill to Broughton, 24 December 1909, GNRP.

15. L. W. Hill to F. A. Patrick, 19 October 1909, GNRP.

16. L. W. Hill to Richard Porter, 25 September 1909, GNRP.

17. L. W. Hill to J. Smith, editor, Judith Gap, 18 October 1909, GNRP; *The Dry Farming Congress Bulletin* (Spokane, Wash.: Dry Farming Congress, 1910), 35, 54–56.

18. *The Dry Farming Congress Bulletin,* 54–56, 102–6.

19. Ibid., 107.

20. Ibid., 105–7.

21. L. W. Hill to Darius Miller, president of CB&Q, 8 September 1910; W. P. Kenney, General Traffic Manager, to Carl R. Gray, Second Vice President, 27 June 1912; Gray to Kenney, 29 November 1913; Miller to Jule M. Hannaford, president of Northern Pacific, 23 September 1913; Hannaford to Miller, 20 September 1913, GNRP.

22. Dickman, "James Jerome Hill," 107, 193–250.

23. Schedule, Fred S. Cooley, Superintendent of Montana Farmers' Institutes, 1909, GNRP; Hargreaves, *Dry Farming,* 180.

24. Hill, *Highways of Progress,* 79–80; Hargreaves, *Dry Farming,* 181–82.

25. Thomas O'Hanlon to L. W. Hill, 2 February 1910; Shaw to L. W. Hill, 1 October 1909, GNRP.

26. O. P. N. Anderson, Office of Commissioners of Railroads, to L. W. Hill, 15 February 1910, GNRP.

27. E. C. Leedy, general immigration agent, to L. W. Hill, 17 February 1910, GNRP.

28. Hargreaves, *Dry Farming,* 170, 180; E. C. Leedy, general immigration agent, to L. W. Hill, 17 February 1910; Shaw to L. W. Hill, 31 December 1912; Leedy to Shaw, 23 February 1913, GNRP.

29. Dickman, "James Jerome Hill," 176; Shaw to L. W. Hill, 31 December 1912, GNRP.

30. *The International Dry-Farming Congress* (Edmonton: Department of Agriculture of the Province of Alberta, 1912), 5; Shaw to L. W. Hill, 31 December 1912, GNRP; Dickman, "James Jerome Hill," 167, 176; Roy V. Scott, *Railroad Development Programs in the Twentieth Century* (Ames: Iowa State University Press, 1985), 35.

31. Scott, *Railroad Development Programs,* 35.

32. L. W. Hill to H. J. Neely, 11 November 1908; to E. F. C. Van Dissel, 12 June 1909; to M. J. Costello, 9 November 1909; Hannaford to L. W. Hill, 30 April and 2 June 1914, GNRP.

33. L. W. Hill to J. C. Stubbs, 12 August 1911; to Leedy, 19 June 1911 and 8 April 1912; Leedy to H. A. Noble, 31 August 1911; to H. H. Parkhouse, 23 August 1912; S. J. Ellison to Broughton, 4 December 1909, GNRP.

34. Douglas M. Edwards, "Exhibiting the Possibilities: Settlement Promotion and the Montana State Fair," paper presented at the Western Historical Association Conference, St. Paul, Minn., October 1997, in possession of author.

35. Dickman, "James Jerome Hill," 107, 193–250.

36. Ibid., 107, 127; Joseph Gilpin Pyle, *The Life of James J. Hill,* vol. 2 (Garden City, N.Y.: Doubleday, Page & Company, 1917), 362.

37. Dickman, "James Jerome Hill," 129–31, 137; Scott, *Railroad Development Programs in the Twentieth Century,* 46; Circular letter to farmers, 21 June 1912; F. R. Crane to Hill, 28 April 1915, General Correspondence, James J. Hill Papers, James J. Hill Library, St. Paul, Minn. (hereafter JJHP).

38. *Minneapolis Morning Tribune,* 16, 17, 20, 22, and 23 September 1912; *St. Paul Dispatch,* 16 September 1912; *St. Paul Pioneer Press,* 17 September 1912.

39. Public letter from Hill, 19 September 1912, General Correspondence, JJHP; see, for example, James C. Carey, *Kansas State University* (Lawrence: Regents' Press of Kansas, 1977), 41–46; Merle Curti and Vernon Carstensen, *The University of Wisconsin, 1848–1925* (Madison: University of Wisconsin Press, 1949): 470–71.

40. James Gray, *The University of Minnesota, 1851–1951* (Minneapolis: University of Minnesota Press, 1951), 96–102.

41. Rosenberg, *No Other Gods,* 159–79.

42. *St. Paul Pioneer Press,* 18 September 1912; *Minneapolis Morning Tribune,* 20 September 1912.

43. David B. Danbom, *The Resisted Revolution: Urban American and the Industrialization of Agriculture, 1900–1930* (Ames: Iowa State University Press, 1979), 75–96; David B. Danbom, *"Our Purpose is to Serve": The First Century of the North Dakota Agricultural Experiment Station* (Fargo: North Dakota Institute for Regional Studies, 1990), 29–52.

44. Danbom, *"Our Purpose is to Serve,"* 61–76; Robert L. Morlan, *Political Prairie Fire: The Nonpartisan League, 1915–1922* (1955; reprint, St. Paul: Minnesota Historical Society Press, 1985), 60–75.

45. Danbom, *"Our Purpose is to Serve,"* 61–76; Morlan, *Political Prairie Fire,* 60–75.

46. The Minnesota Conservation and Agricultural Development Congress being one of the few exceptions, *Saint Paul Pioneer Press,* 19 November 1912; Curtis L. Mosher to L. W. Hill, 26 November 1912, GNRP.

7 / RETIREMENT AND RETREAT, 1912–1916

1. Arthur A. Ekirch Jr., *Progressivism in America: A Study of the Era from Theodore Roosevelt to Woodrow Wilson* (New York: New Viewpoints, 1974), 224–28, 248; R. Laurence Moore, "Directions of Thought in Progressive America," in *The Progressive Era*, ed. Lewis L. Gould (Syracuse: Syracuse University Press, 1974), 47–49; John J. Broesamle, "The Democrats from Bryan to Wilson," in *The Progressive Era*, ed. Gould, 106–8; Arthur S. Link Jr., *Woodrow Wilson and the Progressive Era, 1910–1917* (New York: Harper & Row, 1954), 25–81.

2. Gerald D. Nash, *The American West Transformed: The Impact of the Second World War* (Bloomington: Indiana University Press, 1985), 201–16; Gerald D. Nash, *The American West in the Twentieth Century: A Short History of an Urban Oasis* (Albuquerque: University of New Mexico Press, 1973), 9–11.

3. L. W. Hill to Shaw, 23 February 1913; Shaw to L. W. Hill, 31 December 1912; Kenney to Gray, 27 June 1912, Great Northern Railway Papers, Minnesota Historical Society, St. Paul, Minn. (hereafter GNRP).

4. Circular Letter to farmers, 21 June 1912, General Correspondence, James J. Hill Papers, James J. Hill Library, St. Paul, Minn. (hereafter JJHP); Howard Leigh Dickman, "James Jerome Hill and the Agricultural Development of the Northwest" (Ph.D. diss., University of Michigan, 1977), 137.

5. Theodore M. Porter, *Trust in Numbers: The Pursuit of Objectivity in Science and Public Life* (Princeton: Princeton University Press, 1995).

6. L. W. Hill to Lewis Penwell, 27 October 1912, GNRP.

7. A. E. Chamberlain to L. W. Hill and Kenney, 18 October 1911; to Hill, 8 January 1912; Chamberlain, "Report of Industrial Department, January 1, 1912," 1 January 1912; L. W. Hill to H. H. Parkhouse, 27 August 1912; Thomas Shaw to L. W. Hill, 5 February 1915, GNRP.

8. Chamberlain, "Report of Industrial Department"; Chamberlain to Kenney, 13 December 1912, GNRP.

9. W. F. Gwin to Gray, 12 June 1913; Kenney to Gray, 17 June and 24 November 1913; Gray to L. C. Gilman, 27 November 1913; Gilman to M. J. Costello, 19 December 1913; J. Gruber to L. W. Hill, 9 and 19 March 1914, GNRP.

10. Chamberlain, "Report of Industrial Department," GNRP.

11. Ibid.; Chamberlain to Kenney, 13 December 1912; Gray to Herbert Myrick, 22 August 1913, GNRP.

12. Dickman, "James Jerome Hill," 200–207.

13. W. P. Kenney to Carl R. Gray, 18 December 1913 and 19 January 1914; to L. W. Hill, 6 June 1914; Gray to Kenney, 23 December 1913; L. W. Hill to Kenney, 8 June 1914, GNRP.

14. Fred S. Cooley to subordinate grange masters, 22 December 1913; to O. E. Young, 12 December 1914, Montana State University Archives, Bozeman, Mont. (hereafter MSU).

15. Chamberlain, "Report of Industrial Department"; Chamberlain to Kenney, 13 December 1912, GNRP.

16. L. W. Hill to James A. Murty, 3 June 1915; Jules Hannaford to L. W. Hill, 30 April 1914; Kenney to H. H. Parkhouse, 13 October 1915, GNRP.

17. Douglas Edwards, "Exhibiting the Possibilities: Settlement Promotion and the Montana State Fair," paper presented at the Western Historical Association Conference, St. Paul, October 1997, in possession of author; Chamberlain, "Report of Industrial Department"; Chamberlain to L. W. Hill and Kenney, 18 October 1911, GNRP.

18. J. H. Young, president of Spokane, Portland & Seattle Railway, to Gray, 29 January and 13 March 1913; Shaw to L. W. Hill, 31 December 1912, GNRP; *Oregon Daily Journal* (Portland), 12 May 1913; L. W. Hill to M. R. Brown, 27 March 1913; to E. E. Faville, editor, *Western Farmer,* 19 December, 1916; to H. P. Smith, State College of Washington, 27 December, 1916; to R. D. Hezet, Director of Oregon Extension Service, 27 December 1916; to M. R. Brown, 27 March 1913; telegram from H. H. Parkhouse to L. W. Hill, 13 December 1916; Leedy to Parkhouse, 24 April 1912; George Horace Lorimer to L. W. Hill, 6 May 1912; Kenney to Gray, 18 December 1913, GNRP.

19. L. W. Hill speech in Oregon, 5 June 1913, GNRP.

20. L. W. Hill to Charles Hilles, 13 September 1912, GNRP.

21. L. W. Hill to Hilles, 26 September 1912; Samuel Adams to Hilles, 4, 11, and 12 October 1912; W. H. Manss to L. W. Hill, 23 October 1912; L. W. Hill to Manss, 25 October 1912; William Bole to L. W. Hill, 3 April 1913, GNRP.

22. J. H. Carroll to Gray, 21 May 1913, GNRP; *Tacoma Ledger* (Oregon), 14 May 1913; *Morning Oregonian* (Portland), 14 May 1913; *Irrigation Age* (Chicago), March 1913; *St. Paul Pioneer Press,* 14 May 1913.

23. Gilman to L. W. Hill, 26 October 1912; to Gray, 5 April, 20 and 26 May 1913; telegram, Gilman to Gray, 18 May 1913; H. N. Savage to Gilman, 2 April 1913; telegram, Gray to Gilman, 14 May 1913; telegram, William Bole to Gray, 6 June 1913, GNRP.

24. Savage to Gilman, 17 July 1913, GNRP; Gilman to Gray, 26 September, 1913, GNRP.

25. Donald Worster, *Rivers of Empire: Water, Aridity, and the Growth of the American West* (New York: Pantheon Books, 1985), 176–77; Michael C. Robinson, *Water for the West: The Bureau of Reclamation, 1902–1977* (Chicago: Public Works Historical Society, 1979), 42.

26. Chief Engineer to L. W. Hill, 15 December 1905, GNRP; Charles Ffolliott to J. J. Toomey, 4 February 1920, GNRP; "To the Bondholders of the West Okanogan Valley Irrigation District, n.d., GNRP; Consulting Engineer to Board of Directors, West Okanogan Valley Irrigation District, 12 September 1919, GNRP.

27. Roy V. Scott, *Railroad Development Programs in the Twentieth Century* (Ames: Iowa State University Press, 1985), 54; H. H. Gross to Hill, 29 October 1913, General Correspondence, JJHP; Roy V. Scott, *The Reluctant Farmer: The Rise of Agricultural Extension to 1914* (Urbana: University of Illinois Press, 1970).

28. Letter from Willet Hays, 1 October 1908, University of Minnesota Archives, Minneapolis, Minn. (hereafter UMA). Many of the components of the Dolliver-Davis bill were embodied in the Smith-Hughes Act, passed the year after Hill's death.

29. Hill to Gross, 27 October 1913, General Correspondence, JJHP.

30. Charles Rosenberg, *No Other Gods: On Science and American Social Thought* (Baltimore: Johns Hopkins University Press, 1961), 141–84.

31. John J. Toomey to D. McCleary, superintendent of Humboldt, 14 September 1910, Humboldt Farm Papers, JJHP; Joseph Gilpin Pyle, *The Life of James J. Hill,* vol. 2 (Garden City, N.Y.: Doubleday, Page & Company, 1917), 393–94.

32. In 1911 Northcote lost $12,497.61; in 1912 $12,030.65; in 1913 $22,781.78; and in 1914 $58,968.38. Dickman, "James Jerome Hill," 314.

33. Unbound typed financial records, Humboldt Farm Papers, JJHP.

34. Thomas Shaw, Biography Files, Institute of Agriculture—Director's Office Papers, UMA; Toomey to Robert S. McPheeters, Helena, Minn., 15 August 1899, General Correspondence, JJHP; *Saint Paul Pioneer Press,* 2 March 1914.

35. Pyle, *The Life of James J. Hill,* vol. 2, 350; A. W. Shaw to Toomey, 4, 12, 14, 15, 18, 20, 22, and 24 October and 21 November 1913; Inventory, 1914, North Oaks Papers, JJHP.

36. A livestock register for Suffolk Punch horses was kept from 1911 to 1916, one for Duroc Jersey pigs was kept in 1913, and one for Oxford Down sheep was kept in 1912. Livestock Registers, JJHP.

37. Toomey to Finneman, 3 February, 10 March, and 17 April 1914; Crane to Toomey, 27 April 1914, North Oaks Papers, JJHP; Dickman, "James Jerome Hill," 129. For many years North Oaks had mainly been a family retreat, but by the time of Hill's retirement, his children had lost interest in the property, although this would change after his death. The farm did retain importance in providing supplies to the ever-expanding list of family residences. The farm also retained its intrinsic appeal for Hill and his wife, Mary. When the original wood-frame house burnt down in 1912, Hill replaced it with a large brick dwelling reminiscent of his mansion in St. Paul. He also built new greenhouses and spent $2,556.50 on ornamental landscap-

ing. R. H. Pinnow, gardener, to Toomey, 17 January 1914; Bill from Jewell Nursery Co., Lake City, 3 March 1914 and from Hoyt Nursery Co., St. Paul, 10 April 1914, North Oaks Papers, JJHP.

38. Dickman, "James Jerome Hill," 313; Lohr Bros. to Toomey, 12 September 1915, Humboldt Farm Papers; Hill to K. J. Cahill, 1 March 1913, General Correspondence, JJHP; Bill of Sale, 2 January 1917, Northcote Farm Papers, JJHP. When Hill died in 1916, Humboldt was sold off in sections, and Northcote was sold to John Lohr, who had managed Humboldt since 1909. Lohr paid $208,918 for four thousand acres, which included the Northcote farm, and $75,000 for animals, machinery, and other sundries.

39. Hill to Knute Nelson, 30 March 1914, Letterpress Books, JJHP; Lohr Bros. to Toomey, 10 August 1915, Humboldt Farm Papers, JJHP; J. B. Densmore to Nelson, 13 September, 7 October 1915; to Hill, 7 October 1915, General Correspondence, JJHP.

40. Michael G. Schene, "The Crown of the Continent: Private Enterprise and Public Interest in the Early Development of Glacier National Park, 1910–17," *Forest & Conservation History* 34 (April 1990): 69–75.

8 / "THE VOICE OF THE NORTHWEST"

The chapter title is from Roy V. Scott, *Railroad Development Programs in the Twentieth Century* (Ames: Iowa State University Press, 1985), 35.

1. William G. Robbins, *Colony & Empire: The Capitalist Transformation of the American West* (Lawrence: University Press of Kansas, 1994), 128–29; William G. Robbins, *Landscapes of Promise: The Oregon Story, 1800–1940* (Seattle: University of Washington Press, 1997), 226; Ralph W. Hidy et al., *The Great Northern Railway: A History* (Boston: Harvard Business School Press, 1988), 91.

2. Michael P. Malone, *The Battle for Butte: Mining & Politics on the Northern Frontier, 1864–1906* (Helena: Montana Historical Society Press, 1981), 40–50.

3. Joseph Gilpin Pyle, *The Life of James J. Hill*, vol. 2 (Garden City, N.Y.: Doubleday, Page & Company, 1917), 232–49, 362, 365, 368; Albro Martin, *James J. Hill and the Opening of the Northwest* (1976; reprint, St. Paul: Minnesota Historical Society Press, 1991), 549–55; Howard Leigh Dickman, "James Jerome Hill and the Agricultural Development of the Northwest" (Ph.D. diss., University of Michigan, 1977); Scott, *Railroad Development Programs*, 8, 35; Malone, *James J. Hill*, 197, 250.

4. Joseph Kinsey Howard, *Montana: High, Wide, and Handsome* (New Haven: Yale University Press, 1943), 169; Charles A. Dalich, "Dry Farming Promotion (1907–1916)" (M.A. thesis, University of Montana, 1968), ii; Jonathan Raban, *Bad Land: An American Romance* (London: Picador, 1996).

5. James J. Hill speech, "Great Northern Origins and Growth," 1913, Louis W. Hill Papers, James J. Hill Library, St. Paul, Minn. (hereafter LWHP).

6. Dickman, "James Jerome Hill," 194.

7. Malone, *James J. Hill,* 186, 192–94; Scott, *Railroad Development Programs,* 35; Edward Tuck to Hill, 31 December 1902, General Correspondence, James J. Hill Papers, James J. Hill Library, St. Paul, Minn. (hereafter JJHP).

8. Solon J. Buck, *The Granger Movement* (Cambridge: Harvard University Press, 1913), 159–205; Thomas A. Woods, *Knights of the Plow: Oliver H. Kelley and the Origins of the Grange in Republican Ideology* (Ames: Iowa State University Press, 1991), 147–57; Hill to Kennedy, 5 January 1883, 22 February 1884, 10 and 25 January 1885; to E. T. Nichols, 25 February 1885; to Samuel Thorne, 23 February 1884, Letterpress Books, JJHP; *St. Paul Dispatch,* 19 November 1912; *Warrensburg (N.Y.) News,* 17 February 1910; Robert L. Morlan, *Political Prairie Fire: The Nonpartisan League, 1915–1922,* (1955; reprint, St. Paul: Minnesota Historical Society Press, 1983), 16, 106–7; Thomas Shaw to L. W. Hill, 30 March 1916, Great Northern Railway Papers, Minnesota Historical Society, St. Paul, Minn.

9. Mary Wilma M. Hargreaves, *Dry Farming in the Northern Great Plains, 1900–1925* (Cambridge: Harvard University Press, 1957), 102; Charles A. Dalich, "Dry Farming Promotion in Eastern Montana, 1907–1916" (M.A. thesis, University of Montana, 1968), 35–54.

10. *Havre (Mont.) Plaindealer,* 20 February 1904.

11. *St. Paul Globe,* 14 January 1904.

12. John J. Toomey to James McClure, 24 January 1900, North Oaks Papers; Toomey, 16 February 1899, General Correspondence; Hill to Christopher Stevenson, 17 March 1886; to John M. Martin, 26 November 1886; to H. W. Donaldson, 19 June 1893; to M. S. Merager, 21 May 1889; to C. L. Goodell, 6 June 1908, Letterpress Books, JJHP.

13. James J. Hill speech, "The Mother of All Industry," 1912, LWHP.

14. James J. Hill speech in Williston, N.D., 27 November 1911, LWHP.

BIBLIOGRAPHY

PRIMARY RESOURCES

Archival Material

Agricultural Experiment Station Papers, University of Minnesota Archives, Minneapolis, Minnesota.

Erastus A. Williams Papers, State Historical Society of North Dakota, Bismarck, North Dakota.

Great Northern Railway Papers, Minnesota Historical Society, St. Paul, Minnesota.

Hasslen, John. Oral Interview by Betsy Doermann and Ellen Rosenthal, St. Paul, 24 November 1981. In James J. Hill House, St. Paul, Minnesota.

Institute of Agriculture Files, University of Minnesota Archives, Minneapolis, Minnesota.

James J. Hill Papers, James J. Hill Library, St. Paul, Minnesota.

James J. Hill Papers, University of Washington Archives, Seattle, Washington.

Lindley, Clara. Unpublished Reminiscences, James J. Hill House, St. Paul, Minnesota.

Louis W. Hill Papers, James J. Hill Library, St. Paul, Minnesota.

Montana State Historical Society, Helena, Montana.

Montana State University Archives, Bozeman, Montana.

Northern Pacific Papers, Minnesota Historical Society, St. Paul, Minnesota.

Richard Ballinger Papers, University of Washington Archives, Seattle, Washington.

Thomas Burke Papers, University of Washington Archives, Seattle, Washington.

Newspapers

American Agriculturist (Ithaca, N.Y.)
Anaconda (Mont.) Standard

Ariel (Minneapolis)

Augusta (Ga.) Chronicle

Baltimore American

Billings (Mont.) Daily Gazette

Breeders' Gazette (Chicago)

Butte (Mont.) Evening News

Butte (Mont.) Miner

Chicago Daily Tribune

Chicago News

Chicago Record-Herald

Coast (Seattle)

Crookston (Minn.) Daily Journal

Crookston (Minn.) Daily Times

Daily Minnesota Tribune (Minneapolis)

Daily News (Chicago)

Daily Pioneer Press (St. Paul)

Dakota Farmer (Aberdeen, S.D.)

Fargo (N.D.) Forum and Daily Republican

Farmer (St. Paul and Chicago)

Farmers Advocate and Northwestern Stockman (St. Paul)

Globe Gazette (Wahpeton, N.D.)

Great Falls (Mont.) Daily Tribune

Havre (Mont.) Plaindealer

Helena (Mont.) Independent

Iowa State Register (Des Moines)

Irrigation Age (Chicago)

Leslie's Illustrated Weekly (New York and Chicago)

Madison (Wisc.) Democrat

Michigan Farmer (Detroit)

Milking Shorthorn Journal (Chicago)

Minneapolis Journal

Minneapolis Morning Tribune

Minneapolis Sunday Tribune

Minneapolis Tribune

Minnesota Stockman (St. Paul)

Minot (N.D.) Daily Optic

Minot (N.D.) Daily Reporter

Morning Oregonian (Portland)

National Live Stock Journal (Chicago)
News-Messenger (Marshall, Minn.)
North American (Philadelphia)
North Dakota Magazine (Bismarck)
North Oaks News (Minn.)
Omaha Bee
Omaha Daily News
Orange Judd Farmer (Chicago)
Oregon Daily Journal (Portland)
Philadelphia Press
Philadelphia Record
Post and Record (Rochester, Minn.)
Post-Express (Rochester, N.Y.)
Prairie Leader (Long Prairie, Minn.)
Record (Fargo, N.D.)
Rochester (Minn.) Daily Bulletin
Scott County (Minn.) Argus
Seattle Mail and Herald
Seattle Post-Intelligencer
Seattle Times
Sioux City (S.D.) Tribune
Southern Cultivator (Atlanta)
St. Paul Dispatch
St. Paul Globe
St. Paul Pioneer Press
Sun (New York)
Tacoma Ledger (Oregon)
Times-Enterprise (Albert Lea, Minn.)
Warrensburg (N.Y.) News

Books, Articles, and Pamphlets

Addresses and Proceedings of the First National Conservation Congress Held at Seattle, Washington August 26–28, 1909. National Conservation Congress, 1909.

Boss, Andrew. *Farm Management*. Chicago: Lyons & Carnahan, n.d.

Coulter, John Lee. "Marketing of Agricultural Lands in Minnesota and North Dakota." *American Economic Review*, June 1912, 283–301.

Dry Farming Congress Bulletin. Spokane, Wash.: Dry Farming Congress, 1910.

Dry Farming Congress: Proceedings of the 3rd Congress. N.p., 1909.

Dry Farming Congress: Proceedings of the 4th Congress. N.p., 1910.

Dry Farming Congress: Proceedings of the 5th Congress. N.p., 1911.

Dry Farming Congress: Proceedings of the 6th Congress. N.p., 1912.

Flint, Charles R., James J. Hill, et al. *The Trust: Its Book.* New York: Doubleday, Page & Company, 1902.

Fourth Dry Farming Congress Will Convene in Billings, Montana, U.S.A. October 26th, 27th and 28th, 1909. Helena: Montana Board of Control, 1909.

Hill, James J. *Highways of Progress.* Garden City, N.Y.: Doubleday, Page & Company, 1910.

International Dry Farming Congress: Proceedings of the 4th Congress. N.p., 1909.

International Dry Farming Congress: Proceedings of the 5th Congress. N.p., 1910.

International Dry Farming Congress: Proceedings of the 6th Congress. N.p., 1911.

International Dry Farming Congress: Proceedings of the 7th Congress. N.p., 1912.

International Dry Farming Congress: Proceedings of the 8th Congress. N.p., 1913.

International Dry Farming Congress: Proceedings of the 9th Congress. N.p., 1914.

International Dry Farming Congress: Proceedings of the 10th Congress. N.p., 1915.

Marshall, Duncan. *Shorthorn Cattle in Canada.* N.p.: Dominion Shorthorn Breeders' Association, 1932.

Mills, James, and Thomas Shaw. *The First Principles of Agriculture.* Toronto: J. E. Bryant Co., n.d.

Pinchot, Gifford. *The Fight for Conservation.* New York: Doubleday, Page & Co., 1910.

Proceedings of the First State Irrigation Congress Held at Bismarck, N.D., October 20th and 21st, 1903. Bismarck: State Irrigation Congress, 1903.

Proceedings of the Second National Conservation Congress at Saint Paul, September 5–8, 1910. Washington: National Conservation Congress, 1911.

Proceedings of the Third National Conservation Congress at Kansas City, Missouri, September 25, 26 and 27, 1911. Kansas City: National Conservation Congress, 1912.

Proceedings of the Trans-Missouri Dry Farming Congress. Held at Denver, Colorado, January 24, 25, 26, 1907. Denver: Chamber of Commerce, 1907.

Sanders, Alvin. *Short-Horn Cattle.* Chicago: Sanders Publishing Co., 1918.

Shaw, Thomas. *The Study of Breeds in America: Cattle, Sheep and Swine.* New York: Orange Judd Company, 1902.

Smalley, Victor H. "Wenatchee and the Wonderful Wenatchee Valley." *Northwest Magazine,* March 1902, 1–13.

Swalwell, Joseph A. *Necessity for Continuation of Federal Aid in the Reclamation of Arid Lands.* Spokane: Columbia Basin Irrigation League, n.d.

Trends in the Foreign Trade of the United States. New York: National Industrial Conference Board, 1930.

Veblen, Thorstein. "The Food Supply and the Price of Wheat." *Journal of Political Economy* 1 (1892–93): 365–79.

Government Documents

Atkinson, Alfred, and J. B. Nelson. "Dry Farming Investigations in Montana," *Bulletin 74*. Montana Agricultural College Experiment Station, December 1908.

————. "Dry Farming Investigations in Montana," *Bulletin 83*. Montana Agricultural College Experiment Station, January 1911.

Atkinson, Alfred, and N. C. Donaldson. "Dry Farm Grain Tests in Montana," *Bulletin 110*. Montana Agricultural College Experiment Station, February 1916.

Atkinson, Alfred, H. O. Buckman, and L. F. Gieseker. "Dry Farm Moisture Studies," *Bulletin 87*. Montana Agricultural College Experiment Station, September 1911.

Atkinson, Alfred, J. M. Stephens, and G. W. Morgan. "Dry Farm Crop Rotations and Cultural Methods," *Bulletin 116*. Montana Agricultural College Experiment Station, March 1917.

Bills and Debates in Congress Relating to Trusts. 57th Cong., 2nd sess. Senate. Washington, D.C.: Government Printing Office, 1903.

Boss, Andrew. "Minnesota Agricultural Experiment Station, 1885–1935," *Bulletin 319*. Agricultural Experiment Station, University of Minnesota, May 1935.

Boss, Andrew et al. "Seed Grain; Selection, Treatment, Varieties, Distribution," *Bulletin 115*. Agricultural Experiment Station, University of Minnesota, February 1910.

Columbia River and Tributaries, Northwestern United States—Vol. III. 81st Cong., 2nd sess.: H. Doc. No. 531, 1950.

Commutation of Homestead Entries and Confirming Such Entries in Certain Cases. 60th Cong., 1st sess.: H. Report No. 1555, 1908.

Congressional Record. 1887. 49th Cong., 2nd sess.

Congressional Record. 1888. 50th Cong., 1st sess.

Congressional Record. 1903. 58th Cong., 1st sess.

Congressional Record. 1904. 58th Cong., 2nd sess.

Cooper, Thomas P. "The Cost of Minnesota Dairy Products, 1904–1909," *Bulletin 124*. University of Minnesota, June 1911.

Crickman, C. W., George A. Sallee, and W. H. Peters. "Beef Cattle Production in

Minnesota," *Bulletin 301*. Agricultural Experiment Station, University of Minnesota, February 1934.

"Crop and Live Stock in Ontario," *Bulletin 56*. Ontario Bureau of Industries, November 1895.

Davenport, Eugene. *Circular 123*. University of Illinois Agricultural Experiment Station, 1908.

Eighth and Ninth Annual Reports of the Bureau of Animal Industry for the Years 1891 and 1892. Bureau of Animal Industry, USDA. Washington, D.C.: Government Printing Office, 1893.

Fifth Biennial Report of the Commissioner of Agriculture and Labor to the Governor of North Dakota for the Two Years Ending June 30, 1898. Bismarck: Tribune, State Printers and Binders, 1898.

Fourth and Fifth Annual Reports of the Bureau of Animal Industry for the Years 1887 and 1888. Bureau of Animal Industry, USDA. Washington, D.C.: Government Printing Office, 1889.

General Laws of Minnesota for 1893, Chapter 221, "An Act to Appropriate Moneys for the Purpose of Opening Closed Watercourses."

Grant, Madison. *Early History of Glacier National Park, Montana*. Washington, D.C.: Government Printing Office, 1919.

Hearings Before the Committee on Irrigation of Arid Lands of the House of Representatives Related to Projects for the Irrigation of Arid Lands Under the National Irrigation Act and the Work of the Division of Irrigation Investigations of the Agricultural Department in Connection with Irrigation of Arid Lands. 58th Cong., 3rd sess.: H. Doc. No. 381, 1904.

Hopkins, Cyril. "The Duty of Chemistry to Agriculture," *Circular 106*. University of Illinois Agricultural Experiment Station, November 1906.

———. "Chemical Principles of Soil Fertility," *Circular 124*. University of Illinois Agricultural Experiment Station, November 1908.

House Journal of the Eighth Regular and Extraordinary Sessions of the Legislative Assembly of the State of Montana. Helena: State Publishing Co., 1903.

International Dry Farming Congress. Edmonton: Department of Agriculture of the Province of Alberta, 1912.

Investigation of the Department of the Interior and of the Bureau of Forestry. 61st Cong., 3rd sess.: S. Doc. No. 719, 1911.

James, C. C. "Crops and Live Stock in Ontario," *Bulletin 56*. Ontario Bureau of Industries, November 1895.

Linfield, F. B. "Fourteenth Annual Report for the Fiscal Year Ending June 30, 1907." Montana Agricultural College Experiment Station, February 1908.

Linfield, F. B., and Alfred Atkinson. "Dry Farming in Montana," *Bulletin 63.* Montana Agricultural College Experiment Station, January 1907.

McGee, W. J., ed. *Proceedings of a Conference of Governors in the White House, Washington, D.C. May 13–15, 1908.* Washington, D.C.: Government Printing Office, 1909.

Message From the President of the United States, Submitting the Second Partial Report of the Public Lands Commission, Appointed October 22, 1903, To Report Upon the Condition, Operation, and Effect of the Present Land Laws. 58th Cong., 3d sess.: S. Doc. No. 154, 1905.

Montana Agricultural College Experiment Station: Fourteenth Annual Report. Montana Agricultural College Experiment Station, February 1908.

Montana Agricultural College Experiment Station: Sixteenth Annual Report. Montana Agricultural College Experiment Station, February 1910.

Montana Agricultural College Experiment Station: Eighteenth Annual Report. Montana Agricultural College Experiment Station, February 1912.

Montana Agricultural College Experiment Station: Twentieth Annual Report. Montana Agricultural College Experiment Station, February 1914.

Montana Agricultural Statistics Bulletin, 1995. Helena: State Department of Agriculture, 1996.

Palmer, Ben. "Swamp Land Drainage with Special Reference to Minnesota," *Bulletin 5.* University of Minnesota, Studies in the Social Sciences, March 1915.

Pearson, Murray, Atkinson, Lowe, Harbaugh, Law, Dickson, Mohler, Trumbower, Salmon, Smith, and Stiles. *Special Report on Diseases of Cattle.* USDA, Bureau of Animal Industry. Washington, D.C.: Government Printing Office, 1904.

Pinchot, Gifford, W. A. Richards, and Frederick Haynes Newell. *The Second Partial Report of the Public Lands Commission, appointed October 22, 1903, to Report Upon the Condition, Operation, and Effect of Present Land Laws.* 58th Cong., 3rd sess.: S. Doc. No. 154, 1905.

Report of the National Conservation Commission with Accompanying Papers, February 1909. 60th Cong., 2nd sess.: S. Doc. No. 676, 1909.

Schollander, E. G. "Williston Substation Report for April 1, 1927 to March 31, 1928," *Bulletin 219.* North Dakota Agricultural Experiment Station, May 1928.

Seamans, A. E. "Experiment with Corn on Dry Land at the Huntley Branch Station," *Bulletin 194.* Montana Agricultural College Experiment Station, November 1926.

Selby, H. E. "Statistics of Dry-Land Farming Areas in Montana," *Bulletin 185.* Montana Agricultural College Experiment Station, January 1926.

Seventeenth Annual Report of the North Dakota Agricultural Experiment Station, Agricultural College, North Dakota, to the Governor of North Dakota, 1907. Fargo, N.D.: Walker Bros & Hardy, 1907.

Shaw, Thomas, and C. A. Zavitz. "Roots, Potatoes and Fodder Corn," *Bulletin 72.* Ontario Agricultural College, Experiment Station, 1892.

The Statutes at Large of the United States of America, From March, 1909, to March, 1911, Concurrent Resolutions of the Two Houses of Congress, and Recent Treaties, Conventions, and Executive Proclamations. Washington, D.C.: Government Printing Office, 1911.

Symons, Thomas W. *Report of an Examination of the Upper Columbia River and the Territory in its Vicinity in September and October, 1881, to Determine its Navigability and Adaptability to Steamboat Transportation Made by Direction of the Commanding General of the Department of the Columbia.* 47th Cong., 1st sess.: Ex. Doc. No. 186, 1881.

Tenth and Eleventh Annual Reports of the Bureau of Animal Industry for the Years 1893 and 1894. Bureau of Animal Industry, USDA. Washington, D.C.: Government Printing Office, 1896.

Third Annual Report of the Bureau of Animal Industry for the Year 1886. Bureau of Animal Industry, USDA. Washington, D.C.: Government Printing Office, 1887.

Thompson, Carl W., and G. P. Warber. *Social and Economic Survey of a Rural Township in Southern Minnesota.* Minneapolis: University of Minnesota, 1913.

University of Montana, Agricultural Experiment Station: Twenty-Fourth Annual Report. Montana Agricultural College Experiment Station, February 1918.

U.S. Statutes at Large, Vol. 36, Part I. Washington, D.C.: Government Printing Office, 1911.

Water: The Yearbook of Agriculture, 1955. USDA, 1955.

Whitney, Milton. "The Chemistry of the Soil as Related to Crop Production," *Bulletin 22.* USDA, Bureau of Soils, 1903.

———. "A Study of Crop Yields and Soil Composition in Relation to Soil Productivity," *Bulletin 57.* USDA, Bureau of Soils, October 1909.

SECONDARY SOURCES

Books

Athearn, Robert G. *The Mythic West in Twentieth-Century America.* Lawrence: University Press of Kansas, 1986.

Baker, Gladys et al. *A Century of Service: The First 100 Years of the United States Department of Agriculture.* Washington, D.C.: USDA, 1963.

The Beet Sugar Story. Washington, D.C.: United States Beet Sugar Association, 1959.

Bicha, Karel Denis. *The American Farmer and the Canadian West, 1896–1914.* Lawrence, Kans.: Coronado Press, 1968.

Bledstein, Burton J. *The Culture of Professionalism: The Middle Class and the Development of Higher Education in America.* New York: W. W. Norton & Co., 1976.

Blegen, Theodore C. *Minnesota: A History of the State.* 1963. Reprint, University of Minnesota Press, 1975.

Bowers, William L. *The Country Life Movement in America, 1900–1920.* Port Washington, N.Y.: Kennikat Press, 1974.

Bowling, George Augustus. *A History of Ayrshire Cattle in the United States.* Parsons, W.V.: McClain Printing Co., 1975.

Brengle, K. G. *Principles and Practices of Dryland Farming.* Boulder, Colo.: Associated University Press, 1982.

Buck, Solon J. *The Granger Movement.* Cambridge: Harvard University Press, 1913.

Cady, Edwin Harrison. *The Gentleman in America: A Literary Study in American Culture.* New York: Greenwood Press, 1949.

Carey, James C. *Kansas State University.* Lawrence: Regent's Press of Kansas, 1977.

Cassara, Ernest. *The Enlightenment in America.* Boston: Twayne Publishers, 1975.

Cawelti, John G. *Apostles of the Self-Made Man.* Chicago: University of Chicago Press, 1965.

Clark, George T. *Leland Stanford: War Governor of California, Railroad Builder, and Founder of Stanford University.* Stanford: Stanford University Press, 1931.

Cooper, John Milton, Jr. *Pivotal Decades: The United States, 1900–1920.* New York: W. W. Norton & Co., 1990.

Coulter, John Lee. *Industrial History of the Red River Valley of the North.* St. Paul: Minnesota State Historical Society, 1910.

Craven, Avery. *Edmund Ruffin, Southerner: A Study on Secession.* Baton Rouge: Louisiana State University Press, 1966.

Cronon, William. *Nature's Metropolis: Chicago and the Great West.* New York: W. W. Norton & Co., 1991.

Curti, Merle, and Vernon Carstensen. *The University of Wisconsin, 1848–1925.* Madison: University of Wisconsin Press, 1949.

Cutright, Paul Russell. *Theodore Roosevelt: The Making of a Conservationist.* Urbana: University of Illinois Press, 1985.

Dale, Edward Everett. *The Range Cattle Industry: Ranching on the Great Plains from 1865–1925.* Norman: University of Oklahoma Press, 1960.

Danbom, David B. *The Resisted Revolution: Urban America and the Industrialization of Agriculture, 1900–1930.* Ames: Iowa State University Press, 1979.

———. *"Our Purpose Is to Serve": The First Century of the North Dakota Agricultural Experiment Station.* Fargo: North Dakota Institute for Regional Studies, 1990.

Daniel, Pete. *Breaking the Land: The Transformation of Cotton, Tobacco, and Rice Cultures Since 1880*. Urbana: University of Illinois Press, 1985.

Davis, Clarence B., and Kenneth E. Wilburn Jr., eds. *Railway Imperialism*. New York: Greenwood Press, 1991.

Demaree, Albert Lowther. *The American Agricultural Press, 1819–1860*. New York: Columbia University Press, 1941.

Dies, Edward Jerome. *Titans of the Soil: Great Builders of Agriculture*. Chapel Hill: University of North Carolina Press, 1949.

Drache, Hiram M. *The Day of the Bonanza: A History of Bonanza Farming in the Red River Valley of the North*. Fargo: North Dakota Institute for Regional Studies, 1964.

Dubbert, Joe L. *A Man's Place: Masculinity in Transition*. Englewood Cliffs, N.J.: Prentice-Hall, 1979.

Dunbar, Robert C. *Forging New Rights in Western Waters*. Lincoln: University of Nebraska Press, 1983.

Ekirch, Arthur A., Jr. *Progressivism in America: A Study of the Era from Theodore Roosevelt to Woodrow Wilson*. New York: New Viewpoints, 1974.

Erickson, T. A. *My Sixty Years with Rural Youth*. Minneapolis: University of Minnesota Press, 1956.

Fahey, John. *The Inland Empire: Unfolding Years, 1879–1929*. Seattle: University of Washington Press, 1986.

Fite, Gilbert C. *The Farmers' Frontier, 1865–1900*. New York: Holt, Rinehart and Winston, 1966.

———. *American Farmers: The New Minority*. Bloomington: Indiana University Press, 1981.

Furner, Mary O. *Advocacy & Objectivity: A Crisis in the Professionalization of American Social Science, 1865–1905*. Lexington: University Press of Kentucky, 1975.

Fussell, G. E. *Jethro Tull: His Influence on Mechanized Agriculture*. Reading, U.K.: Osprey Publishing, 1973.

Geiger, Louis G. *University of the Northern Plains*. Fargo: University of North Dakota Press, 1958.

Getman, A. K., and R. W. Gregory, eds. *Contributions of Leading Americans to Agriculture*. Des Moines: Meredith Publishing Company, 1940.

Gilman, Rhoda R., Carolyn Gilman, and Deborah M. Stulz. *The Red River Trails: Oxcart Routes Between St. Paul and the Selkirk Settlement, 1820–1870*. St. Paul: Minnesota Historical Society Press, 1979.

Good, Henry, and James Teller. *A History of American Education.* New York: MacMillan Co., 1973.

Goodwyn, Lawrence. *The Populist Moment: A Short History of Agrarian Revolt in America.* New York: Oxford University Press, 1978.

Gould, Lewis L. *The Presidency of Theodore Roosevelt.* Lawrence: University Press of Kansas, 1991.

————, ed. *The Progressive Era.* Syracuse: Syracuse University Press, 1974.

Gray, James. *The University of Minnesota, 1851–1951.* Minneapolis: University of Minnesota Press, 1951.

Grodinsky, Julius. *Transcontinental Railway Strategy, 1869–1893: A Study of Businessmen.* Philadelphia: University of Pennsylvania Press, 1962.

Hall, Darwin S., and R. I. Holcombe. *History of the Minnesota State Agricultural Society from Its Organization in 1854 to the Annual Meeting of 1910.* St. Paul: McGill-Warner Company, 1910.

Hancock, Jane, Sheila Ffolliott, and Thomas O'Sullivan. *Homecoming: The Art Collection of James J. Hill.* St. Paul: Minnesota Historical Society Press, 1991.

Hargreaves, Mary Wilma M. *Dry Farming in the Northern Great Plains, 1900–1925.* Cambridge: Harvard University Press, 1957.

Hays, Samuel P. *The Response to Industrialism, 1885–1914.* Chicago: University of Chicago Press, 1931.

————. *Conservation and the Gospel of Efficiency: The Progressive Conservation Movement, 1890–1920.* Cambridge: Harvard University Press, 1959.

Hibbard, Benjamin Horace. *A History of Public Land Policies.* Madison: University of Wisconsin Press, 1965.

Hidy, Ralph W., Muriel E. Hidy, Roy V. Scott, and Don L. Hofsommer. *The Great Northern Railway: A History.* Cambridge: Harvard Business School Press, 1988.

Hofsommer, Donovan L., comp. *Railroads of the Trans-Mississippi West: A Selected Bibliography.* Plainview, Tex.: Wayland College, 1974.

Hollon, Eugene W. *The Great American Desert Then and Now.* New York: Oxford University Press, 1966.

Howard, Joseph Kinsey. *Montana: High, Wide, and Handsome.* New Haven: Yale University Press, 1943.

Howard, Stanley W. *Green Fields of Montana: A Brief History of Irrigation.* Manhattan, Kans.: Sunflower University Press, 1974.

Hull, Lindley M., ed. *A History of Central Washington Including the Famous Wenatchee, Entiat, Chelan and the Columbia Valleys with an Index and Eighty Scenic Historical Illustrations.* Spokane, Wash.: Shaw & Borden Co., 1929.

Hunter, William C. *Beacon Across the Prairie: North Dakota's Land-Grant College.* Fargo: North Dakota Institute for Regional Studies, 1961.

Jesness, Oscar B., ed. *Andrew Boss: Agricultural Pioneer and Builder, 1867–1947.* St. Paul: Itasca Press, 1950.

Johnson, E. Bird, ed. *Forty Years of the University of Minnesota.* Minneapolis: General Alumni Association, 1916.

Judd, Denis. *Radical Joe: A Life of Joseph Chamberlain.* London: Hamish Hamilton, 1977.

Kapferer, Jean-Noel. *Strategic Brand Management: New Approaches to Creating and Evaluating Brand Equity.* New York: Free Press, 1992.

Kerridge, Eric. *The Farmers of Old England.* Totowa, N.J.: Rowman and Littlefield, 1973.

Klein, Maury. *The Life and Legend of E. H. Harriman.* Chapel Hill: University of North Dakota, 2000.

Kolko, Gabriel. *The Triumph of Conservatism: A Reinterpretation of American History, 1900–1916.* New York: Free Press, 1963.

Lasch, Christopher. *The True and Only Heaven: Progress and Its Critics.* New York: W. W. Norton & Co., 1991.

Layton, Stanford J. *To No Privileged Class: The Rationalization of Homesteading and Rural Life in the Early Twentieth-Century American West.* Salt Lake City: Charles Redd Center for Western Studies, Brigham Young University, 1988.

Limerick, Patricia Nelson. *The Legacy of Conquest: The Unbroken Past of the American West.* New York: W. W. Norton & Co., 1987.

Link, Arthur S., Jr. *Woodrow Wilson and the Progressive Era, 1910–1917.* New York: Harper & Row, 1954.

Lyman, W. D. *History of the Yakima Valley, Washington, Comprising Yakima, Kittitas and Benton Counties. N.p.:* S. J. Clarke Publishing, 1919.

Malone, Michael P. *The Battle for Butte: Mining & Politics on the Northern Frontier, 1864–1906.* Helena: Montana Historical Society Press, 1981.

―――. *James J. Hill: Empire Builder of the Northwest.* Norman: University of Oklahoma Press, 1996.

Malone, Michael P., and Richard B. Roeder. *Montana: A History of Two Centuries.* Seattle: University of Washington Press, 1976.

Marcus, Alan I. *Agricultural Science and the Quest for Legitimacy: Farmers, Agricultural Colleges, and Experiment Stations, 1870–1890.* Ames: Iowa State University Press, 1985.

Marcus, Alan I, and Howard P. Segal. *Technology in American Life: A Brief History.* Fort Worth: Harcourt Brace Jovanovich, 1989.

Marling, Karal Ann. *Blue Ribbon: A History of the Minnesota State Fair.* St. Paul: Minnesota Historical Society Press, 1990.

Marshall, Duncan. *Shorthorn Cattle in Canada.* Dominion Shorthorn Breeders' Association, 1932.

Martin, Albro. *James J. Hill and the Opening of the Northwest.* 1976. Reprint, St. Paul: Minnesota Historical Society Press, 1991.

May, Henry F. *The Enlightenment in America.* New York: Oxford University Press, 1976.

McGinnis, R. A., ed. *Beet-Sugar Technology.* New York: Reinhold Publishing Corporation, 1951.

McMath, Robert C., Jr. *American Populism: A Social History, 1877–1898.* New York: Hill and Wang, 1993.

Meinig, Donald W. *The Great Columbia Plain: A Historical Geography, 1805–1910.* Seattle: University of Washington Press, 1968.

Mercer, Lloyd J. *Railroads and Land Grant Policy: A Study in Government Intervention.* New York: Academic Press, 1982.

Minchinton, W. E. *Essays in Agrarian History: Volume I.* New York: Augustus M. Kelley, 1968.

Morlan, Robert L. *Political Prairie Fire: The Nonpartisan League, 1915–1922.* 1955. Reprint, St. Paul: Minnesota Historical Society Press, 1983.

Morris, James M. *Our Maritime Heritage: Maritime Developments and Their Impact on American Life.* Washington, D.C.: University Press of America, 1979.

Mowry, George E. *The Era of Theodore Roosevelt: 1900–1912.* New York: Harper & Row, 1958.

Murray, Stanley Norman. *The Valley Comes of Age: A History of Agriculture in the Valley of the Red River of the North 1812–1920.* Fargo: North Dakota Institute for Regional Studies, 1967.

Myers, Rex C., and Harry W. Fritz. *Montana and the West: Essays in Honor of K. Ross Toole.* Boulder, Colo.: Pruett Publishing Co., 1984.

Nash, Gerald D. *The American West in the Twentieth Century: A Short History of an Urban Oasis.* Englewood Cliffs, N.J.: Prentice-Hall, Inc., 1973. Reprint, Albuquerque: University of New Mexico Press, 1984.

———. *The American West Transformed: The Impact of the Second World War.* Bloomington: Indiana University Press, 1985.

Nash, Roderick. *Wilderness and the American Mind.* New Haven: Yale University Press, 1973.

Noble, David. *The Progressive Mind, 1890–1917.* Chicago: Rand McNally & Co., 1970.

Nicosia, Francesco M., ed. *Advertising, Management, and Society: A Business Point of View.* New York: McGraw-Hill, 1974.

Oglivie, William Edward. *Pioneer Agricultural Journalists: Brief Biographical Sketches of Some of the Early Editors in the Field of Agricultural Journalism.* Chicago: Arthur C. Leonard, 1927.

Oleson, Alexandra, and John Voss, eds. *The Organization of Knowledge in Modern America, 1860–1920.* Baltimore: Johns Hopkins University Press, 1979.

Osgood, Ernest Staples. *The Day of the Cattleman.* 1929. Reprint, Chicago: University of Chicago Press, 1970.

Patterson, Jerry E. *The Vanderbilts.* New York: Harry N. Abrams, Inc., 1989.

Peffer, E. Louise. *The Closing of the Public Domain: Disposal and Reservation Policies, 1900–1950.* Stanford: Stanford University Press, 1951.

Persons, Stow. *The Decline of American Gentility.* New York: Columbia University Press, 1973.

Pisani, Donald J. *To Reclaim a Divided West: Water, Law, and Public Policy, 1848–1902.* Albuquerque: University of New Mexico Press, 1992.

Pleck, Elizabeth H., and Joseph H. Pleck, eds. *The American Man.* Englewood Cliffs, N.J.: Prentice-Hall, 1980.

Porter, A. R., J. A. Sims, and C. F. Foreman. *Dairy Cattle in American Agriculture.* Ames: Iowa State University Press, 1965.

Porter, Theodore M. *Trust in Numbers: The Pursuit of Objectivity in Science and Public Life.* Princeton: Princeton University Press, 1995.

Pringle, Henry F. *Theodore Roosevelt: A Biography.* New York: Harcourt, Brace and Company, 1931.

Pugh, David G. *Sons of Liberty: The Masculine Mind in Nineteenth-Century America.* Westport, Conn.: Greenwood Press, 1983.

Pusateri, C. Joseph. *A History of American Business.* Arlington Heights, Ill.: Harlan Davidson, Inc., 1984.

Pyle, Joseph Gilpin. *The Life of James J. Hill.* 2 vols. Garden City, N.Y.: Doubleday, Page & Company, 1917.

Raban, Jonathan. *Bad Land: An American Romance.* London: Picador, 1996.

The Red River Aggie. Crookston, Minn.: Senior Class of the Northwest School of Agriculture, 1926.

Richardson, Elmo R. *The Politics of Conservation: Crusades and Controversies, 1897–1913.* Berkeley: University of California Press, 1962.

Rischin, Moses, ed. *The American Gospel of Success: Individualism and Beyond.* Chicago: Quadrangle Books, 1965.

Robbins, William G. *Colony & Empire: The Capitalist Transformation of the American West.* Lawrence: University Press of Kansas, 1994.

———. *Landscapes of Promise: The Oregon Story, 1800–1940.* Seattle: University of Washington Press, 1997.

Robinson, Elwyn B. *History of North Dakota.* Lincoln: University of Nebraska Press, 1966.

Robinson, Michael C. *Water for the West: The Bureau of Reclamation, 1902–1977.* Chicago: Public Works Historical Society, 1979.

Rohrbough, Malcolm. *The Land Office Business: The Settlement and Administration of American Public Lands, 1789–1837.* New York: Oxford University Press, 1968.

Rosenberg, Charles. *No Other Gods: On Science and American Social Thought.* Baltimore: Johns Hopkins University Press, 1961.

Ross, Alexander M. *The College on the Hill: A History of the Ontario Agricultural College, 1874–1974.* Vancouver: Copp Clark Publishing, 1974.

Ross, Alexander M., and Terry Crowley. *The College on the Hill: A New History of the Ontario Agricultural College, 1874–1999.* Toronto: Dundurn Press, 1999.

Ross, Earle. *A History of Iowa State College.* Ames: Iowa State College Press, 1942.

Rouse, John. *World Cattle III: Cattle of North America.* Norman: University of Oklahoma Press, 1973.

Rowley, William D. *Reclaiming the Arid West: The Career of Francis G. Newlands.* Bloomington: Indiana University Press, 1996.

Runte, Alfred. *Trains of Discovery: Western Railroads and the National Parks.* Flagstaff, Ariz.: Northland Press, 1984.

Scott, Roy V. *The Reluctant Farmer: The Rise of Agricultural Extension to 1914.* Urbana: University of Illinois Press, 1970.

———. *Railroad Development Programs in the Twentieth Century.* Ames: Iowa State University Press, 1985.

Shoptaugh, Terry L. *Roots of Success: A History of the Red River Valley Sugarbeet Growers.* Fargo, N.D.: Institute for Regional Studies, 1997.

Shurts, John. *Indian Reserved Water Rights: The Winters Doctrine in Its Social and Legal Context, 1880s–1930s.* Norman: University of Oklahoma Press, 2000.

Smith, Guy-Harold, ed. *Conservation of Natural Resources.* New York: John Wiley & Sons, 1950.

Speer, Ray, and Harry Frost. *Minnesota State Fair: The History and Heritage of 100 Years.* Argus Publishing, 1964.

Steen, Harold K. *The U.S. Forest Service: A History.* Seattle: University of Washington Press, 1976.

Stoll, Steven. *The Fruits of Natural Advantage: Making the Industrial Countryside in California.* Berkeley: University of California Press, 1998.

Stover, John E. *American Railroads.* 1961. Reprint, Chicago: University of Chicago Press, 1997.

Strouse, Jean. *Morgan: American Financier.* New York: Random House, 1999.

Taylor, Jeffery. *Fashioning Farmers.* Regina: Canadian Plains Research Centre, 1994.

Thornton, Tamara Plakins. *Cultivating Gentlemen: The Meaning of Country Life Among the Boston Elite, 1785–1860.* New Haven: Yale University Press, 1989.

Toole, K. Ross. *Montana: An Uncommon Land.* Norman: University of Oklahoma Press, 1959.

———. *Twentieth-Century Montana: A State of Extremes.* Norman: University of Oklahoma Press, 1972.

Trachtenberg, Alan. *The Incorporation of America: Culture and Society in the Gilded Age.* New York: Hill and Wang, 1982.

Ulanoff, Stanley M. *Advertising in America: An Introduction to Persuasive Communication.* New York: Hastings House, 1977.

U.S. Shipping and Shipbuilding: Trends and Policy Choices. Washington, D.C.: Government Printing Office, 1984.

Vaught, David. *Cultivating California: Growers, Specialty Crops, and Labor, 1875–1920.* Baltimore: Johns Hopkins University Press, 1999.

Vileisis, Ann. *Discovering the Unknown Landscape: A History of America's Wetlands.* Washington, D.C.: Island Press, 1997.

Walters, Ronald G., ed. *Scientific Authority and Twentieth Century America.* Baltimore: Johns Hopkins University Press, 1997.

Warburg, Frieda Schiff. *Reminiscences of a Long Life.* New York: n.p., 1956.

Watson, J. A. Scott, and May Elliot Hobbs. *Great Farmers.* London: Selwyn & Blount, 1937.

Webb, Walter Prescott. *The Great Plains.* 1931. Reprint, Lincoln: University of Nebraska Press, 1959.

White, Richard. *"It's Your Misfortune and None of My Own": A New History of the American West.* Norman: University of Oklahoma Press, 1991.

Wiebe, Robert H. *The Search for Order, 1877–1920.* New York: Hill and Wang, 1967.

Willard, Daniel E. *Montana: The Geological Story.* Lancaster, Penn.: Science Press, 1935.

Woods, Thomas A. *Knights of the Plow: Oliver H. Kelley and the Origins of the Grange in Republican Ideology.* Ames: Iowa State University Press, 1991.

Worster, Donald. *Rivers of Empire: Water, Aridity, and the Growth of the American West.* New York: Pantheon Books, 1985.

Wyllie, Irvin G. *The Self-Made Man in America: The Myth of Rags to Riches.* New York: Macmillan Company, 1954.

Articles

Ankli, Robert. "Ontario's Dairy Industry, 1880–1920." *Canadian Papers in Rural History* 8 (1992): 261–76.

Appleby, Joyce. "Commercial Farming and the 'Agrarian Myth' in the Early Republic." *Journal of American History* 64 (March 1982): 833–49.

Belyk, Ralph. "The Midway Railway War." *Canadian West* 6 (1986): 34–38.

Bender, Barbara L. "Historic 'Sisters' on Puget Sound." *Portage* 8 (summer 1986): 14–17.

Berg, Carol J. "'Dear Mr. Hill. . . .' Letters to the Empire Builder, 1876–95." *Minnesota History* 50 (summer 1986): 71–77.

Bergman, H. J. "The Reluctant Dissenter: Governor Hay of Washington and the Conservation Problem." *Pacific Northwest Quarterly* 62 (January 1971): 27–33.

Bicha, Karel Denis. "The American Farmer and the Canadian West, 1896–1914: A Revised View." *Agricultural History* 38 (January 1964): 43–46.

Burrows, G. T. "How Dual-Purpose Shorthorns Reached America." *Milking Shorthorn Journal* 38 (March 1947).

Chapple, Oliver. "Avalanche in the Cascades: A Deadly Trap on the Great Northern Line." *American West* 20 (Jan./Feb. 1983): 60–67.

Costello, Gladys R. "Irrigation History and Resettlement on the Milk River Project, Montana." *Reclamation Era* 40 (May 1940): 136–42.

Cotroneo, Ross. "Selling the Land on the Montana Plains: Northern Pacific Railway's Land-Grant Sales Policies." *Montana* 37 (spring 1987): 40–49.

Danbom, David B. "The Agricultural Experiment Station and Professionalization: Scientists' Goals for Agriculture." *Agricultural History* 60 (spring 1986): 246–55.

———. "The North Dakota Agricultural College Controversy of 1893: Scientific Professionalism and Political Patronage." *North Dakota History* 53 (winter 1986): 12–23.

———. "The North Dakota Agricultural Experiment Station and the Struggle to Create a Dairy State." *Agricultural History* 63 (spring 1989): 174–86.

———. "Politics, Science, and the Changing Nature of Research at the North Dakota Agricultural Experiment Station, 1900–1930." *North Dakota History* 56 (fall 1989): 16–29.

Edwards, Everett E. "T. L. Haecker, The Father of Dairying in Minnesota." *Minnesota History* 19 (June 1938): 148–61.

Everitt, John, Roberta Kempthorne, and Charles Schafer. "Controlled Aggression: James J. Hill and the Brandon, Saskatchewan and Hudson's Bay Railway." *North Dakota History* 56 (spring 1989): 3–19.

Farrell, Richard. "Advice to Farmers: The Content of Agricultural Newspapers, 1860–1910." *Agricultural History* 51 (January 1977): 209–17.

Ferlerger, Lou. "Uplifting American Agriculture: Experiment Station Scientists and the Office of Experiment Stations in the Early Years After the Hatch Act." *Agricultural History* 64 (spring 1990): 5–23.

Grant, H. Roger. "A. B. Stickney and James J. Hill: The Railroad Relationship." *Railroad History* 146 (fall 1982): 9–22.

Hafermehl, Louis N. "To Make the Desert Bloom: The Politics and Promotion of Early Irrigation Schemes in North Dakota." *North Dakota History* 59 (summer 1992): 13–27.

Hargreaves, Mary W. M. "Dry Farming Alias Scientific Farming." *Agricultural History* 23 (January 1948): 39–55.

———. "The Dry-Farming Movement in Retrospect." *Agricultural History* 51 (winter 1977): 149–65.

Hickcox, David H. "The Impact of the Great Northern Railway on Settlement in Northern Montana, 1880–1920." *Railroad History* 148 (spring 1983): 58–67.

Hofsommer, Don L. "Rivals for California: The Great Northern and the Southern Pacific, 1905–1931." *Montana* 38 (spring 1988): 58–67.

———. "Hill's Dream Realized: The Burlington Northern's Eight-Decade Gestation." *Pacific Northwest Quarterly* 79 (October 1988): 138–46.

———. "For Territorial Dominion in California and the Pacific Northwest: Edward H. Harriman and James J. Hill." *California History* 70 (spring 1991): 31–45.

Hudanick, Andrew, Jr. "George Hebard Maxwell: Reclamation's Militant Evangelist." *Journal of the West* 14 (July 1975): 108–21.

Hudson, John C. "North Dakota's Railway War of 1905." *North Dakota History* 48 (winter 1981): 4–19.

Hundley, Norris, Jr. "Water and the West in Historical Imagination." *Western Historical Quarterly* 27 (spring 1996): 5–31.

Isherwood, J. H. "Great Northern Liner: 'Minnesota of 1904.'" *Sea Breezes* 53 (November 1970): 670–75.

Jones, David C. "'We'll All Be Buried Down Here in This Dry Belt. . . .'" *Saskatchewan History* 35 (spring 1982): 41–54.

Kirby, Russell S. "Nineteenth-Century Patterns of Railroad Development on the Great Plains." *Great Plains Quarterly* 3 (summer 1983): 157–70.

Lang, William L. "Charles A. Broadwater and the Main Chance in Montana." *Montana* 39 (summer 1989): 30–36.

———. "Corporate Point Men and the Creation of the Montana Central Railroad, 1882–87." *Great Plains Quarterly* 10 (summer 1990): 152–66.

Lovin, Hugh T. "'Duty of Water' in Idaho: A 'New West' Irrigation Controversy, 1890–1920." *Arizona and the West* 23 (spring 1981): 5–28.

Lowitt, Richard. "George W. Norris, James J. Hill, and the Railroad Rate Bill." *Nebraska History* 40 (1959): 137–246.

———. "Henry A. Wallace and Irrigation Agriculture." *Agricultural History* 66 (fall 1992): 1–10.

Marcus, Alan I. "The Ivory Silo: Farmer-Agricultural College Tensions in the 1870s and 1880s." *Agricultural History* 60 (spring 1986): 22–36.

———. "The Wisdom of the Body Politic: The Changing Nature of Publicly Sponsored American Agricultural Research Since the 1830s." *Agricultural History* 62 (spring 1988): 4–26.

Martin, Dale. "Railroading on the Great Divide: Images of the Milwaukee Road's Western Main Line." *Montana* 43 (spring 1993): 52–61.

McDean, Harry. "Professionalism in the Rural Social Sciences." *Agricultural History* 58 (July 1984): 373–92.

McInnis, Marvin. "The Changing Structure of Canadian Agriculture, 1867–1897." *Journal of Economic History* 42 (March 1982): 191–98.

Miller, August C., Jr. "Jefferson as an Agriculturist." *Agricultural History* 16 (April 1942): 65–78.

Mitchell, F. Stewart. "The Chicago, Milwaukee & St. Paul Railway and James J. Hill in Dakota Territory, 1879–1885." *North Dakota History* 47 (fall 1980): 11–19.

Moore, Gary E. "The Involvement of Experiment Stations in Secondary Education, 1887–1917." *Agricultural History* 62 (spring 1988): 164–76.

Murray, Keith A. "The Highline Canal: Irrigation Comes to Wenatchee." *Columbia* 9 (winter 1995/96): 17–23.

Murray, Stanley N. "Railroads and the Agricultural Development of the Red River Valley of the North, 1870–1890." *Agricultural History* 31 (October 1957): 57–66.

Norrie, Kenneth H. "Cultivation Techniques as a Response to Risk in Early Canadian Prairie Agriculture." *Explorations in Economic History* 17 (fall 1980): 386–99.

Otter, A. A. Den. "Adapting the Environment: Ranching, Irrigation, and Dry Land Farming in Southern Alberta, 1880–1914." *Great Plains Quarterly* 6 (summer 1986): 171–89.

Percy, Michael B., and Tamara Woroby. "American Homesteaders and the Canadian Prairies, 1899 and 1909." *Explorations in Economic History* 24 (winter 1987): 77–100.

Quisenberry, Karl. "The Dry Land Stations: Their Mission and Their Men." *Agricultural History* 51 (January 1977): 218–28.

Rakestraw, Lawrence. "The West, States' Rights, and Conservation: A Study of Six Public Land Conferences." *Pacific Northwest Quarterly* 48 (July 1957): 89–99.

Robbins, William G. "'At the End of the Cracked Whip': The Northern West, 1880–1920." *Montana* 38 (autumn 1988): 2–11.

Roeder, Richard. "Thomas H. Carter, Spokesman for Western Development." *Montana* 39 (spring 1989): 23–29.

Schene, Michael G. "The Crown of the Continent: Private Enterprise and Public Interest in the Early Development of Glacier National Park, 1910–1917." *Forest & Conservation History* 34 (April 1990): 69–75.

Schonberger, Howard. "James J. Hill and the Trade with the Orient." *Minnesota History* 41 (winter 1968): 178–90.

Schutz, Howard. "Giants in Collision: The Northern Pacific Panic of 1901." *American History Illustrated* 21 (May 1986): 28–32.

Schwantes, Carlos A. "Problems of Empire Building: The Oregon Trunk Railway Survey of Disappointed Homeseekers, 1911." *Oregon Historical Quarterly* 83 (winter 1982): 371–90.

———. "Landscapes of Opportunity: Phases of Railroad Promotion of the Pacific Northwest." *Montana* 43 (spring 1993): 38–51.

Shaw, Douglas V. "Ralph Budd, the Great Northern Railway, and the Advent of the Motor Bus." *Railroad History* 166 (1992): 57–79.

Smith, Burton M. "Business, Politics and Indian Land Settlements in Montana, 1882–1904." *Canadian Journal of History* 20 (April 1985): 45–64.

Tanner, Scott. "The Completion of the Great Northern Railway: What It Meant to Everett." *Great Northern Railway Historical Society Reference Sheet #212* (December 1993).

Tonsfeldt, Ward. "Railroads and Politics, 1890–1931." *Journal of the Shaw Historical Library* 3 (spring 1989): 10–16.

"Wall Street Looks at the Agricultural Northwest." *Minnesota History* 33 (summer 1952): 61–63.

Walter, David. "Simon Pepin, A Quiet Capitalist." *Montana* 39 (winter 1989): 34–38.

White, W. Thomas. "Paris Gibson, James J. Hill & the 'New Minneapolis': The Great Falls Water Power and Townsite Company, 1882–1908." *Montana* 33 (summer 1983): 60–69.

———. "Main Street on the Irrigation Frontier: Sub-Urban Community Building in the Yakima Valley, 1900–1910." *Pacific Northwest Quarterly* 77 (July 1986): 94–103.

———. "A Gilded Age Businessman in Politics: James J. Hill, the Northwest, and the American Presidency, 1884–1912." *Pacific Historical Review* 57 (November 1988): 439–56.

———. "Commonwealth or Colony? Montana and the Railroads in the First Decade of Statehood." *Montana* 38 (autumn 1988): 12–23.

Wieffering, Eric. "A Legacy of Wealth and Pain." *Corporate Report Minnesota* 26 (February 1995): 22–33.

Zeidel, Robert F. "Peopling the Empire: The Great Northern Railroad and the Recruitment of Immigrant Settlers to North Dakota." *North Dakota History* 60 (spring 1993): 14–23.

Zeisler-Vralsted, Dorothy. "Reclaiming the Arid West: The Role of the Northern Pacific Railway in Irrigating Kennewick, Washington." *Pacific Northwest Quarterly* 84 (October 1993): 130–39.

Unpublished Materials

Bryans, William Samuel. "A History of Transcontinental Railroads and Coal Mining on the Northern Great Plains to 1920." Ph.D. diss., University of Wyoming, 1987.

Colburn, Carol Ann. "The Dress of the James J. Hill Family, 1863–1916." Ph.D. diss., University of Minnesota, 1989.

Dalich, Charles A. "Dry Farming Promotion in Eastern Montana, 1907–1916." M.A. thesis, University of Montana, 1968.

Dickman, Howard Leigh. "James Jerome Hill and the Agricultural Development of the Northwest." Ph.D. diss., University of Michigan, 1977.

Edwards, Douglas M. "Visions of Virtue and Efficiency: Promoting Agricultural Settlement in Montana, 1909–1916." Paper presented at American Heritage Center, Fifth Annual History Symposium, Laramie, Wyoming, September 1996. In possession of author.

———. "Exhibiting the Possibilities: Settlement Promotion and the Montana State Fair." Paper presented at the Western Historical Association Conference, St. Paul, Minnesota, October 1997. In possession of author.

Gilman, Rhoda R. "The Fur Trade in the Red River Valley." Paper presented at Teacher Conference at the Minnesota Historical Society, St. Paul, July 1993.

Irwin, Thomas W. "Government Funding of Agricultural Associations in Late Nineteenth-Century Ontario." Ph.D. diss., University of Western Ontario, 1998.

Kelly, Paul Edward. "Under the Ditch: Irrigation and the Garrison Diversion Controversy." M.A. thesis, North Dakota State University, 1989.

Luecke, John. "Minnesota Railroads." Paper presented at Teacher Conference at the Minnesota Historical Society, St. Paul, July 1993.

Nesmith, Tom. "The Philosophy of Agriculture: The Promise of Intellect in Ontario Farming, 1835–1914." Ph.D. diss., Carleton University, Ontario, 1988.

Roet, Jeffrey B. "Agricultural Settlement on the Dry Farming Frontier, 1900–1920." Ph.D. diss., Northwestern University, 1982.

Roberts, Norene, and Claire Strom. "Statement of Content, National Register Nomination for the University of Minnesota." State Historic Preservation Office, Minnesota Historical Society, St. Paul, Minnesota.

Smith, Dennis J. "Procuring a Right-of-Way: James J. Hill and Indian Reservations, 1886–1888." M.A. thesis, University of Montana, 1983.

INDEX